D1645741

3.99
4/29

THE WILD GOSPEL

What does it mean to live by truth? What *is* truth? We live in a world which has lost touch with truth, which has reduced it to the merely rational and then discarded it as inadequate to explain the complexity of our lives.

But truth is more than fact or concept. Truth is the living force of reality itself, the power of God in the universe. Incarnate in the person of Jesus Christ, truth is not just factual but personal, not just intellectual but profoundly emotional. Reality is not just to be explained but discovered, not to be understood so much as experienced. Can we burst free from the inherited framework of our culture, and learn not just to know truth but to feel it and live it, in such a way that it becomes real to those around us?

In this highly original book, Alison Morgan shows that Jesus himself lived free from the culturally imposed norms which restrict our understanding of truth. Offering a challenge to the world into which he came, Jesus overturned every assumption which kept people from experiencing the living reality of God. Examining church history, prophecy past and present, the state of our culture and of the church today, and drawing both on personal experience and the experience of others, Alison blends analysis and imagination, history and poetry in this prophetic challenge to the Western church.

The Revd Dr Alison Morgan has written a number of books, including an internationally recognised work on the poet Dante. She is on the staff of Holy Trinity, Leicester, where she lives with her husband Roger and their three children. She is a member of the Council of SOMA UK, and an Associate of ReSource, an Anglican agency for the encouragement and renewal of the church for mission. Her website is www.alisonmorgan.co.uk

ReSource works for the renewal of people and churches for mission in the power of the Holy Spirit – across all traditions, Churches and denominations, and with an Anglican distinctive. It publishes resources and a regular magazine, and offers a team ministry which works at all levels of the Church, and especially with the local and the ordinary. Its strategy includes the prophetic, the pastoral and the missionary. It is based at 4 Old Station Yard, Abingdon, Oxon OX14 3LD – phone: 01235 553722 – email: office@resource-arm.net – website: www.resource-arm.net.

The Wild Gospel

Bringing truth to life

We are the music makers,
And we are the dreamers of dreams,
Wandering by lone sea breakers,
And sitting by desolate streams:
World losers and world forsakers
On whom the pale moon gleams;
Yet we are the movers and shakers
Of the world forever it seems.

– A O'Shaughnessy

ALISON MORGAN

MONARCH
BOOKS

Oxford, UK & Grand Rapids, Michigan

Copyright © Alison Morgan 2004
The right of Alison Morgan to be identified
as the author of this work has been asserted by her in
accordance with the Copyright, Designs
and Patents Act 1988.

All rights reserved.
No part of this publication may be reproduced or
transmitted in any form or by any means, electronic
or mechanical, including photocopy, recording or any
information storage and retrieval system, without
permission in writing from the publisher.

First published in 2004 by Monarch Books,
(a publishing imprint of Lion Hudson plc),
Mayfield House, 256 Banbury Road, Oxford OX2 7DH
Tel: +44 (0)1865 302750 Fax: +44 (0)1865 302757
Email: monarch@lionhudson.com
www.lionhudson.com

Reprinted 2005

Published in conjunction with ReSource,
4 Old Station Yard, Abingdon, Oxon OX14 3LD

Distributed by:
UK: Marston Book Services Ltd, PO Box 269,
Abingdon, Oxon OX14 4YN;
USA: Kregel Publications, PO Box 2607
Grand Rapids, Michigan 49501.

UK-10: ISBN 1 85424 672 0
UK-13: ISBN 978 1 85424 672 1
US-10: ISBN 0 8254 6070 0
US-13: ISBN 978 0 8254 6070 8

Unless otherwise stated, Scripture quotations are
taken from the New Revised Standard Version (NRSV) of the Bible,
copyright © 1989 by the Division of Education of the National
Council of Churches of Christ in the United States of America
and are used by permission. All rights reserved.

British Library Cataloguing Data
A catalogue record for this book is available
from the British Library.

Printed in Great Britain.

To Roger, Edward, Bethy and Katy

CONTENTS

ACKNOWLEDGEMENTS

My thanks are due to those who have stood alongside me as I have written. I am especially indebted to Jenny Ridge, who has prayed faithfully with me throughout; to Martin Cavender, for his constant challenge and encouragement; to John Woolmer, for leadership and inspiration in Africa; and to Tony Collins, my publisher, for his early belief in the book. Meriel Cullen, Nicola Vollkommer and my father Bill Keymer have read from first draft to final version and offered me many helpful remarks over the five years it has taken me to produce the book; and Roger Coleman, Jonathan Hesketh, Bob Jackson, Laurence Singlehurst, Laurie White, and Sue Young have all made invaluable comments and observations at various stages. They haven't of course been able to rescue me from the fact that I am me, and errors and infelicities are therefore mine alone (as is the at times deliberately idiosyncratic typesetting). I am grateful to those who have allowed me to share their story, either by name or under a pseudonym. Of all that I have read, I have benefited most particularly from the writings of Walter Brueggemann.

More widely I would like to thank the people of northern Zambia and of the Diocese of Mount Kilimanjaro in Tanzania, who have welcomed me amongst them and shared their world with me, to my immeasurable benefit; and the members of Holy Trinity, Leicester, amongst whom I live, work and grow.

But most of all I would like to thank my husband Roger, for all these things and more.

FOREWORD

This remarkable book is about renewal in body, mind and spirit. It is eloquent and beautiful, about the re-creation of people, self-discovery and fullness of life, both individual and corporate. It is a book about God and his beloved people, God and his Church in its mission to his world. Most profoundly it is a book about life, which reminds me of those words of Dietrich Bonhoeffer, "Christianity is not about religion – it is about making humanity, and making it as God intended it to be"; or St Irenaeus in the second century, "The glory of God is a human being fully alive".

There is a moment in Mel Gibson's film *The Passion of the Christ* when Jesus is depicted as falling, yet again, under the weight of the cross as he makes his bloody, battered, death-imminent way along what we have named the Via Dolorosa. His mother presses through the crowd and the flailing soldiers to cup his face in her hands for one last time. The figure of Jesus utters in that snatched second the glorious words, "Behold, I make all things new".

It may not be biblically accurate in its timing – the words actually appear in Revelation 21:5, given to St John on Patmos – but the exchange is vital to our understanding of what Jesus Christ was doing for the world he had made as he gave his life, covered with blood and sweat and spit. In his death all humankind was made new. In this book Alison Morgan shows us brilliantly what that renewal means.

Bishop Tom Wright in his commentary on the gospel of St Mark speaks about the renewal in Jesus himself, as he was baptised by John in the Jordan at the beginning of his ministry. He speaks about the experience for Jesus as the Holy Spirit descended upon him in the form of a dove, and its intimate connection with the experience of the Christian believer – whether for the first time or in a constant remaking on the road. Mark says, "This is how it happened... he saw the heavens open". Tom Wright responds from the biblical roots of the phrase, "It doesn't mean that Jesus saw a little door ajar miles up in the sky. It's more as though an invisible curtain, right in front of us, was suddenly pulled back, so that instead of the trees and flowers and buildings, or in Jesus' case the river, the sandy desert and the crowds, we are stand- ing in the presence of a different reality altogether". Behold, I make all things new – or, in the words of St Paul, "So if anyone is in Christ, there is a new creation: everything old has passed away; see, everything has become new!" (2 Corinthians 5:17).

Part of that work of opening to "a different reality" consists in examining with real honesty ourselves and the culture in which we live, under the arc-light of the gospel of Jesus Christ. It calls for clear sight and sacrificial truth in speaking and writing. "First catch your prophet", as Archdeacon Bernard Pawley once said to the General Synod, as the Church of England was contemplating its Decade of Evangelism. He saw how crucial was the work of the prophet in clearing the way and pointing the direction. Prophecy is a gift of the Holy Spirit which has never been more in need than at this time.

People ask, "Who are the prophets, the clear speakers of our day?" They point to C S Lewis, T S Eliot, Dorothy Sayers, Archbishop William Temple and others from the last century. I believe Alison Morgan is prophetic in her reach and desire for truth. Maybe that follows from being a Medievalist, like Lewis, Eliot and Sayers. However it comes about, this is a clearly drawn map of a lucid exploration, a rigorous intellectual search for the answer to Pilate's question, "What is truth?".

The journey leads us away from merely holding to something finite and adjusting one's lifestyle to it, away from the courtroom's "whole truth and nothing but the truth". The discovery is bigger by far, taking us by the shoulders and facing us in another direction altogether. Truth, says Alison, is the living force of a different reality, God himself. The key to travelling with God in his world is to grasp that it's an attitude, an outlook, a matter of floating upwards in his hot-air balloon for a God's-eye view of life and living, remaking humanity in the power of the Holy Spirit of truth.

Here is the answer to Pilate, and to anyone who has ever said, "There must be more to life than . . ." Here is the **good** news. The gospel of Jesus Christ is the fixed horizon for the giddy flightpath of a world of change and uncertainty.

John Keats spoke well when he said, "Beauty is truth, truth beauty; that is all ye know on earth, and all ye need to know" (Ode on a Grecian Urn). This book about truth is one which carries beauty as well, in its words about life, renewal and that different reality. I am very grateful to Alison. She has taken my blithe assumptions, my lawyer's formulations about meaning and shaken them without mercy. I believe this prophet for today has spoken God's truth in her writing. I am profoundly thankful for the chance to stop and listen, to see afresh, and to be remade.

Martin Cavender
ReSource, Abingdon, Oxon
June 2004

INTRODUCTION

*The most real in this world is the most invisible;
but because the most invisible the most easily
forgotten. Reading about these invisible realities of
our Faith corrects the tendency for our hold on the
invisible to lessen. It feeds our minds with the
Truth.*

John Dalrymple[1]

This book is the mid point on a journey of discovery. It began
a quarter of a century ago, when as a 16-year-old faced with
the prospect of trying to map a path through the tangled
growth of the adult world looming up before me, I first set
out to acquire the tools that would make my journey possible. I began then with a question, and the question was this:
What is truth? It seemed to me that if I could find the answer
to this question, I would be standing on some kind of basic
platform from which it would be possible to try and build the
building that would be my life. And so, not knowing where
else to begin, I took myself to the philosophy section of the
school library and got out everything I could find on truth.
Some of these books I took to Italy on the first of what were
to become many trips there; and as I walked by black lava
shores and surveyed the horizons of this new world, I learned

the difference between contingent truth and absolute truth, despaired of ever reaching out into the latter, if indeed there was such a thing as absolute truth, and settled for the prospect of constructing my platform on a foundation of contingent truth. Contingent truth doesn't bother itself with the absolutes of the universe; contingent truth is man-made truth, and it can be managed. Contingent truth declares that the 9:15 train for Sheffield will leave from Platform 1, and that when I sit on my chair it will hold my weight. Contingent truth offers a framework for life, a framework of predictability. You can build with contingent truth.

Back in England, I did two things. Because it seemed to me that to believe any contingent truth was an act of faith, and because I remembered from going to church parade as a Brownie that faith was what Christianity was supposed to be about, I went out and bought myself a Bible. The problem was that I couldn't understand it. Chairs and trains I was familiar with, but this book didn't seem to speak my language. So I returned to the philosophy section of the school library, and discovered Jean-Paul Sartre and existentialism. And I found that Sartre did speak my language. In fact he offered precisely what I was looking for: the suggestion that in the absence of the existence of any absolute truth the only way to make sense of life was to create one's own meaning.

So I did just that. I began the task of forming the world around me into the shape I wanted it to take. I set myself aims and targets and achieved them. I got a place at Cambridge to read modern languages, and embraced the opportunities of university life. My horizons broadened, and what had seemed to be the forbidding tangled growth of the adult world became, once parted with the tools of my new philosophy, not just manageable but exciting. Released from the confines of home and school, I flung myself into new activities. I cycled through the mist of frosty mornings to row on the River Cam. I took the little orange tent of my child-hood into the fens, and spent summer weekends amongst the hum of mosquitoes and the grating of sedge warblers. I discovered 2,000 years of literature, and explored new modes of thought and expression. I spent a year in Florence, study-ing in shuttered libraries with curved wooden seats, watching shafts of sunlight slant through the darkened air, specks of dust dancing in their beam, and intruded upon by the hum of different sounding buses and the hooting of motorcycles hot in the world outside. I wandered through the flower-specked olive groves of Tuscany in spring, and watched the solid yellow light of the afternoon sun spread itself like butter on the thick clods of the freshly ploughed fields in autumn. I stayed in the snow-blanketed valleys of Romansch-speaking Switzerland with one friend, surrounded by white peaks and enjoying the silence of crackling icicles and the warm breath of domestic cattle sheltered in wooden winter chalets; and I drove through the undulating vines of Bordeaux with another, pausing to taste the round oak warmth of the red and the laundry-crisp freshness of the white wines offered us at the end of tree-lined drives by sun-smiling viticultors. I returned to Cambridge victorious in my conquering of this new world, fluent in Italian and confident in my abilities to ride the wave of the challenges I had embraced. A year later, and with a First to my name, I decided to stay on in this wonderful world of stimulus and opportunity, building on my platform of existentialism, creating my own meaning, making my own decisions, achieving my ambitions. I chose as the subject of my research the *Divine Comedy* of Dante Alighieri, foremost writer of the Italian Middle Ages and one of the greatest poets who has ever lived, and set out on a voyage through 2,000 years of painting and writing in the attempt to discover why Dante had portrayed the other world as he had.

Then my friend died. Her name was Ruth, and she had been my director of studies as an undergraduate. They told me one day, as I walked from the library back to my college for lunch, that the cancer had returned. She was 41, dark-haired, intelligent and vivacious, with everything to live for. She inhabited a square, chaos-filled room with a big window overlooking the sunlit grass of the college quadrangle, pictures by her school-age children pinned crookedly to the walls, books and papers piled high on the desk, stimulus and encouragement oozing out of the brickwork for those who reached the mark of her high standards. I had spent many hours there breathing it all in, and she had changed me. Over the next few months, I was to spend many hours with her again, shorter visits this time, sharing the jokes I'd picked up from my fellow-researchers at lunchtime, and watching her die. And as I found myself forced to face the fact that that was what was going to happen, the universe that I had so carefully arranged around me fell apart. As the cancer consumed her body and dimmed her spirit, an earthquake rumbled beneath my platform of contingent truth, and the bricks of my self-constructed meaning began to totter and slide. Fresh back from Italy, I felt like the tower of Pisa: a magnificent edifice, the source of endless satisfaction to those who had built it, and the object of wonder and envy to the lesser buildings around it, now lurching over because it turned out to have been built on an unstable foundation. Ruth herself, by contrast, was more worried about the lectures she was supposed to be writing than about the prospect of impending death. She was a Christian. She didn't want to die; but she knew where she was going, and she felt quite capable of going there. We talked about it. The strength of Christianity, she said, lay for her in the fact that it had been found to make sense in many different cultures. It had a universality about it; it was not subject to history or geography. And so she took me back to the Middle Ages we'd spent so many hours discussing in that sun-filled room three years previously, and asked me a simple question: Could I imagine existentialism making sense in the thirteenth century? And almost before she'd got the words out, dynamite exploded beneath my unsteady marble tower and blew it to smithereens. Of course I couldn't. I left the house that day drained and empty. You cannot construct your own reality. There are absolute truths, and one of them is death. Build what you like, but you're building it in a bubble. And sooner or later the bubble will meet a pin. Mine just had.

Ruth died on 31 March 1983. I saw her the evening before she died. She wished me a happy Easter, and I think those were the last coherent words she spoke. A week before, she'd given me a book. It was a beautiful copy of the *Visconti Hours*, a fifteenth-century Italian illuminated prayer book, and in it she had written, in Latin, the following words: "I know two masters: Christ and letters".

So as I boarded the train to Florence a few days after her funeral, I knew it was back to the drawing board. What is truth? Well, I'd watched Ruth die, unperturbed and in peace, a peace that had contrasted so sharply with my own turmoil, and I knew that her building had stood on a platform which had not subsided when faced with the intrusion of death into our seemingly immortal lives. "Two masters: Christ and letters", she'd written. I remembered my attempt years previously to look at the Bible, and it occurred to me that perhaps I should look at it again. Back in my familiar Florence, I went one day into Santa Croce, the big thirteenth-century Franciscan church that stands near the river, just up the road from my old student digs, and round the corner from the National Library where I had watched the dust dance in the sunbeams. E M Forster compared it to a barn, and it offers a strange impression of emptiness, the footsteps of visitors clattering on the stone floor and echoing up to the high wooden roof, and frescoes of the saints glowing on the walls in the chapels at the east end when you put 200 lire into the little slot machine that provides measured seconds of light. In the

thirteenth century, before the days of the university, Santa
Croce was a centre of learning, and Dante probably studied
there – Dante, the poet who told the tale of his own journey
from the tangled wood of confusion to faith in God, and in
whose quest I was beginning to see my own. So as I gazed at
the simple solidity of Giotto's paintings of St Francis I
resolved that wherever truth was to be found, it had to be
capable of providing a framework of meaning for then as
well as for now. It had to meet Ruth's criterion and stand
outside the language and assumptions of a particular culture.
I'd had enough of contingent truth. This time it had to be the
absolute version.

And so my journey began again. I read John's gospel, and
admired the broad sweep of his philosophical concepts, but
failed to understand any of his references to the Holy Spirit.
My world didn't have a space for the Holy Spirit; my world
was the tangible world of libraries and relationships, ambitions and bicycles. I took my Spiritless summary of John back
to Ruth's husband in Cambridge. How would I like to pursue
my quest, he asked. I could look at Christianity as a philosophy, and think about whether it made sense of the world I
lived in – whether Ruth was right, and it would do a better
job of offering meaning and purpose to any culture and any
society than had my existentialism. Or I could look at it
historically, and think about Jesus, the man who stood at its
centre – for although the Christian faith was just that, a faith,
it claimed to be founded on a fact, the fact of the life, death
and resurrection of Jesus, and a fact furthermore which if it
was indeed accepted as a fact would change the whole shape
of the universe for me yet again. Or I could look at it experi-
entially, and think about the lives of people like Ruth who
had lived and died by it, and seemed to find it satisfactory. In
the end I did all three. And I arrived, some months later, at
the conviction that I had at last found absolute truth.
Absolute truth was God, and it came incarnate in his Son,

Jesus. It made sense of life both personally and universally. It offered a framework of meaning that could not be shattered by anything I could think of that life might throw at it; and it extended beyond my material and psychological world into a new world, a second, overlay world, a world of spiritual reality, a world of truth in a different dimension. And so it was that my journey began.

In the beginning

When Jesus was taken by the council of the Sanhedrin to give an account of himself before Pontius Pilate, the Roman governor of Judea, this is what he said:

> "For this I was born, and for this I have come into the world, to bear witness to the truth."[2]

But what is truth? That was the question I had first asked myself at 16 as I stood on the threshold of the adult world, and it was the question with which Pilate immediately responded to Jesus. For me it remains the crucial question of all time. It is a simple question. And yet, as often with simple questions, I find it admits of no simple answer. Jesus, of course, was the truth. "I am the way, the truth and the life."[3] But what could such a statement possibly mean? For me it has been like a pebble dropped into a pond: it lands, splash, in the centre, clear and visible, at the moment of first encounter with Jesus; and yet its arrival is a beginning, not an end, for from the point of impact spring concentric ripples which slowly move over the surface of the pond in ever-increasing and interdependent circles. God is at the centre; but then it turns out that God is at the circumference also. So the truth starts with God and has to work its way out over the surface of the pond from God, only to find that its destination is also God. From the moment of impact, there begins a dialogue, a dialogue between you and God, a dialogue which never ends, a dialogue which if honestly conducted will spread out into all areas of your life, into your relationships, and ultimately into the world you inhabit. This dialogue takes place, as dialogues must, in words; and it reflects and repeats a process that began at the beginning of time with the creation of the world itself.

> In the beginning was the Word, and the Word was with God, and the Word was God. He was in the beginning with God. All things came into being through him, and without him not one thing came into being . . . And the Word became flesh and lived among us, and we have seen his glory, the glory as of a father's only son, full of grace and truth.
>
> John 1:1–3, 14

God spoke, and the universe sprang into being. In the beginning, we read in Genesis, when God created the heavens and the earth, the earth was a formless void and darkness covered the face of the deep. And what did God do? God spoke. *And God said*, Let there be light. Let there be a dome in the midst of the waters. Let the waters under the sky be gathered together into one place, and let the dry land appear. Let the earth put forth vegetation. God spoke; *and it was so*.[4]

Now for us this is tantalising but confusing. For us, words don't do this. For us, the spoken word is merely a vehicle, a vehicle for information. We live in a world of words, and words have become devalued. Millions of words sit locked up in books on the shelves of my study, ready to serve me and inform me the moment I take them down from the shelf. Words obey me as I sit at my desk and make them appear on the screen in front of me by a mere movement of my fingers. The very air is thick with words, words throbbing from radio masts and through mobile phones. Everything we do generates yet more words: reports, files, letters, newspapers. We have invented the internet, a world word machine where words jiggle and dance before your eyes the moment you log on. Everywhere there are words. We use them, abuse them, and ultimately flee from them; one of the essential skills of modern life is to know how to filter out words.

But for the writers of Genesis and John it was not so. For them, words are the expression of truth; and truth is the very principle of reality. For them, a word does not just exist, as it does for us. It isn't that the truth *is*, but rather that the truth *does*. When John wrote in Greek that Jesus was the Word, he used the word *logos*. And *logos* does not mean "word" in the sense that we mean "word". For us, a word is no more than a unit of speech, a soundbite in the air or a splatter of ink on a page. *Logos* is not this. *Logos* is a philosophical term, and it means something more like Reason than like Word. For the Greek philosophers who used it, *logos* was a principle or force, a statement about the universe.[5] When Jerome translated the Greek Bible into Latin some 300 years after John first wrote his gospel, he translated the Greek *logos* by the Latin *verbum*, from which we take our word "verb". And it has always seemed to me that in many ways "verb" would be a better translation. A verb, as we learn at school, is a *doing* word. And through the verb, conjugated as we learnt to conjugate it at school, God does. God did, God does and God will do.

So Jesus is the Word, the word that spoke the world in the first place, and the word that became flesh and lived among us as truth, a truth that, like the pebble dropped in the centre of the pond, is not static but dynamic; a truth that *does* something. This is the absolute truth I first started to look for at the age of 16. This truth is a force, the creative force which comes from God, through Christ, into the matter of the universe and into the spirit of man. This truth is the ultimate principle of reality. It pulses through the universe. It has to be engaged with for our life as we experience it to come into contact with that reality, to be transformed by it and to stay in contact with it for eternity. This is the truth that created the cosmos, the truth that sets us free, the truth in which we find ourselves and in the power of which we too become part of God's continued speaking into our world. But all that happens only as we appropriate the truth for ourselves and proclaim it to others. Truth is the gospel. Pilate couldn't take it in.

In a sense none of this was new with Jesus. It couldn't have been, of course, for the Word that God spoke in the incarnation of his Son was the same as the Word which he spoke when he created the universe. God has always spoken. Before Jesus, he spoke through the prophets of the Old Testament. Since Jesus, he has spoken through the Holy Spirit, the Spirit of truth, as Jesus called him. And always his words have been not just vehicles for information but carriers of power, the power of the Creator himself.

This has enormous implications for us today. If the world was spoken by God, if Jesus was the word he spoke, and if the words that Jesus spoke are the truth, then it must surely follow that we, also spoken by God in the moment of our creation, spoken to by Jesus in the moment or moments of our conversion, and spoken to by the Spirit of truth who lives within us, we too must speak. What then are the words that we must speak?

> In the beginning was the Word, and the Word was with God, and the Word was God. He was in the beginning with God. All things came into being through him, and without him not one thing came into being. What has come into being in him was life, and the life was the light of all people. The light shines in the darkness, and the darkness did not overcome it.
>
> John 1:1–5

God spoke, and what he spoke was life, the life of a living

universe. Jesus spoke, and what he spoke was life, the life of a living faith. God spoke, and there was light, and God separated the light from the darkness. Jesus spoke, and the light shone in the darkness, and the darkness did not overcome it. The power of the creative word is a principle of the universe, in both its physical and spiritual aspects. And we, who are made in the image of God, and heirs to the kingdom of God, we are to speak also. What we are to speak are the words of the gospel, the truth of the good news which brings light into darkness. We have the key to the universe and therefore the power to change it – an outrageous claim, but one which lies at the heart of our faith.

The prophets of the Old Testament knew this. The task of the Old Testament prophets, like the task of their successors, was to speak the word of God to the people. It was not primarily to foretell the future, but to speak into the present – not to foretell, but to forthtell. The Old Testament prophet spoke the "now" word of God to the people.[6] What did these prophets understand by a word? A word for us is merely a tool, which can be used for framing laws or explaining computers or advertising sunflower margarine or a whole host of other things. But in the mouth of an Old Testament prophet, words were much more than that. Words didn't just contain meaning, they contained power. The Hebrew word *dabar* means both "word" and "deed". The two were inseparable. So the prophet didn't merely pass on a message; his very enunciation of that message was itself the beginning of its fulfilment. He expected his God-given words to have the creative power of their originator – not just to be, but to *do* something. As the word was spoken, so it began to happen. The spoken word of God is invested with the creative energy of God. It isn't just a verbal noise; it is a living and powerful thing.[7]

And so it is with us. Since the ascension of Jesus and the subsequent coming of the Holy Spirit, we all have the potential to speak out the word of God, and in so doing to be part of his creative purposes. The Old Testament prophets knew that this would happen. Moses had expressed the wish that everyone might be a prophet, able to listen to God and to speak his word. Isaiah promised that God would pour his Spirit one day not just on his chosen prophets but on all people. Joel confirmed it in his famous declaration that sons and daughters would prophesy, old men dream dreams and young men see visions, and even menservants and maidservants receive the power of the Holy Spirit.[8] We are the heirs of these ancient prophets. We, like them, are charged with the task of speaking the "now" word of God into the lives of the people around us, of reintroducing the power of the Word into the lifeless, garbled and printed shapes of our information age, of bringing the creative force of God into the formless void of empty souls, and light into the darkness of a world which has disconnected itself from truth. This is what it means to preach and to minister the gospel; this is what it means to live by truth. It means nothing short of learning to live plugged in to the energy that sparked the Big Bang itself. And just as the energy of that explosion brought light into darkness and created the matter of the universe, so the energy available to us now brings light into the darkness of people's lives. One day, that same energy will create a new universe, a new heaven and a new earth, and the old will pass away. That will be the day that we pass from Genesis and from John to Revelation.[9] That will be the day that our task as ministers of the word of God is complete – then, and only then.

So: I had begun at 16 with the question "What is truth?". And I came at 24 to the conclusion that the answer lies in Jesus. Jesus is the way, the truth and the life. Jesus is the Word of God, the word which created the universe and which created me. Jesus is the Word spoken by God into his spoken universe, to bear witness to the truth of its creation and purpose, and to draw humankind back into relationship with that truth. And I too am to speak that word. Everything I now do and am comes out of that single conviction. As Christians we do not speak words of information. We speak words of truth, and therefore words of power; and like Jesus we don't just speak them, we *do* them. When Paul tells the Ephesian church to "speak the truth in love", the verb he uses in fact means not just to *speak* the truth but rather to *do*, to *maintain*, to *live* the truth.[10] And that is our task too. Of ourselves, we can change nothing. But when we speak and live the truth, we find that our words and our deeds have the power of God himself: for a verb, as we saw, is a doing word.

But often the power of God has not been noticeably present amongst Christians. As I have pursued my question, and sought to watch and understand the ripples which spread out over the waters of life as I have experienced it and known others to experience it, I have found myself asking, in some anguish, a second question. Truth is the power of God in the universe. But is it the force that pulses through the church? Have we Christians learnt to appropriate that power in our own lives and to make it visible to others? Are we showing them the splash of the pebble and inviting them to allow the healing and liberating power of the ripples to flow through their lives? Is the truth, in all its life-changing power, what we have on offer?

And sadly I conclude that often it is not. We live in a culture which by and large is not receptive to the gospel. But we do not help the gospel, because we ourselves have lost touch with its dynamic power. We live by the truth; but it is a truth which has been stripped of its energy. The gospel burst into the world 2,000 years ago as a word spoken with all the power of the creator God. It changed everything. People embraced it all over the Roman empire and beyond, many facing persecution and death rather than renounce their new, life-changing relationship with God. It is likely that within 50 years of Jesus's death nearly 30 per cent of the world's population had been exposed to the gospel, and by the early fourth century the whole Roman empire was officially Christian.[11] The gospel has been a force for change throughout history and all over the world, wherever and whenever it has been effectively preached and wholeheartedly embraced, both in the lives of individuals and through them of the societies of which they form part. And yet that is not the case, by and large, in the West today. There have been exceptions, but on the whole the last 300 years have been a period of decline, of loss of confidence in the power of the word, and of decreasing ability in the church to proclaim it. We stand, in the church, at the end of a long process of accommodation in which we have unconsciously sought to harmonise the gospel with the assumptions of our culture, a culture which in abandoning the quest for absolute truth has embraced a new set of values – rationalist, materialist, technological, and reductionist.[12] The effect has been that we have gradually turned the gospel from something subversive and life-changing to something tamed, packaged and institutionalised; from something expressed in words of power to something conveyed, if it is conveyed at all, in words of information. The gospel has been squeezed out from under the platform of our lives and become merely a picture on the wall, familiar but essentially unrelated to everyday reality. We must learn again to turn the word into a language, a living language that can speak into the assumptions of our culture just as Jesus spoke into the assumptions of his, and in so doing can do what he promised it would do:

> If you continue in my word, you are truly my disciples; and you will know the truth, and the truth will make you free.
>
> John 8:31–32

I think there is great hope that we can do this. We stand on the threshold of a new millennium. We have hailed it as the gateway to a new era of peace and plenty. Maybe it is; maybe it isn't. But one thing is sure: we are living at a time of cultural change. We are seeing a turning away from the technological and reductionist certainties of the recent past, and the beginnings of a search for a renewed spirituality. That spirituality is often not sought in the church; for the church stands for the old certainties of a reduced truth, certainties of dogma and religious practice and set ways of doing and being. As Christians we have an opportunity: the opportunity to reconnect with the truth, to reassess the way in which we live and proclaim the gospel, and to allow God to burst into the third millennium with the same force with which he burst into the first. But we will do that only if we are prepared to abandon the values and certainties of our culture, to learn to look at it afresh in the same way that Jesus looked at the culture of 2,000 years ago; and then to have the courage to reach out from that new place and proclaim the truth into the lives of the individuals around us.

This is an exciting prospect. We have the opportunity to seize and inspire a new vision of the potential of the gospel in contemporary society. Let's watch the pebble fall, and let's follow the ripples outwards. This isn't going to be a how-to book; my aim is rather to paint a picture of new possibilities, and invite you, the reader, to enter into it; to impart the confidence to undress the gospel from its dull, restricting clothes, and reclothe it in the eye-catching colours of its original garb. Four centuries ago Michelangelo painted the Sistine chapel ceiling. With the common usage of the chapel the protective varnish became discoloured until, although the power of the figures could still be seen, the bright colours of the original were lost. It took the Japanese to restore it, to clean away the grime and return it to a glow of colour so bright that many were horrified by the unfamiliar intrusion of life into what had become reassuringly muted. And so it is with the gospel.

Jesus burst into the world with a power and a dynamism which turned the settled ways of doing and being upside down. Many didn't like it; but its impact could not be denied, and the world was transformed. Then gradually the colours dimmed with usage, and now the Christian faith is familiar, still accepted by many, but given no real place in the way things are. In other parts of the world this is not so; and perhaps just as it took the Japanese to bring Michelangelo back to life, so we should look to Argentina or South Korea, Uganda or China, to see what restoration can look like for the gospel. For we live in exciting times; times of change, times of opportunity. There is, as Shakespeare perceived, "a tide in the affairs of men which, taken at the flood, leads on to fortune; omitted, all the voyage of their life is bound in shallows and in miseries". And, to continue in his words, ". . . on such a full sea are we now afloat, and we must take the current when it serves, or lose our ventures".[13]

If we are to ride this current I think there are two things we must do. Firstly, we must take a close look at the assumptions of our culture in the light of the gospel. The gospel is not a sealed and timeless package, fixed in a set form of words and lived out in a particular way. The gospel is the word of God, spoken before time but spoken also into time, spoken therefore in a particular language and into a particular culture, and yet containing universal truth which can be carried by any language and be understood in any culture. If it is to be successfully appropriated by anyone other than a first-century Jew, it therefore has to be translated – not just verbally, from Aramaic to English or Bemba or Punjabi, but conceptually, so that it speaks to the needs and values of a given people. In order to do this for our generation and our culture, we need first to examine the way in which Jesus spoke the gospel into the cultural context of first-century Palestine, and then to try and look at the assumptions and values of our own society and see how he might have spoken it to us. If the gospel is about truth, it follows that it must be focussed into untruth; and each generation must challenge the untruths amongst which they live with the same blunt force with which Jesus challenged the untruths of his day. And so in this book we will look both at the challenge Jesus mounted to the culture of his time and, drawing on the work of what we refer to as the gospel and culture movement, at the challenge he might have mounted to ours.

It is, however, my conviction that essential though this process is, it is no more than a precondition, a necessary first stage in what we have to do. Jesus spoke words of radical criticism into the culture of his day: but not, I suggest, with the fundamental intention of changing it. His target was not society but the individual, and his critique of the values and practices of his society was directed to that end. His aim was to open the eyes of the individuals and groups with whom he spoke to the shaky foundations on which they had built their lives, and on which their whole society was founded – just as Ruth opened mine with her one simple question about the dubious universality of my late-twentieth-century Western European existentialist philosophy. Jesus criticised the culture in order to get people out of the culture, out of the world of empty words and truthless practices, and into – to use the traditional language – the kingdom of God, the alternative world of spiritual reality, the world of truth. So once we have learned to look with God's eyes at our man-made world, we must learn to speak with God's words into the lives of the people who belong to it. That is the real aim: to let people know the truth, so that the truth can set them free. Then, and then only, can the two worlds begin to fit back together; then only can we talk about what it will mean to live out the gospel in our own particular setting.

Notes

1 *Simple Prayer*, p.48. Full details of the works cited in the notes are given in the bibliography.
2 John 18:37 (RSV). All Bible quotations are from the New Revised Standard Version (NRSV) unless otherwise stated.
3 John 14:6.
4 See Genesis 1:1–2, 3, 6, 9, 11.
5 For a discussion of this, see Leon Morris, *The Gospel According to John*, pp.115–26.
6 "The prophetic task in any age is to perceive the word of God in its contemporary relevance so that it may be proclaimed with prophetic authority as the 'Now' word of God". C Hill, *Prophecy Past and Present*, p.5.
7 See for example Isaiah 55:10–11, where God says through the prophet that the word which goes out from his mouth shall not return to him empty, but shall accomplish that which he purposes.
8 Numbers 11:29; Isaiah 44:1–4; Joel 2:28–29.
9 See Revelation 21:1.
10 Ephesians 4:15. See J Stott, *The Message of Ephesians*, pp.171–72.
11 Statistics given by P Johnstone, *The Church is Bigger Than You Think*, p.68. Christianity was made the official religion of the empire by Constantine in 312 AD.
12 This is a theme developed with particular power by Walter Brueggemann; see especially *Finally Comes the Poet: Daring Speech for Proclamation*. For a recent discussion of our concept of truth, see Os Guinness, *Time for Truth*.
13 Julius Caesar, IV iii 215.

PART ONE:
THE MINISTRY OF JESUS

CHAPTER ONE:

JESUS AND THE CULTURE OF HIS DAY

We live within a particular culture. By that I mean that we are a particular people living in a particular place at a particular time in history, and that together we have developed a particular way of interpreting and handling life as we experience it. To live within a culture is to be human; the least erudite but perhaps one of the most compelling definitions of culture is this: "Culture is everything monkeys don't do".[1] A culture is a shared way of thinking and living, different in England and India and sub-Saharan Africa. It encompasses beliefs, values and practices. It is reflected in our social, political, economic and religious lives as well as in our interpersonal relationships. And it is within the parameters of our culture that we find our own sense of identity. Culture is the framework of meaning within which we manage the complexity and diversity of our lives.

And yet culture excludes as well as includes. To live within a culture is to live within a bubble, a bubble which encloses the manageable within its translucent walls, and fences off the threatening world of naked reality which lies outside. Our culture enables us to live; it offers a pre-ordered, pre-interpreted world which removes the need for questions. And yet sometimes it is only by asking those questions, and allowing ourselves to look beyond the bubble's fragile walls, that we can reconnect with the living God who alone holds the key to the meaning of life.

Jesus was born into a particular culture. It was very different from ours. And yet it had in common with ours, and with all other cultures, the fact that it was built on a set of assumptions. What Jesus did was to overturn those assumptions. Through both his behaviour and his teaching he challenged every norm of the culture into which he had come. Jesus was a revolutionary – not the political revolutionary many people were waiting for, but rather a social and cultural revolutionary who mounted a single-handed but complete challenge to the prevailing worldview of contemporary Judaism. Jesus was profoundly subversive – so subversive that even his own family doubted his sanity at times.[2]

And yet that is not how we normally see him. It is hard to break out of our own assumptions and enter into those of a bygone era. Most of the information we have about Jesus comes from the pages of the New Testament. But the New Testament is written in the language of a culture we don't understand, and it assumes a framework which we do not share. The consequence is that we easily adopt a watered-down Christianity in which Jesus is viewed through our own particular spectacles and made to fit with the values of our culture; those aspects of his life and teaching which conflict with our accepted values are placed firmly on the outside of the bubble. And so the New Testament becomes a kind of religious fairy story which we read with the dull eyes of familiarity, the once-upon-a-time minds of incomprehension; and Jesus himself becomes a Christmas-card figure striding into a legendary world, speaking a mythical language of repentance, baptism, sacrifice and kingdom of heaven which fails completely to connect with our own language of postmodernism, consumerism, and pluralism. In our confusion we rely on tradition to mediate his words; and we almost completely lose touch with the subversive character of the gospel message as he first brought it.

So I think that before we can address the question of how best to appropriate and communicate the gospel in our own world we need to reconnect with what Jesus was doing in his. We need to think our way back into the skin of a bygone age, and try and understand what it must have been like to be a member of that culture and to encounter Jesus. This is not as straightforward a task as it might seem; although great strides forward are being made in archaeology and in the cross-disciplinary studies which enable us to evaluate new findings, it remains the case that there is much we simply do not know, and research has necessarily been characterised by disagreement and speculation. Even the written sources cannot always be taken at face value.[3] But let us try.

Daily life in Palestine at the time of Jesus

Jewish Palestine covered an area of 7,000 square miles, stretching from the Mediterranean coastal plain in the west, over a mountain ridge into the Rift Valley and up again onto a high plateau in the east. In many ways it was a pleasant place to live. This is the Roman historian Josephus, describing the northern province of Galilee, where Jesus was brought up:

> The land is everywhere so rich in soil and pasturage and produces such variety of trees, that even the most indolent are tempted by these facilities to devote themselves to agriculture. In fact, every inch of the soil has been cultivated by the inhabitants . . . The towns are thickly distributed, and even the villages, thanks to the fertility of the soil, are . . . densely populated . . . In short, Galilee . . . is entirely under cultivation and produces crops from one end to the other.[4]

Most people lived by subsistence farming, growing a varied

crop of grain, olives, dates, figs, walnuts, fruit and vegetables, keeping sheep and goats and, for those near the Sea of Galilee, fishing. Home industry included the manufacture of pottery, weaving, leather and stone goods, baskets, ropes and silk. The land was fertile, and most families were able to produce everything they needed themselves.

But the rural idyll was not without its tensions. Immigration meant that pressure on the land was intense, and often the biennial rains would fail and food shortages result. The vast majority of the people paid high rent to distant land-lords as well as taxes and tithes to both the Roman and the Jewish authorities, and were at constant risk of being forced off the land through debt to eke out a precarious existence as beggars, outlaws, day labourers and slaves. Life expectancy was a mere 29 years, lower than anywhere in the world today. And in Galilee as they struggled to survive, they watched the new Roman cities of Sepphoris and Tiberias take shape, financed by their taxes and maintained by the produce of their labours, paid in kind as tributes, tolls, rents and inter-est charges. In Judea the story had long since been the same; Herod the Great had embarked on an ambitious building programme, paid for entirely through peasant taxation. It is estimated that up to 40 per cent of provincial income went as tax of one kind or another; and discontent ran high.[5]

That they should be subject to an occupying power was of course nothing new to the people of Palestine. For centuries they had been governed by a series of foreign empires, even-tually regaining political independence with the Maccabean revolt of the second century BC, but losing it again to the Romans in 63 BC when rival claimants to the throne invited the general Pompey to support them, resulting in a Roman invasion in which 12,000 people died. For the next 60 years Palestine was governed by a series of puppet rulers, last of whom was Herod the Great. On Herod's death in 4 BC the land was divided into three provinces, to be ruled over by his three sons – but not before there had been widespread social and political rebellion, crushed this time by the Roman governor of Syria with the public crucifixion of 2,000 rebels outside Jerusalem. The brutality of one of the sons, Archelaus, led to his deposition in 4 AD, after which Judea came under direct Roman rule. The others, Philip and Herod Antipas, remained in office throughout Jesus' lifetime. A census in 6 AD provoked another rebellion, led by Judas the Galilean and his resistance fighters, who became known as Zealots; and increasing unrest over the following years culminated in a fullscale and disastrous uprising against Roman rule in 66 AD, in the course of which Jerusalem was sacked and the temple destroyed.[6]

It was in the context of all this that Israel sought to maintain her identity as a nation chosen by God. For us there is little conflict between religion and politics. But for Israel there was a continuous interaction between them. Religion had always been both her source of identity and her means of maintaining it under the pressures of foreign rule; and it offered not the private spirituality with which we are familiar, but a total system providing for all aspects of daily living, in much the same way that Islamic law does today. Israel, in fact, regarded herself not as a province of Rome but as a theocratic state. And so there was a constant tension between the religious and secular authorities, each of whom operated their own legal, fiscal and administrative system of government. It was in this tension that Jesus was to die. But meanwhile, the Jews had to find a way of preserving their national identity as the people of God.[7]

This was achieved by what has been dubbed "the politics of holiness".[8] God was holy, Israel was holy, and she was to express her holiness in clinging to God and keeping herself separate from anything that would threaten her identity as his chosen people. In practice this came to mean a rigid adherence to a body of social and religious observances designed to prevent assimilation between the Jewish nation and her Roman masters. A system of polarities grew up, foremost amongst which was the distinction (to do with ritual, not with hygiene) between clean and unclean. Daily life, for the observant, was governed by the endeavour to remain ritually clean. And so strict laws developed covering diet, the cleansing of self and personal effects, the offering of sacrifices, social relationships and even permitted occupation. The concept was not a new one; but as the political tensions deepened, so did the determination to preserve national identity, and a number of renewal movements had grown up with this aim in view, each with their own strategy.

Foremost amongst these were the Pharisees, whose name means "separatists". They were a lay movement of men committed to the preservation of holiness by devotion to all aspects of religious law, which for ease of access they had expanded into a system of 248 commands, 365 prohibitions and 1,521 amendments. They tend to get a bad press today because Jesus treated them so scathingly; but Pharisaism began as a sincere attempt to do all that was humanly possible to live in a way that was pleasing to God. To this end they drew support from the scribes, scholars trained in the law, with whom they are frequently associated in the gospels.[9]

Another group, the Sadducees, shared the Pharisaic emphasis on the law, but focussed on the written law only, to the exclusion of the vast corpus of oral law which had grown up around it. More literal-minded than the Pharisees, they also denied the survival of the soul after death and the existence of non-human spiritual powers. Aristocratic and conservative, they occupied most of the seats on the ruling council of the Sanhedrin.

A third group, the Essenes, pursued their determination to live a pure and holy life by withdrawing from the pressures of society altogether into a pre-monastic community by the Dead Sea; in accordance with the politics of holiness, entrance requirements were strict, excluding those with mental or physical handicaps of any kind as well as women and minors, and the rules of life were stringent.[10]

Finally there were the Zealots. It is not known to what extent they were an organised movement, but they proclaimed that national identity could be preserved only through political means, and from the initial uprising led by Judas the Galilean in 6 AD they pursued a campaign of armed resistance against Roman rule. Their central claim was that the people of God should not pay taxes to Caesar. Many people were to interpret Jesus's teaching in the light of this movement.[11]

For most people, however, the religious life of the nation was centred, as it always had been, on the temple and on the festivals associated with it. Overseen by the priests, the key to the temple was purity. Sacrifices were made, unblemished animals being bought from the temple flocks with temple coinage specially changed for the purpose; persons with skin diseases, or ritually unclean after menstruation, sex or childbirth, were excluded; and only the high priest was allowed into the inmost sanctuary, and then only once a year and with a bell and rope attached to his ankle so that his body could be safely withdrawn should he make a mistake and be struck dead inside. Everyone was expected to pay an annual temple tax, to give a tenth of their produce, and to come to the temple at key moments in their lives to perform the appropriate rituals. The entire male population was required to attend the three major festivals each year, and there were many other minor festivals, all of which were celebrated with a pomp and pageantry scarcely imaginable today.[12]

This then was the framework within which the ordinary people pursued their lives. Within this framework a strong and clearly defined set of social norms prevailed. Society was organised into a rigid hierarchy, and everyone knew their place within it. Upward mobility was frowned upon, hard work respected, and honour and prestige were the main social values. The basic unit of society was the family, and the main vehicle of social interaction was the shared meal. Certain occupations rendered their participants "outcasts", to be excluded from normal interaction with the rest of society, as did the non-payment of tithes and failure to observe the religious norms. Non-ethnic Jews were also regarded as outcasts. Children were the least important members of society, and women lived a home-bound and socially circumscribed life in which they were subject at all times to the will of their fathers or husbands. Social boundaries were rigid, and to our eyes intolerably and outrageously restrictive. And yet perhaps for most people they were protective; the main tension lay not here but in the day to day struggle to feed themselves. And as is often the case, a vibrant popular spirituality had grown up alongside the institutional one, and served to sustain the people in the difficulties of their everyday lives. Astrology and numerology were widely practised, unseen forces believed to affect the whole of life, disease thought to be caused by sin, and miracles known to be performed by itinerant charismatic healers.[13] And, above all, it was known and expected that one day the "Messiah" promised in the holy scriptures would come and save God's chosen people. Whatever that might mean.

Jesus and religion

Into the midst of all this came Joshua, son of Joseph, a carpenter of Nazareth. For 30 years he had excited no more attention than one would expect of a village carpenter. But one day he gave up his job, recruited a small band of followers, and began to travel the land. Within three years he had achieved such fame and notoriety that the religious leaders of the nation found it necessary to demand his execution. Why?

The essential reason is that Jesus stuck a pin into the

bubble. Armed only with words, but speaking with an authority that astonished all who heard him, he mounted a radical and threatening challenge to the existing world order, overturning the assumptions of the culture, inviting his hearers to embrace a new way of thinking and being, and proclaiming the beginning of a new era in human history. "Gospel", or "good news", they called it; news that the confining walls of the bubble had been breached, and that beyond its boundaries lay not the swirling waters of chaos which they so much feared, but a realm of light and life in which they could enter into a personal relationship with God himself. Those whose job it had been to maintain the religious life of the people within the parameters of the bubble could scarcely be expected to embrace the opportunity. And yet that was precisely what Jesus was inviting them to do.

The people of Palestine regarded themselves as the people of God, and their daily lives were governed by a set of religious rules and practices designed to protect them from falling short of God's expectations of them. One of the most noticeable things about Jesus, in his role as bubble-buster, was his complete disregard for these rules and practices. From the very beginning of their history, the Jewish people had observed the sabbath by abstaining from work, and every person knew exactly what that meant in practice, for it had been drawn up in the most minute and literal detail by the rabbis. Jesus and his followers picked and ate ears of wheat on the sabbath, thus contravening the rules on "harvesting"; and Jesus healed a man with a withered hand, thus contravening those on healing. There were similarly strict rules governing ritual hand-washing before meals: Jesus and his followers not only ignored them but made aggressive speeches about it being dirty hearts that needed worrying about, not dirty hands. Fasting was a recognised spiritual discipline; Jesus and his followers were conspicuous for their enjoyment of eating and drinking. Proper burial of the dead was one of the highest duties of surviving relatives, and yet Jesus scornfully rejected a would-be follower who wished to bury his father before joining him. All these things drew forth savage criticism from the Pharisees, and in turn sharp ripostes from Jesus.[14]

Now to us these rules seem very odd. But to Israel they were not. "You shall be holy, for I am holy", God had declared to them centuries earlier.[15] The rules were part of a holiness code, a way of life based on God-given commandments designed to preserve the Jews in their identity as the people of God, but developed in recent years into a politics of holiness which was becoming increasingly oppressive, though rarely challenged. The anger Jesus aroused by these apparently simple actions was not due to the actions themselves, but to the radical undermining of a whole set of values which they carried within them. "Which is the greatest commandment?" a clever lawyer asked him, hoping he would deny the special relationship between the people and God that the politics of holiness aimed to protect. "To love the Lord your God, and your neighbour as yourself", Jesus replied, summarising the historic commandments and failing to fall into the trap; and then adding, ". . . and how is it that David calls the Christ 'Lord', if the Christ is the son of David?" – with the devastating implication that when it comes to the special relationship, it is he who knows more than they.[16]

Jesus was, however, not content to leave it at that. In addition to breaking the rules of the politics of holiness, he mounted a fullscale verbal attack on the beliefs and lifestyles of those most dedicated to upholding it. In a series of blistering assaults on the Pharisees, respected for their dedication to God, he accused them of being like dirty washing up, sparkling clean on the outside, but filthy with greed and self-indulgence on the inside; he compared them to a brood of vipers, to whitewashed tombs beautiful in appearance but full of rotting bones underneath; and to hypocrites tithing herbs but ignoring justice, mercy and faith, and straining gnats to purify their drinking water whilst swallowing camels whole. He denounced them as blind guides keeping people out of heaven, loading their followers with burdens and leading them astray, and said they would find extortioners and prostitutes being let in before them. And finally, in a crescendo of fury, Jesus shouted that they would be sentenced to hell, the blood of the righteous upon their heads.[17] So much for the politics of holiness.

But even that wasn't the limit of it. Jesus broke the rules and insulted the guardians of the rules. But even more profoundly, he challenged the role of the temple. Perhaps the ordinary people had breathed a sigh of relief at the thought of being exonerated from keeping some of the more oppressive rules, incompatible with the realities of the peasant economy as they were. Perhaps they had not been altogether displeased at the slating of the moral Pharisees, with their public displays of prayer, fasting and almsgiving. But not even they could have predicted that anyone in his right mind would consider undermining the role of the temple. Ever since the first one had been built in Jerusalem by Solomon, the temple had stood for everything that was special about Israel. It was the focus of their national life, the place where everything began and ended.[18]

And yet undermine it Jesus did, both directly and indirectly. On one occasion he stormed into the temple, overturning the tables of the moneychangers and the sellers of sacrificial doves and animals, both of whom exercised monopolies and took advantage of the rules disallowing Roman coinage and the sacrifice of "blemished" birds and animals to make fat profits.[19] On another he predicted (correctly) its destruction; an almost sacrilegious thought, horrifying in its audacity, given the vast expense to which Herod had recently gone to rebuild it, and bearing in mind that the entire economy of the city depended upon it.[20]

But the real challenge Jesus mounted to the temple was more profound even than that. The temple was the place where the people were able, through the proper intermediaries, to meet with God; and the primary purpose of that meeting was to seek his forgiveness for their sins. It had been so for centuries, and however unsatisfactory the details, the temple's role was unquestioned. Yet question it Jesus did. A paralysed man was brought by his friends to a meeting in Jesus's home. "Take heart, son, your sins are forgiven", said Jesus, healing him as proof of his authority, and failing to send him to the temple to make the appropriate offerings. On another occasion he made the incredible announcement that the many sins of a prostitute were forgiven – just because he said so. On another he seems to have drawn a specific analogy between the temple and his own body, foretelling that it would be knocked down and raised up again in three days. "Something greater than the temple is here", he said on yet another, in case they weren't getting the point. In all these ways Jesus was effectively taking to himself the role of the temple as the intermediary between man and God, and declaring it, and its many priests and retainers, redundant. Jesus was claiming to be and do exactly what the temple was and did.[21]

This carried enormous implications, for in redefining the appropriate relations between man and God, Jesus was effectively redefining their concept of God, and thus of reality itself. Every culture, including our own, rests on a view of reality which it knows, consciously or unconsciously, as its religion.[22] The Greeks and Romans had populated their world with fickle and unpredictable gods, indifferent or hostile to humanity, mostly preoccupied with their own affairs, and convenient as scapegoats for human failings and misfortunes. The Jews, on the other hand, believed in a God who was the sole creator of the universe and everything in it, loving Father of his chosen people, but absolute in justice and holiness, and therefore separated from a sinful humanity by a great gulf which could be crossed only by careful observance of the appropriate procedures. God was to be feared. God was judge. This was why they needed a temple, and priests, and sacrifices.[23]

But Jesus appeared to want to do away with all these things. To do so would make sense only if in abolishing the temple and the structures which supported it he was also abolishing the concept of God, and therefore of reality itself, which made it necessary. It would make sense only if somehow the gulf between God and man could be bridged, only if God could be seen no longer as judge but somehow as friend. Man couldn't do it, for he was too far removed from the perfect holiness of God. Only God could do it.[24]

And so we have arrived at the central claim Jesus made. To this intellectually sophisticated and profoundly religious culture Joshua the carpenter made the announcement that he was God. "Before Abraham was, I am", he said, using the forbidden phrase for the divinity. "Who do you say that I am?" he asked the disciples later. "You are the Messiah, the Son of the living God", Peter replied. "Blessed are you", came the response. Why then had God sent his Son? "So that everyone who believes in him may not perish but may have eternal life", he said to Nicodemus. And what of the temple, which was supposed to achieve just that? "God desires mercy, not sacrifice", he said bluntly to the Pharisees.[25] Time and again he claimed to be one with God, to have the authority of God, and to be the means by which all who wished to could enter into a new and personal relationship with God. Reality had been redefined, a whole worldview had been cast off, and a new way of doing things was on offer. Christians would call it grace. But the claim was so countercultural, so offensive to the religious authorities, guardians of the old order, that Jesus was accused of blasphemy, of making himself equal with

God, and brought before the Roman authorities with a demand for the death sentence.

Jesus and politics

It was Roman policy to allow its occupied territories as much jurisdiction over their own affairs as was compatible with social and political stability. This meant that whereas law and order was ultimately maintained by the Roman army, many of the functions of government were effectively entrusted to the puppet rulers and, in the province of Judea where Archelaus had had to be replaced by a Roman governor, to the Sanhedrin, a council of elders made up of chief priests and representatives of the lay nobility (many of whom were Sadducees), and scribes (some of whom were Pharisees). Thus it was that much of the legal, administrative and judicial authority in the region was exercised by the religious leaders.[26]

However, the Romans did place limits on their powers. In particular, they were not allowed to pass a death sentence on any citizen without the authorisation of the Roman governor. So when Jesus was found guilty of blasphemy by the Sanhedrin, an offence punishable by death under Jewish but not Roman law, he had to be brought before Pilate under a political charge for which he could be given the death sentence. The charge was to be sedition: "We found this man perverting our nation, forbidding us to pay taxes to the emperor, and saying that he himself is the Messiah, a king . . . He stirs up the people by teaching throughout all Judea, from Galilee where he began even to this place".[27] Pilate clearly couldn't see much evidence of supposed kingship in Jesus, nor could Herod Antipas to whom he sent him, as a Galilean. But he did fear unrest, and unrest there definitely was; so he had him crucified, under the Latin inscription *INRI* – "Jesus of Nazareth, King of the Jews". Since then there has been much debate concerning Jesus' political agenda. Was Jesus a political revolutionary as well as a religious one; and should we therefore be looking for a political edge to our faith? Or was that just the charge with which they knew they had to frame him?

To understand this we need to go back to Jesus himself. These are the words with which he began his ministry:

> The Spirit of the Lord is upon me, because he has anointed me to bring good news to the poor. He has sent me to proclaim release to the captives and recovery of sight to the blind, to let the oppressed go free, to proclaim the year of the Lord's favour . . . Today this scripture has been fulfilled in your hearing.
>
> Luke 4:18–21

They were surprising words. Surprising to the local people present at the Nazareth synagogue where he spoke them, because this was the familiar figure of Joshua, son of Joseph, who had grown up amongst them, and the claim seemed peculiarly inappropriate. Surprising also to the rabbis who presided over the meeting, because these were the words of the prophet Isaiah, long understood within the messianic tradition as part of God's promise of intervention in the ailing affairs of the Jewish people, and scarcely to be expected in the figure of this untrained artisan. And finally, surprising in the exclusivist statements with which Jesus followed them, stating baldly that the year of the Lord's favour would not see that favour bestowed on all – and not, perhaps, on those present. Surprise turned rapidly to fury, and Joshua the carpenter was driven from the synagogue.

Surprising though they may have been, Jesus' words were spoken into a context of long expectation. For centuries Israel had been dominated by foreign powers, and the Hebrew scriptures had foretold the coming of a Saviour or "Messiah", one who would restore her fortunes, lead her out of the social and political enthralment and relative alienation from God into which she had fallen, and restore her as a sovereign people.[28] The task of John the Baptist was to announce the imminent arrival of this Messiah, and so it was appropriate that Jesus should begin his ministry by declaring from the scriptures that he himself was the one. It was a claim he often repeated. To a Samaritan woman who expressed the view that he was the Messiah, who is called the Christ, he replied, "I am he". To some Jews who begged him, "If you are the Messiah, tell us plainly", he answered, "I have told you, and you do not believe". When the high priest Caiaphas asked him whether he was the Messiah, the Son of the Blessed One, he said simply, "I am". And on many other occasions he claimed to have come in fulfilment of the scriptural prophecies concerning the Messiah.[29]

What then was the Messiah, or Saviour, expected to do? What, to be precise, was he going to save them *from*? This was not a simple question, for the concept of salvation encompassed a related cluster of ideas, political, social and religious; but dominant among them was that of kingship. They were expecting a king. And this is precisely the framework within which Jesus' ministry was often understood by the people of his time. Matthew states that Jesus was born king of the Jews, and that this sufficiently alarmed Herod, the actual holder of that title, to cause him to order the immediate execution of every baby boy in the region. Jesus himself makes frequent references to a new kingdom and, at the climax of his ministry, rides into Jerusalem in what has become known as the "triumphal entry" in recognition of its relationship to the established tradition of victorious kings entering a city on horseback to the accompaniment of a celebrating crowd. And finally, Jesus is brought before Pilate as the King of the Jews, and crucifixion is demanded on the grounds that in making himself a king he is setting himself against Caesar.[30]

And yet this never quite seemed to fit what Jesus was doing. Firstly, he himself sometimes behaved in peculiar ways which weren't really compatible with the idea that he had come as a political saviour, walking away when the crowd wished to take him by force and make him king, and remarking that he was not leading a rebellion when soldiers came to arrest him in Jerusalem.[31] Secondly, the charge was not taken seriously by the Romans, who took delight in taunting him, dressing him in the purple robe of kingship, giving him a crown of thorns, and then crucifying him under the plainly sardonic inscription *INRI* whilst letting his followers go free. And thirdly, and apparently conclusively, there he died, defeated by the system like many would-be revolutionaries before and since, and leaving his followers consumed with disappointment and facing the failure of their dreams.[32] So Jesus' language of kingship has to be evaluated in non-obvious ways if we are to make sense of it.

Jesus came from Galilee, and Galilee had long been known as a hotbed of revolutionaries. With a different political history from Judea, and a hilly terrain conducive to secret hideouts, Galilee had seen strong resistance to Roman rule, most recently in the rebellion led by Judas son of Hezekiah. One of Jesus' disciples was known as Simon the Zealot, and it is clear from the demands of some of the others that for a long time they assumed that Jesus' kingdom was to be an earthly one, centred in Jerusalem, with themselves as members of his ruling council. Yet Jesus was at pains to explain that although "kingdom" was the best term for what he had in mind, it would be a kingdom of a kind hitherto quite unknown. It would be a kingdom in which servanthood would be the model for leadership, in which armed resistance was out of the question, and in which the most important people would be the least important people – children, the marginalised, the destitute. It would be one in which wealth brought no status, and the established authority structures were an irrelevance which might as well be obeyed as not obeyed. His decree that it is appropriate to pay Caesar's taxes with Caesar's coins must have come as a profound disappointment to the Zealots, whose politics were rooted in the conviction that to do so showed disloyalty to God, their true ruler; and his statement to Peter that although he was under no obligation to do so, it was as well to pay the temple tax must have come as a surprise to the disciples, given his attitude to the temple itself. But Jesus' kingship was, as he eventually explained to Pilate, not a kingship of this world. "So you *are* a king?" asked Pilate, confused. "You say so", came the reply. And then this: "For this I was born, and for this I came into the world, to testify to the truth". His kingdom would turn out to be, as we shall see when we look more closely at his teaching in Chapter 3, something quite mind-blowing in its scope, something not subject to the vagaries of local politics, something which would make Pilate, Herod and even Augustus Caesar himself seem little more than passing blips on the horizon of time. No, Jesus was not a Zealot.[33]

And yet many commentators agree that both Herod and Pilate would have done well to take the threat to the established political order more seriously than they did. Jesus was clearly not interested in seizing power, but it was nonetheless the case that he did not envisage the new kingdom he talked about as simply a nice thought for the hereafter, but rather as present reality, and that it was profoundly subversive of the values and assumptions on which the existing order was founded. Jesus was not concerned with the overthrow of a regime; but had his followers lived as he did, with the values he had, it would nevertheless have radically altered the social and political order of the empire.[34] Jesus, the Word of God, was speaking a new language, undermining the assumptions of the old one, calling people to abandon the values which had enslaved them, and urging them to enter into a new kingdom, a kingdom not of this world, a kingdom that is mysteriously both already present and yet to come, a kingdom in which they would discover the reality of God's forgiveness and mercy. That is why he told Pilate he had come to testify to the truth, to burst the bubble which safely enclosed the known and manageable. Jesus spoke as a prophet – and the prophetic purpose, as Walter Brueggemann remarks, is much more radical than social change.[35]

Jesus and the created world

Now this was all very well, but perhaps it was a bit academic. Jesus would burst aggressively into the temple and speak words of biting criticism to the Pharisees, and later he would stand fearless and uncooperative before the governing representative of the most powerful ruler in history. But the majority of the people to whom he spoke were neither rabbis nor Romans; they were peasants or, in our terms, ordinary people. And the major concern of the ordinary people, as for the majority of the world's population today, was not religion or politics, but the daily struggle against hunger and disease. To be sure, that struggle was made harder by virtue of the rules of the rabbis and the taxes of the Romans, and many had given up and fallen into non-observance or destitution. But most struggled on. And for them the question must have been this: Did this remote God who apparently required so much appeasement, and who had allowed them to fall into servitude to a harsh occupying power – did this God care? And how was he going to show it? Or, to put it in the words of a man in Gillingham: "That's all very well, but what about my ulcer?".[36]

The unforgettable thing about Jesus, Son of God, is that these were the people he wanted to be with and for whom he cared. Far from being the unperturbed individual whom we often imagine, free from the passions which we know to reign within us, Jesus entered fully into the emotional lives of those around him. Reduced to tears at the grief of his bereaved friends Mary and Martha, often filled with compassion at the plight of the sick, willing to pray for hours with each one individually, and overcome with the cold dread of anguish at the thought of his own death and the manner of it, Jesus marched straight into the middle of the peasant world as one who belonged to it in every way.[37] And a hard world it was, a world of tight-knit community, and yet a world also of hunger, fear and grinding poverty, where children played between the beggars crouched in the village dirt, where soldiers were never far away, where adults worked from dawn to dusk in the relentless attempt to provide for their families, and where disease and death were daily intrusions into Josephus' would-be country idyll of sunlit green pastures and heavily laden fruit trees.

Once he had given up his job, faced a time of spiritual testing, and chosen some disciples, we learn that Jesus began to travel around Galilee, teaching in the synagogues, proclaiming the good news of the kingdom, and curing every disease and every sickness among the people. And this, as we well know, was the hallmark of his ministry. Jesus performed miracles. He healed people. The results were spectacular; according to Matthew his fame spread by word of mouth throughout Syria, and everyone brought the sick – those suffering from disease, pain, demon possession, epilepsy, paralysis – to him. Apparently he healed them all, and crowds followed him from Galilee, the Decapolis, Jerusalem, Judea and beyond the Jordan. They didn't come by bus; they walked, many of them for days over arid and mountainous territory they can never have crossed before, and carrying the sick with them. Luke, Mark and John tell the same story: wherever Jesus went, he was followed by crowds who had seen him healing people. On one occasion so many pressed around him that he had to get into a boat to escape being crushed; sometimes it all got too much, and he swore those whom he had healed to secrecy.[38]

Some of the people he healed stand out amongst the others. There was, for example, the man born blind. Jesus spat on the ground and put some of the mud on the man's eyes, telling him to go and wash it off. He did; and returned sighted. Unfortunately this was a sabbath day, and the furious Pharisees insisted on taking an immediate case history. In front of the neighbours and those who had seen the man begging, they summoned his parents for confirmation that he had indeed been blind since birth, and subjected the man himself to a hostile cross-examination. The man stuck to the facts: all he knew was that he hadn't been able to see, and now he could. Eventually he exclaimed in frustration: "Here is an astonishing thing! You do not know where he comes from, and yet he opened my eyes . . . Never since the world began has it been heard that anyone opened the eyes of a person born blind. If this man were not from God, he could do nothing."[39]

Then there was the woman who had been bleeding for twelve years. She'd spent all her money on doctors and got no better; and of course she also had to endure exclusion as ritually unclean. Jesus was on his way to see the dying daughter of one of the synagogue elders, so she pushed her way through the crowd and touched his cloak – superstitious, it would seem. But Mark says that immediately her bleeding stopped, and she felt in her body that she was free of her disease. Jesus, however, turned in the throng of people around him and asked who had touched his clothes. The short and obvious answer, as the disciples pointed out, was that everyone was touching his clothes. But he had felt power going out of him. The woman comes forward, and he tells her she is healed of her disease.[40]

A third story is even more remarkable. Jesus was in Capernaum when a Roman centurion came to ask him to heal his paralysed and anguished servant. Jesus agreed to accompany him to his house. But the centurion said that wouldn't be necessary. He has heard about Jesus' ability to heal with only a word, and a word is all he requires. He is, after all, used to giving commands and having them carried out, and he is confident that it will be enough for Jesus to speak for the deed to be done. Jesus, amazed at his faith, speaks the word which is both word and deed, and the servant is later found to have been healed at that precise moment.[41]

What then was going on? For, remembering that this is not a fairy-tale world of bygone legend, but the real world of a peasant people in a particular place and at a particular time in history, we must assume that something, rather than nothing, was happening. Jesus was not crucified because he was a good listener.

The facts seem to have been that Jesus's relationship with the created world was of an unprecedented kind. His healings were spectacular, and cannot easily be explained away. He himself accounted for them like this:

> Do you not believe that I am in the Father and the Father is in me? The words that I say to you I do not speak on my own; but the Father who dwells in me does his works. Believe me that I am in the Father and the Father is in me; but if you do not, then believe me because of the works themselves.
>
> John 14:10–11

So Jesus attributes the power of his works and his words to God himself, God who at the beginning of time spoke the words that created the world, and God who now through him seems to be creating a new world. And it wasn't just the healings; Jesus's authority over the created world appears to have extended to its inanimate as well as to its animate components. He calmed a storm at sea with a simple word, causing the astonished disciples to ask, "Who is this, that he commands even wind and water, and they obey him?" He turned water into wine at a wedding. He cursed a fig tree and caused it to wither. He knew precisely where Peter should put down his nets after a night of fruitless fishing for a full catch. Most famously, he walked three to four kilometres over the Sea of Galilee, having missed the boat in which the disciples had set sail, terrifying them when he appeared, and mystifying those left on the shore who next morning could not find him, although no boats were gone other than the one they'd seen the disciples leave in.[42]

So Jesus stood outside the laws of nature; and he claimed that his followers would be empowered to do the same. This was not expected. It caused as much consternation then as it would now. It was deeply surprising and, to some, profoundly threatening. And it is presented, by those who wrote it down in the generation or two which followed, not as myth, as a symbolic recasting of mere concepts, but as history. We aren't meant to read about Jesus walking on the Sea of Galilee as we read about George and the dragon, or about all those who touched the fringe of his garment and were made well as we read about Midas turning all he touched to gold. We may wish to dismiss it as fraud, although there is sound evidence for not doing so; but the claim of the text is that it was actually happening.[43] It is a claim consistent with the idea that this man was, as John later wrote of him, the eternal word, the word through whom the universe was made; the word who spoke the laws which govern it, and who had no hesitation when occasion demanded in speaking them again, but according to a different formula.

The man in Gillingham was healed of his ulcer.

Jesus and the spiritual world

He is the image of the invisible God, the firstborn of all creation; for in him all things in heaven and on earth were created, things visible and invisible, whether thrones or dominions or rulers or powers – all things have been created through him and for him.

Colossians 1:15–16

In the beginning God spoke, and he spoke a world, a world that was both material and spiritual, visible and invisible. The material world is the world we see and in which we live. But it is intertwined with an invisible world, a world where God is the ultimate reality, a world which lies outside the confines of time and place. Two thousand years ago God spoke again, sending the Word whom he had spoken from the spiritual into the material world, to shatter the parameters which humankind had sought to build round the unfenceable chaos of the invisible, and to reconnect us with the reality of life above and beyond the material. "My kingdom is not of this world," said Jesus. And it was inconceivable that he would confine his earthly speaking to the visible world, the world of the seen. He spoke also into the invisible world, the most real world because eternal, the world into which the new kingdom was extending its light.[44] He spoke into it when he redefined the relationship between the people and God. He spoke into it when he announced that their sins were forgiven, thus healing them not only of physical disease but of spiritual disease as well. He spoke into it with words of truth, overcoming the power of the lies on which they had come to base their lives, and declaring that the truth would set them free.[45]

Now for us in the twenty-first-century West this is an almost inaccessible concept. Officially, we do not believe in the existence of an unseen world, a spiritual world of strange powers and forces. Our world is the world we see, the world we can investigate and manipulate. It is the world of science and technology, of materialism and consumerism. It is a world in which we understand things by taking them apart, and our philosophy is based on our relationship with the material. And yet there are signs that our certainties are cracking. Postmodern science increasingly recognises that the fixed laws of modernism no longer provide an adequate explanation for the phenomena we observe, and an increasingly vibrant popular spirituality pays tribute to a whole host of occult and New Age powers and practices which take us far from the see-it world of the rationalist framework within which we are supposedly still straining to find our meaning.[46]

But perhaps it was not so very different for the first-century Jew. The Sadducees firmly rejected any possibility that there might be an eternal, non-visible world, whilst the Pharisees were primarily absorbed with the endeavour to define and keep the law in this one. The scriptures were mostly centred on the relationship between man and God in the here and now, although with a strong historical perspective; only latterly had an otherworld dimension crept into the words of the prophets, and the glimmerings of a belief in a life which would continue after death and into eternity. But, as with our own culture, when an essentially material world-view is upheld by the intellectuals, an undercurrent of protest tends to swirl amongst the people. So a whole host of popular works had been composed purporting to describe the world of the hereafter, a world populated by angels and demons, a world of compartmentalised heavens and gradated degrees of hell. Herod consulted wise men or "magi" when Jesus was born, and Pilate's wife was spoken to in a dream. Belief in palmistry, astrology, numerology and clairvoyance was normal, physical and mental illness were attributed to the influence of demonic forces, and miracles were part of the accepted order of things.[47]

This was the world into which Jesus came, and the fury of the religious leaders was due in no small measure to the fact that he appeared to endorse it. They saw themselves as the people of God, labouring to keep his commandments and hopeful of gaining his approval; Jesus opened a window and showed them a spiritual dimension to life of which they had no understanding, and for which they had very little room in their philosophy. He showed them a world in which a spiritual battle was raging, unseen but devastating in its effects; a world in which evil spirits seek to ensnare people, to bring them into captivity and draw them away from God. He demonstrated the existence of this world by delivering people from the influence of these evil spirits and by warning of the need for vigilance against them; and he told of a future where the world would meet destruction, where those who were with God would enjoy their relationship with him for ever in a kingdom prepared especially for them, and where those who were not with him would remain separated from him for ever.[48] Life, Jesus declared, is as much about the unseen as about the seen. Of course this did not make him popular with those who wished to make it about the seen, and to exercise their own control over that seen world. It was, however, consistent with the idea that this man was, as Paul later wrote, the image of the invisible God, in whom all things were created, in heaven and on earth, visible and invisible, whether thrones or dominions or principalities or authorities, and through whom one day all these things would be reconciled. Jesus, the truth, showed the world that its boundaries were not in the safe and predictable places it had thought they were; one world had become two, and reality was more real, and power more powerful, in the spiritual realm than in the material.

What then did this irruption of Jesus into the invisible world look like in practice? From the beginning of his ministry, it seems that Jesus' very presence in a synagogue would provoke evil spirits to cry out from within the person they were afflicting; and that they, in contrast to the startled people present, had no difficulty in recognising Jesus as "the Holy One of God" and "the Son of God". And it continued to be the case that wherever he went, light shone into darkness, the spirits of darkness were forced to show themselves in a way and on a scale which had never previously been known, and the "occult" – which just means "hidden" – was exposed. Once exposed, it was summarily despatched. As crowds gathered, Jesus freed many from evil spirits. He dismissed a demon from a boy who went into convulsions the moment he saw him, and sent seven out from Mary Magdalene. Most famously, he removed a legion of demons from a notorious madman; they addressed him as "Jesus, Son of the Most High God", fled into a herd of pigs and threw themselves – and the pigs – down a steep bank and into the Sea of Galilee, filling the local farmers with dismay and causing them to request Jesus' immediate departure. And it is noticeable that not even his opponents suggested that there was any other explanation for what was happening than that Jesus was bursting into the spiritual realm with an authority that was quite outside human experience; although they did suggest that this authority derived not from God but from the devil himself.[49]

And yet this is obviously not how Jesus was doing it. He did it, in fact, by simple command; by the power of the Word itself. Time and time again Jesus told the demons to go, and they went. On one occasion he even dismissed a demon from a Syro-Phoenician woman's daughter at a distance, just as he had healed the centurion's servant at a distance.[50] And he gave this same authority to his astonished disciples.

Jesus was the Word of God. He spoke light into darkness, and truth into untruth. And it was in the light that the powers of darkness were exposed, in the visible world that the battles of the invisible one were played out, and into the realm of lies that the power of the truth brought freedom. For if truth is a force, the ultimate force of reality itself, so is untruth a force, a dark dynamism which brings destruction to people's lives, a counter-reality which has held sway since Jesus first saw Satan fall like lightning from heaven.[51]

It is in this counter-reality that we find the explanation for human sin and disaster, for the bondage we see around us as we survey the wreckage of individual and global human affairs. And it was in this counter-reality that Jesus came to proclaim his identity as image of the invisible God, maker of heaven and earth, and incarnation of the truth. He came to bear witness to "a reality so real that it alone has gravity and weight – the only 'really real reality' in the universe". And yet they crucified him. For, as T S Eliot remarked, humankind cannot bear very much reality.[52] Bubbles are, on the whole, safer.

Conclusion

Jesus, then, was profoundly at odds with the world into which he came. Far from being the meek and humble stereotype with a star-spangled, angel-attended and really rather magical stable birth whom we are taught to revere in school, Jesus was a difficult and uncooperative revolutionary who so threatened the established order of the day that there seemed to be no option but to have him executed. By turn irascible, compassionate, exhausted and stubbornly silent, Jesus was not the "fitting household pet for pale curates and pious old ladies" that Dorothy Sayers once declared we had made him.[53] He was abrasive, rude and cuttingly clever when confronted with the religious leaders of the day; he regarded the existing political order as an irrelevance; he paid astonishingly scant attention to the binding nature of the laws of the physical universe; and wherever he went he brought an explosion of light into darkness and a release of people from the unseen powers that had bound them. Perhaps the biggest shock of all was that he had the unnerving audacity to claim a unique intimacy with God, his Father, in a world where even to mention the holy name of God was forbidden. This was the passion and the heartbeat that lay at the very core of his ministry, a godly passion with which they were familiar from the pages of scripture, but which was blasphemous in a mere man. And it was this perhaps more than anything else that grated on the senses of the professional theologians whose faith had increasingly taken the form of endless debates about sacral trivialities. Jesus, Son of God, didn't fit into the disinfected, orderly environment of their buttoned-up doctrine; and that is why they wanted him crucified. Jesus, in the words of a modern rabbi, imperilled Jewish civilisation; "To adopt his teaching means no less than to remove oneself from the whole sphere of ordered national and human existence."[54]

So Jesus clashed with his culture. And yet he showed no apparent desire to reform it. Rather, he ignored it – and nowhere more effectively and purposefully than in his dealings with individuals, as we shall see in the next chapter. The outcry was not because he *did*, but because he *spoke*. If Marx, apparently a timid man, could change the course of history merely by sitting in the British Library and writing, how much more could Jesus, the incarnate Word of God, change it by speaking the truth, and speaking it with all the power which first made the universe itself? And he spoke it into a culture which did not underestimate its power. He spoke a new kingdom, and so he had to be crucified. His death was a triumph for the establishment – the Word of God had been rubbed out, and life could get back to normal.[55]

But it didn't work out that way. For we know how the story ended. Just as Jesus had shown that he was indeed the way, the truth and the life by raising people from the dead, so too he himself rose from the dead.[56] And in his resurrection we find God's certification of the alternative world, the kingdom that stands outside time and outside culture. The resurrection cannot be explained out of the previously existing reality.[57] The resurrection is the beginning of a new world. This is the world we are being invited to enter, now as then.

And we will enter it not as a society, not even as a church, but first and foremost as individuals.

Notes

1 A more precise definition is offered by Richard Niebuhr: "Culture is the artificial, secondary environment which man superimposes on the natural. It comprises language, habits, ideas, beliefs, customs, social organization, inherited artifacts, technical processes, and values", *Christ and Culture*, p.46.

2 Mk 3:21–22.

3 Major written sources are the works of philosopher Philo of Alexandria, Jewish historian Flavius Josephus (known for his tendency to exaggerate when it suited his own agenda), and Roman historians Tacitus and Suetonius, alongside the scriptures themselves and the Jewish Mishnah, a summary of the oral tradition drawn up in 200 AD.

4 *The Jewish War*, III 42–43.

5 See F F Bruce, "Render to Caesar", in E Bammel and C F D Moule (eds), *Jesus and the Politics of his Day*. For an analysis of the economic situation of the time, see R A Horsley, *Archaeology, History and Society in Galilee*, especially ch.3, "Trade or tribute: the political economy of Roman Galilee". For social structures, see J D Crossan, *Jesus: A Revolutionary Biography*, pp.23–26; and M Borg, *Jesus: A New Vision*, ch.5, "The social world of Jesus". For the peasant economy, see J Riches, *Jesus and the Transformation of Judaism*, pp.80–82.

6 For an analysis of the political situation of the time, see R J Cassidy, *Jesus, Politics and Society*; E Bammel and C F D Moule (eds), *Jesus and the Politics of his Day*; and, cast in fictional form, G Theissen, *The Shadow of the Galilean*. An excellent introduction to all these issues is to

be found in C J Roetzel, *The World that Shaped the New Testament*.

7 J D M Derrett, *Jesus's Audience*, ch.2, "The economic and political scene".

8 M J Borg, *Jesus: a New Vision*, p.86.

9 For the Pharisees, see P Yancey, *The Jesus I Never Knew*, p.130; for all these groups, see R J Cassidy, *Jesus, Politics and Society*, pp.121–25.

10 For the Sadducees, see C J Roetzel, *The World that Shaped the New Testament*, pp.29–32. For the rules of the Essenes, see A T Dale, *Portrait of Jesus*, p.55: "No madman, or lunatic, or simpleton, or fool, no blind man, or maimed, or lame, or deaf man, and no minor shall enter the community."

11 For the Zealots, see G Theissen, *The Shadow of the Galilean*, p.66.

12 The atmosphere of the temple is evoked by A Punton, *The World Jesus Knew*, ch.11, and J Bowker (ed.), *The Complete Bible Handbook*, pp.286–87. See also P Yancey, *The Jesus I Never Knew*, p.264.

13 For popular spirituality, see J D M Derrett, *Jesus's Audience*, pp.114–28. The best-known healers were Honi the Circle-Drawer and Hanina ben Dosa; see M J Borg, *Jesus: A New Vision*, p.31.

14 For harvesting and healing, see Matthew 12:1–14. Healing was permitted on the sabbath only when the condition was life-threatening. See W Hendriksen, *The Gospel of Matthew*, p.511. Other refs: Matthew 15:1–12 (hands and hearts); Matthew 9:14–15, Matthew 11:19 (eating and drinking); Matthew 8:21–22 (burial).

15 Leviticus 11:45.

16 Matthew 22:41–46.

17 For Jesus' diatribes against the Pharisees, see Matthew chs.12, 15, 21 and especially 23.

18 For the significance of the temple, see C J Roetzel, *The*

World that Shaped the New Testament, pp.55–64.

19 Matthew 21:12–13; and see M J Borg, *Jesus: A New Vision*, p.175. On the impact of this act, see the remark of B Meyer: "To disrupt temple operations and to do so at the head of a crowd of messianic-minded pilgrims come to Jerusalem for Passover, was to perform an explosive act", *The Aims of Jesus*, p.170.

20 For the destruction of the temple, see Matthew 24:1–2. For the economic activity associated with the temple, see G Theissen, *The Shadow of the Galilean*, p.169. Cassidy estimates that 18,000 lambs were reared and sacrificed in the temple each year; *Jesus, Politics and Society*, App.II.

21 Matthew 9:2–8 (paralysed man); Luke 7:36–50 (prostitute); John 2:19–22 (destruction of temple); Matthew 12:6 (Jesus as temple). For the identification of Jesus with the temple, see G Theissen, *The Shadow of the Galilean*, p.145, and T Wright, *The Original Jesus*, p.84. In John's description of the heavenly kingdom in Revelation he stresses that he did not see a temple in the city, because the Lord God Almighty and the Lamb are its temple (21:22).

22 See T S Eliot: "the culture of a people [is the] incarnation of its religion", "Notes towards the definition of culture" in *Selected Prose*, p.299.

23 For the difference between the classical outlook ("shame culture") and the Judaeo-Christian outlook ("guilt culture"), see E R Dodds, *Pagan and Christian in an Age of Anxiety*.

24 In *The Responsible Self*, H R Niebuhr draws the distinction between reality seen as hostile, indifferent, requiring appeasement, and friend; see M J Borg, *Jesus: A New Vision*, p.102–03.

25 John 8:58 (I am); Matthew 16:16 (the Messiah); John 3:16 (the Son); Matthew 12:7 (mercy not sacrifice).

26 See R J Cassidy, *Jesus, Politics and Society*, App. I.

27 Luke 23:1–5.

28 For the history of the concept of a messiah, see the article "Messiah" by E Jenni in *The Interpreter's Dictionary of the Bible III*, ed. G A Buttrick, pp.360–65.

29 Mark 14:62 (I am). For other claims, see for example Matthew 13:13–17; 26:31; Luke 4:18–21; 24:27; 18:31–34.

30 For the expectation of a king, see C J Roetzel, *The World that Shaped the New Testament*, p.21; and D Wenham, *The Parables of Jesus*, p. 22–23. For the messiah as king, see for example Zechariah 14:9: "The Lord will be king over the whole earth." Carroll summarises thus: "In essence messiah . . . would be a great warrior of Davidic proportions who would free the Jewish people from the yoke of foreign domination (i.e. Rome), restore power to the temple-city of Jerusalem, and make the nations subservient to Israel", R P Carroll, *Wolf in the Sheepfold*, p.106. See also D R Catchpole, "The 'triumphal' entry", in E Bammel and C F D Moule (eds), *Jesus and the Politics of his Day*; and Zechariah 9:9. For the accusation of kingship, see John 19:22.

31 See John 6:15 and Luke 22:52 (NIV).

32 See the comment of Cleopas, Luke 24:18–22.

33 There has been much debate about Jesus' relationship with the Zealots. For the history, see the various contributions in *Jesus and the Politics of his Day*, ed: E Bammel and C F D Moule. For the disciples' expectations of secular power, see Matthew 18:1; 20:20–21; Mark 10:35–45. For the reversal of values in the kingdom, see Mark 10:42–43, Matthew 26:51–54, and especially the Sermon on the Mount (Matthew 5). For the temple tax, see Matthew 22:15–22; Matthew 17:24–26. For the conversation with Pilate, see John 18:33–38.

34 See R J Cassidy, *Jesus, Politics and Society*, ch.6, "Was Jesus dangerous to the Roman empire?"

35 See W Brueggemann, *The Prophetic Imagination*, p.28.

36 Words spoken at an evangelistic meeting led by John Collins.

37 John 11:35; Luke 4:40; Matthew 26:37–46.

38 See Matthew 4:23–25 (crowds); Mark 1:28–34, Luke 6:17–19, John 6:2 (healings); Mark 3:9, Matthew 9:27–31 (escape by boat, injunction to silence).

39 John 9.

40 Mark 5:25–34.

41 Matthew 8:5–13.

42 Luke 8:22–25 (storm); John 2:1–11 (wine); Matthew 21:18–22 (fig tree); Luke 5:1–7 (fishing); John 6:16–25 (walking on water).

43 For the reliability of the New Testament texts, see F F Bruce, *The New Testament Documents*, and N Anderson, *Jesus Christ: The Witness of History*. Summary in A Morgan, *What Happens When We Die*, ch.6.

44 See the opening quote from John Dalrymple; and 2 Corinthians 4:18. "We fix our eyes not on what is seen, but on what is unseen. For what is seen is temporary, but what is unseen is eternal."

45 John 8:31–32.

46 "There has grown up a widespread feeling, especially among those who study fundamental physics, that there is more to the world than meets the eye", John Polkinghorne, *Science and Creation*, p.15. See also Paul Davies, *God and the New Physics*.

47 For the beginnings of a belief in an afterlife, see Isaiah 25:8, 26:19; Daniel 12:2–3, Ezekiel 26. For the beliefs of the Sadduccees and Pharisees, see Josephus, *The Jewish War*, II 154–58, VII 343–44. The most important of the popular texts describing the other world are the *Book of Enoch, Apocalypse of Esdras, Apocalypse of Baruch* and *Testament of Abraham*. For Herod and Pilate's wife, see Matthew 2:1–8 and Matthew 27:19. For the popular

belief in an occult world, see J D M Derrett, *Jesus's Audience*, pp.114–28, and C J Roetzel, *The World that Shaped the New Testament*, pp.95–107. Evidence for popular occultic activity is to be found in Acts 13:6–12, 19:18–20, and Galatians 5:20.

48 Peter and Paul develop the theme of the spiritual battle in their letters to the churches; see 1 Peter 5:8, "Like a roaring lion your adversary the devil prowls around, looking for someone to devour", and Ephesians 6:10–17, and especially verse 12: "Our struggle is not against enemies of blood and flesh, but against the rulers, against the authorities, against the cosmic powers of this present darkness, against the spiritual forces of evil in the heavenly places." For Jesus' account of a Last Judgement, see Matthew 25:31–46.

49 See Luke 4:34, 41 (evil spirits recognise Jesus); Mark 1–3 (casting out of evil spirits); Mark 9:14–28 (boy); Luke 8:2 (Mary) and 26–39 (pigs); Luke 11:14–23 (accusation of working with the devil).

50 Mark 7:24–30.

51 Luke 10:17–20.

52 Quotations from Os Guinness, "Mission in the face of modernity", in M Eden and D F Wells (eds): *The Gospel in the Modern World*, p.88, and T S Eliot: "Burnt Norton", in *Collected Poems* 1909–62, p.190.

53 Quoted by P Yancey, *The Jesus I Never Knew*, p.21.

54 Rabbi Klausner, quoted by R Niebuhr, *Christ and Culture*, p.18; and by E Bammel, *Jesus and the Politics of his Day*, p.44.

55 "The death of Jesus certified both temple religion and the rightness of Roman legal justice for, after all, as everyone knew, cruel death was a sure sign of God's own displeasure. The cross branded Jesus Christ an impostor, a dealer in false dreams, indeed both a heretic and a socially dangerous insurrectionist." D Buttrick, *Preaching the*

New and the Now, p.58.

56 The people Jesus restored to life were the daughter of Jairus (Matthew 9), the son of the widow of Nain (Luke 7) and his friend Lazarus (John 11).

57 W Brueggemann, *The Prophetic Imagination*, p.107.

CHAPTER TWO:

JESUS AND THE INDIVIDUAL

Come to him, a living stone, though rejected by mortals yet chosen and precious in God's sight, and like living stones, let yourselves be built into a spiritual house, to be a holy priesthood, to offer spiritual sacrifices acceptable to God through Jesus Christ.

1 Peter 2:4–5

For us the concept of the individual is a familiar one. In 1776 the American Declaration of Independence asserted the right of every person to life, liberty and the pursuit of happiness; and thus, perhaps, began the modern age. Two hundred years later we find ourselves living in a society of free individuals, each setting out on the journey of life with rights in one hand, hopes in the other, only to find that rights do not guarantee happiness, and that hopes are all too often swept away in the dry desert wind which swirls round those who would find their way to the destination of their dreams. We have higher aspirations and greater choices than at any time in human history; and yet more of our young people kill themselves than in any previous society.[1] Individualism has brought fragmentation, and the dream of personal fulfilment all too often becomes a reality of insecurity, isolation and competition.

In first-century Palestine the opposite was true. In Jewish society what mattered was not the individual, but the collectivity of which he or she formed part. Each individual was a member of the people of God, identified by genealogical history and named according to tradition.[2] Each was bound to the others by a set of norms which gave him or her a specific hierarchical and lateral location in society. Most lived and died in the place of their birth, following the occupation of their ancestors and raising their children to respect the traditions of the elders. To be sure, the gradual encroachment of the Roman world into daily life offered new possibilities and choices to some; but the Jewish people had protected themselves against such encroachments for centuries, and the national consciousness remained one of obedience to the laws and traditions which had faithfully preserved their identity as the people of God.[3] The result was a cohesive society with a clear sense of collective identity; but the reality for the individual was, as we shall see, often crushingly restrictive and exclusive.

A greater contrast between two societies can scarcely be imagined. And yet they have one thing in common. Throughout human history there has been a tension between the individual and the society of which he or she forms part. Always present, the tension becomes acute at particular times; and we live, as did they, at such a time. The tension can be expressed by borrowing a common biblical metaphor. Let us imagine a wall. It is an old wall, with bricks evenly worn, and mortar which has settled over the years to sit comfortably between them. England is built of such walls, and many of them have been there for hundreds of years, silent but stable witnesses to the quiet living of life as it has always been lived, mellowed by the passage of time and stamped by the changing shadows of the events that pass them by. There are periods in every society when life is like this. But there are also times when the winds of change lash fiercely against the wall, and harsh conditions cause it to wear unevenly. In one place, weathered bricks flake, crumble and fall when the mortar which holds them in place does not match their decline but remains strong and inflexible. In another, weak and loosened mortar places in jeopardy a wall whose bricks preserve the sharp angles and smooth surfaces they had when first placed one upon another. In both places the survival of the wall is in doubt.

In this image we find a picture of our two societies. The people of first-century Palestine were the weathered bricks of conflict and poverty. Fragile, resentful, looking for new ways to cohere together in the face of harsh conditions, they were nonetheless bound by the rigid form of the unyielding mortar offered by their social and religious traditions. Crumbled, needing repair, squashed as they may have been, many still stood as part of the wall; but increasingly they felt trapped, chafed by the sharp edges of the firm structures which held them in place. Many more, cracked by frost, had fallen from the wall, leaving gaping holes framed by the mortar which remained. We, by contrast, have almost lost the mortar which once bound us together. In our individualistic society, bricks of different shapes and sizes sit between mortar which has been so loosened that it has become little more than rubble. Whole sections of the wall are falling down, old bricks lie scattered in the nettles, and piles of new ones, red and purple and yellow, lie abandoned in field corners, unable to find a place in the disintegrating wall. Different causes bring the same effect: tension between individual and society, brick and wall, is running high; and something, sooner or later, is likely to give.

Social norms in first-century Palestine

So life in Jewish Palestine was governed by a strong theoretical framework made up of social and religious norms and values. Based on the law and on the interpretation of the law, and intertwined with the peculiar consciousness which makes up the character of a people, these values can scarcely be separated one from another. Rigid though the resultant structures were, honoured as much in the breach as in the observance though by necessity they had often become, nonetheless they held sway. Caught between the pressures of Roman rule and the impossible requirements of the law as it was taught, the people were increasingly at odds with the system.

The criteria for acceptability in this society were as straightforward as they were, for the majority, unattainable. The common assumption was that you had to be Jewish. You had to be male. And you had to express your faith in God by your obedience and good works in accordance with the law.[4] Persons of mixed race (this included the inhabitants of whole regions), women (who were not instructed in the law), and the non-observant (those for whom the daily struggle for survival left no time for good works and hours of prayer) were not thought pleasing to God. These were the bricks, acceptable and unacceptable, which made up the wall of human society, and they were cemented together by a web of values which found expression in set forms of religious observance and a clear code of social intercourse. Let us look at them in a little more detail.

The rejected and damaged bricks

Prominent amongst the rejected bricks of Palestinian society were the Samaritans. Lying between Judea and Galilee, Samaria had been populated since the eighth century BC by a people of mixed Jewish and Assyrian descent. After a period of polytheism they had returned to the worship of God, but instead of joining the faithful in Jerusalem they had built a rival temple on their own Mount Gerizim. Furthermore, they acknowledged only the first five books of the scriptures. To the Jews they were thus stained by both racial and religious impurity, and the most devout took the long way round when travelling between Judea and Galilee so as to avoid entering Samaria.[5]

If the Samaritans were to be excluded from social and religious intercourse with the people of God, so of course were the other nationalities whose members lived in and around Palestine. Roman rule was regarded as an especial threat to the people's religious and political identity, and the introduction of land tax, pagan images and violations of the temple had all caused violent riots in recent times. Jesus himself initially refused to speak to a Syro-Phoenician woman whom he met in the cosmopolitan city of Tyre, on the grounds that she was not Jewish, and the bustling new imperial cities of Sepphoris and Tiberias with their Greek-speaking cultures are scarcely mentioned by the gospel writers.[6]

Other members of Palestinian society were treated as outcasts by virtue not of their race but of their occupation. Foremost amongst these were the infamous tax collectors. In order to avoid the expense of a state-sponsored and empire-wide inland revenue, the Romans had put tax collection out for private tender, accepting the lowest bid without enquiring too closely as to the methods adopted. In order to make a profit, tax collectors therefore routinely overcharged and cheated the taxpayers, arousing loathing on the double grounds of treachery and dishonesty.[7] Immorality of other kinds incurred the same disapproval: for women the main ground of social exclusion was prostitution. These people were "sinners", not in the shameful Victorian sense of living in the gutter beyond the pale of middle-class respectability, but in the much more profound sense that they had violated the law of God and thus endangered the standing of a whole people – wealthy and influential though they may have been. Their tithes were unacceptable, because unacceptably gained, and their company shunned by the "righteous" – those who did seek to live according to the law of God.[8]

A particularly battered part of the wall was made up of the non-observant, some for reasons of social or political rebellion, but most simply because of poverty. Found mostly amongst the so-called "people of the land", these were the struggling peasants who at best lived at subsistence level, at worst below it, and who were in no position to observe the economically demanding niceties of the law. Unable to tithe, compelled to work seven days a week, and ignorant of the scriptures, they were regarded by the rabbis as little better than non-Jews. Below them in the social hierarchy lay the 10 per cent of the population who had failed altogether to make ends meet: day labourers, beggars, robbers, outlaws, and slaves. These were the ordinary people of rural Palestine; but measured by the standards of the law they too were failures.[9]

Alongside these groups were the unclean, those who temporarily or permanently were regarded as unfit to approach the holy God. Uncleanness was contagious, and the law laid down elaborate rules for separating that which was clean, and perfect, and holy, from that which was not. These laws extended even to the stones of a house: stones flaked with mildew were to be removed and cast on the city dump, and the inhabitants of the house were required to purify themselves before rejoining the worshipping community. Similarly, persons with the flaking skin of leprous diseases (the word used is the same) were to be regarded as unclean, as were women and men with normal or abnormal bodily emissions, and after childbirth or contact with a dead body.[10] All these were excluded from the community of the faithful in its relationship to God for the duration of their affliction, as were those affected by unclean spirits, mental illness and physical disability.

And then there were women. "Blessed art thou, O Lord, who has not made me a woman", began the synagogue prayers. Women sat in a separate, screened-off section in synagogues, and in the temple were admitted only as far as the Court of the Gentiles and the Court of Women. They were not counted in quora (witness the feeding of the 4,000, where the 4,000 are men, "besides women and children"). They could be divorced at will, although they themselves had no right of divorce, and were automatically disinherited from a husband or father's will where there was a male heir. Social intercourse with women was frowned on; the rabbis ruled that "one should not talk with a woman on the street, not even with his own wife, and certainly not with someone else's wife"; and that "it is forbidden to give a woman any greeting". Inferior in status, women were temptingly dangerous to the righteous male; the Pharisees had developed the practice of lowering their heads to avoid looking at passing women, and the most scrupulous were known as "bleeding Pharisees" due to the frequency with which they collided with walls and other obstacles. Perhaps in practice it was not always as bad as that; realism suggests that half of what went on in this rural society was in fact determined by women.[11] But nonetheless the social and religious status of women was not high. Women were not wanted in the wall.

Finally, there were children. Children were nobodies, non-persons in the Mediterranean world of paternal power, slaughtered by kings and exposed to die throughout the empire if supernumerary to requirements. Children were potential bricks; but not actual ones.[12]

The response of Jesus

Into this world strode Jesus. And one of the things that is immediately striking as we read through the gospel stories is the apparent disregard he showed for these time-honoured norms: the distinctions between righteous and sinners, clean and unclean, pillars of society and outcasts seemed to pass him by completely, for he associated freely and persistently with persons from every single one of the categories mentioned above.

Take, for example, his attitude to Samaritans and other foreign nationals. He saw no reason not to travel through Samaria, and on at least one occasion cleansed a Samaritan leper. He had a long conversation with a Samaritan woman whom he met at a well, and he had no hesitation in healing the servant of a Roman centurion. Far from avoiding tax collectors, he seemed to seek them out, calling one, Matthew, to be his disciple, initiating a conversation with another, Zacchaeus, and accepting the hospitality of both – in flagrant and immediately controversial defiance of the rule which forbade table fellowship between the clean and the unclean, righteous and sinners. He did it again in the house of Simon the leper.[13] On another occasion he allowed a sinful woman to pour ointment over his feet, and on yet another gently released a woman caught in adultery from the vengeful condemnation of an angry crowd. He included a member of the resistance movement amongst his disciples, and promised a place in paradise to a condemned criminal. He did not hesitate to touch a leper in order to heal him, and made no complaint when a woman with uterine bleeding fingered his cloak. He had compassion on the spiritually unclean, releasing one man from the non-Jewish side of the Sea of Galilee from a legion of demons, and receiving a woman from whom he had banished seven demons as his friend and disciple. He accepted the financial support of women and welcomed them amongst those who travelled with him – an arrangement which according to the mores of the time would have been regarded as little short of scandalous.[14] He condemned the readiness of men to divorce their wives. And not only did he encounter women, healing, delivering, befriending and teaching them; his sayings and parables are drawn equally from the male and female worlds, and still stand today in gender-symmetrical pairs – astonishing in an androcentric and patri-archal culture where women were officially invisible. It was to a woman – and an adulterous Samaritan woman at that –

that he first chose to reveal his identity as the Messiah; from a woman that he accepted the anointing of kingship in preparation for his burial; and to a woman that he first appeared after his resurrection. Finally, Jesus not only allowed children to be brought to him but insisted that they should be taken as role models of faith.[15]

In all these encounters Jesus showed scant regard for the socio-religious conventions of his culture. He simply seemed to have no sense of what was socially appropriate. He insisted on treating everyone he met as an individual of equal value, pouring scorn on the hysterical objections from the religious establishment that he was breaking the God-given laws of the Jewish people by speaking to the wrong individuals (women, children, outcasts, foreigners, sinners) in the wrong places (at parties, in ordinary people's houses) at the wrong times (on the sabbath) and in the wrong way (without the involvement of the priests). Instead of being made unclean through contact with lepers and the sick, he made them clean; instead of being distanced from God by the company of sinners, he drew them into relationship with him.[16] If Jesus was a "brickie" sent to mend the wall, he seemed to be setting about it in a very peculiar way.

Manifesto for a new society?

So what exactly did Jesus mean by all this? He had appeared to offer political revolution and the promise of a new kingdom, and yet he died in disgrace. He had appeared to offer religious reform, and yet he said he had come not to abolish the law but to fulfil it.[17] And now we see that he appeared to offer social reform, and to model a new society in which the rejected would be accepted and outcasts included. Many over the centuries have risen to the challenge, seeking to model their own faith and to express the mission of the church according to this vision. One of our foremost New Testament scholars writes that Jesus brought a social programme which sought to rebuild a society upwards from its grass roots, on principles of religious and economic egalitarianism, and that he "did not invite a political revolution, but envisaged a social one at the imagination's most dangerous depths". And yet still we hear the cry of Walter Brueggemann that the prophetic purpose is more radical than social change; and we wonder whether perhaps things are not quite as simple as they would appear.[18]

What are we to make, for example, of the fact that Jesus combined an undoubted readiness to speak to the poor and the destitute with an apparently equal willingness to talk to the rich and the respectable, offering them the same opportunities and challenges that he offered to the marginalised? He invited a rich young ruler to leave his wealth and become his disciple, promising him eternal life if he would do so. When Jairus, ruler of the synagogue and holder of the highest civic office in the community, asked him to come to his house and heal his daughter, Jesus did not hesitate; and this time he laid no conditions and asked nothing in return. Amongst his followers he included Joanna, the wife of Chuza, royal steward to Herod Antipas, accepting her financial support along with that of Mary of Magdalene and another woman named Susanna; we do not know how or where he met these well-to-do women, but it surely wasn't in the homes of the fishermen of Capernaum.[19] Nor did he shun the religious leaders. He accepted the hospitality of Simon the Pharisee, and attended a sabbath meal at the house of another "leader of the Pharisees". He explained the gospel to Nicodemus, also a Pharisee and a member of the ruling council of the Sanhedrin; Nicodemus later defended him to his fellow Pharisees and with Joseph of Arimathea took responsibility for the preparation for burial of Jesus' body. Joseph, another rich and powerful member of the Sanhedrin, had also become a disciple of Jesus, and it was he who asked Pilate for custody of the body and provided the tomb. Jesus, it seemed, had friends in high places as well as amongst the common people. Even the agents of imperial Rome had received his care – in Capernaum both the centurion and a royal official had received healing for their dependants.[20] It would seem that he was not so much overturning the social hierarchy as ignoring it altogether.

And then what are we to make of the fact that if he did have a social manifesto, it seemed to be a singularly confusing one? He assaulted the social norms in many ways; but always there was an ambiguity to his actions. He presented himself as a rabbi, but without the proper training and with no respect for the other rabbis. He appeared as the leader of a revolutionary band of Galileans, but failed to produce the expected manifesto of armed resistance. He lived as a beggar without home or family, and yet somehow his eyes lacked the proper cringe, and his voice the proper whine. He clearly wished to make a statement, a subversive statement which would undermine the shared values of a whole society. But what was it? In his conversations with individuals Jesus said nothing which could be formulated into any kind of coherent social ethic; his statements about the kingdom and how to enter it were shot through with surprises and contradictions.

Take family values. This is a man who is remembered for his insistence that his followers should love one another; a man who three times raised the dead out of compassion for their grieving relatives; and a man who, dying, entrusted his presumably widowed mother to the care of his closest disciple.[21] And yet before we cast him too readily as Minister for the Family, we would do well to reflect that this is also a man who said he had come to bring not peace between the generations, but a sword; who urged his followers to hate father and mother, wife and children and brothers and sisters; who refused to let a would-be disciple say goodbye to his nearest and dearest; and who would not go to his mother and brothers who were looking for him, defining his own family as those who do the will of God, irrespective of the ties of kinship.[22]

Or consider his attitude to money. This is the man who told a rich young ruler to give away all his wealth, and who taught that the kingdom of God would belong to the poor. This is the man who insisted on the importance of giving food, drink and clothing to the destitute; who warned his disciples to lay up treasure in heaven rather than on earth; and who said that if a beggar asks you for your coat, you should give him your shirt as well. This is the man, indeed, who inspired Mother Teresa. And yet it wasn't quite as simple as that. The rich young ruler was told to give away all he had; but Zacchaeus, the dishonest tax collector, was apparently permitted to keep half his considerable capital. The disciples were taught to donate their money to the poor; and yet immediately afterwards a woman who had spent a vast sum on a jar of costly ointment was praised for pouring it over Jesus' head as an act of homage. Mary, Joanna and Susanna used their wealth to support Jesus and the other disciples, and Joseph of Arimathea provided Jesus' tomb out of his means; there is no suggestion that Jesus had asked them to give away their money.[23] So whatever it was that he was advocating, it clearly wasn't the restructuring of society on the basis of the simple redistribution of wealth to the poor. We shall look in more detail at Jesus' teaching in the next chapter; but it is already clear that if his aim was to present a new manifesto for social and cultural change, it was a very odd one indeed. It would seem that it was not, after all, socialism that was being invented here.

The ministry of Jesus: into the culture but for the individual

We saw in Chapter 1 that Jesus spoke words of subversion into his culture, challenging its every norm, assaulting the social and religious framework which held it together, and speaking everywhere he went of a new world and a new reality which would bring freedom to the poor, the imprisoned, the blind and the oppressed.[24] To describe this new order he used the political word "kingdom"; and yet he sought neither to overthrow the existing puppet king Herod and his Roman masters, nor to offer any kind of coherent alternative social manifesto. He didn't come with handouts for the poor, he didn't break down the doors of the prisons or demand improvements in working conditions, and he didn't chain himself to the railings of political protest. He was not found standing on soapboxes in Tiberias and Sepphoris, or demanding audiences in the palaces of Jerusalem and Caesarea, or seeking election to the council of the Sanhedrin.[25] Rather he was found speaking to individuals whenever and wherever he encountered them – in their homes, on their sickbeds, at their tables; in the street, in the fields, in the synagogue; out on the lake as they fished, and by the well as they drew water.

Of what then did he speak to these individuals? The astonishing answer is that to each one he spoke the truth. And that for each one, the truth was different, because it penetrated differently into the untruth by which they were bound. I suggest that Jesus assaulted the norms of his culture not as an end in itself, but in order to reach out to individuals within the culture, to shake the faulty foundations on which they were building their lives, and to issue a new challenge for thinking and living. He ministered *into* the culture, but *for* the individual. He came to replace a chafing framework of untruth with a liberating one of truth. To the culture, and to its representatives, he offered only criticism. But to the individual he offered an invitation. And so he set up a choice between two competing worlds. The first was the familiar world of a culture built on the clearly drawn lines, boundaries, hierarchies and discriminations which spring readily from the human spirit; a world which is structured and ordered, but ultimately not able to meet the needs of people's souls. The second was a spiritual world, a world of a different reality, a world which the Creator himself had decided it was time to offer to his chosen people, and through them to others, as the ultimate fulfilment of the law-bound existence they had struggled increasingly painfully to maintain.

And so to the individuals whom he met on his travels, Jesus didn't talk about religion or society at all. He talked about relationship, the relationship between them and God. For different people that meant different things, as it does today; but always it meant change. Above all it meant repentance: "thinking again", turning away from old thought patterns, beliefs and habits in order to turn to God and live in a new way. For some that meant a particular course of action: abandoning wealth and status, abandoning dishonesty and immorality, stepping outside the bonds of family. For others it meant receiving healing, or deliverance from evil spirits. But always it meant an encounter with the truth, a listening to the word, and a response of faith. It meant receiving the truth which sets people free, the light which comes into darkness, and the life which is to be found in relationship with God, the source of life itself. So Jesus' focus was on the individual, but the individual within a precise set of circumstances.

Jesus' encounters with individuals

For every individual there is an issue. That is so today as it was then. We each live our life, consciously or unconsciously, within a certain set of parameters and according to a certain set of values. We shelter, to return to the image of Chapter 1, inside a bubble whose shining walls are the assumptions which enclose the familiar, fence out the uncomfortable, and offer us a strategy for making the unmanageable manageable. These were the assumptions which Jesus challenged in his encounters with individuals, and for each one the challenge was slightly different. Many of these encounters are recorded only briefly in the gospels, and of those most are described in terms of the effect that they had on those who witnessed them rather than of the issues raised for the individuals concerned. But often it seems that for each person Jesus exposed a different barrier to a full relationship with God. The rich young ruler desperately wanted to enter into such a relationship. He claimed to have kept all the commandments, and asked what else he should do in order to inherit eternal life. Jesus did not dispute his claim. But he did ask him to sell his possessions and give the money to the poor – finding the hidden obstacle at once, for this the man could not bring himself to do; his security, his identity and his position at the pinnacle of Jewish society lay in his wealth. On another occasion a scribe wished to follow Jesus, who warned him that this meant leaving his home and his professional standing in a society which accorded the highest respect to those who had spent years studying the law. It was a status he was unable to give up, for it stood at the heart of his inherited value system. Another disciple wished to be true to his responsibility to bury his father before setting off, only to be told to let the dead bury their own dead. A fourth wished merely to bid his family goodbye, a request which met with scorn. And yet these were the chief values of the everyday world in which they lived. For each of these people, the thing to be relinquished and the value to be overturned was different; and none of them was willing to do it.[26]

And yet others were. The twelve themselves had all accepted Jesus' invitation to step beyond the fixed boundaries of the known, to ignore the screaming commonsense voices which must surely have threatened them with ruined livelihoods and destitute dependants, and to look beyond the limits of the bubble. They accepted; and to them, and those who would be like them, Jesus promised eternal life and a place in the kingdom of heaven.[27]

These brief examples all come from the gospels of Matthew, Mark and Luke. But it is John's book which is the gospel of the individual *par excellence*. The others record many of the same incidents described by John, but always in compressed form; their spotlight falls on Jesus himself, for their purpose is to set down the main elements of his life and teaching for the benefit of the early church. But John, writing slightly later than the other gospel authors, can perhaps afford to take much of that for granted. And so he introduces us to Jesus' interlocutors as real people, and for the first time the encounters come alive as they seek to get their minds round what it means, for them, that they are talking with the incarnate Word of God.

One of Jesus' earliest encounters in the gospel of John is that with Nicodemus, a leading Pharisee, respected teacher, and member of the Sanhedrin. Nicodemus' position as a man of God is assured; and yet on meeting Jesus, it seems that for the first time this teacher of Israel finds himself asking questions to which he has no answer. Unwilling to risk his reputation, he comes to this ragged and recently violent rabbi under cover of darkness, and in answer to his crescendo of fumbling questions Jesus offers the first explanation of the gospel. Jesus speaks to Nicodemus, a man of the intellect, a man of the law, and explains that he must be born again of the Spirit, saying that in doing so he will step out of the darkness in which he has come, and in which for all his learning he lives, and come into the light of God. John is of course echoing the words with which he began his gospel: "What has come into being in him was life, and the life was the light of all people. The light shines in the darkness, and the darkness did not overcome it." Nicodemus, startled to find his impeccable Jewish faith inadequate, is left to ponder Jesus' words and, as we learn later, to respond to them.[28]

The next major encounter described by John is one

between Jesus and a Samaritan woman.[29] No greater contrast could be imagined than that between the respectable Nicodemus and this person who suffers from the descending disadvantages of being Samaritan, being woman, and being irregular in her relationships with the opposite sex. Jesus meets her at a well. He is thirsty; she has a bucket. He asks for a drink. Unlike Nicodemus, this woman has nothing to lose, and so she teases him – male Jews don't ask female Samaritans for water, particularly when they have no bucket. But before she knows where she is, he has revealed that she has had five men and is now on her sixth, and he has offered her living water, the water of life, in exchange for the still water of the well from which she draws in her misguided attempts to get her needs met. Her social assumptions shattered and her status unmasked, she raises the major bone of contention between Samaritans and Jews – should God be worshipped on Mount Gerizim, as held by the Samaritans, or in Jerusalem, as maintained by the Jews? But here too Jesus fails to conform to her expectations, remarking that location is irrelevant, for true worship is worship in spirit and in truth, not in temples or on mountains; and that he is the Messiah come to show these things. Confronted not just with the truth about herself, but with the Truth himself, and overwhelmed with the enormity of the fact that the Messiah had consented to reveal himself to her, a social and religious misfit, she drops the bucket and runs to tell her neighbours.

In the following chapter John introduces us to a rather unattractive individual, a man who for 38 years has been lying paralysed by the healing waters of the pool of Bethesda in Jerusalem. "Do you *want* to be made well?" Jesus asks him – not an idle question, for often it is easier to stay ill and dependent on others than to be made well and have to take responsibility for oneself. Lacking the energy to reply to the question, the man listlessly complains that he can't be made well, because he has no one to put him into the water at the crucial moments when it stirs, and someone else always gets there first. Jesus tells him to stand, pick up his mat and walk. Used to dependence, he does, wasting no words on thanks, and merely shrugging, when he receives the inevitable challenge from some Pharisees (it is once again the sabbath), that he is doing what he was told. And yet even now it seems that he still hasn't really grasped the issue; his healing, like his illness, had merely happened to him. Jesus finds him later in the temple and warns him to change his attitude before something worse befalls him.[30]

The same message is given to a woman brought triumphantly to Jesus by the scribes and Pharisees because she has been found committing adultery, an undeniable infringement of the law for which the prescribed punishment is death.[31] Here Jesus manages to trounce the expectations of both parties. Refusing to go against the law, he nonetheless prevents its enforcement by inviting anyone who has not sinned to throw the first stone at the woman. A motionless silence falls over the gathering. Then, as the implications of Jesus' words gradually sink in, the men slope off, one by one, in inverse order of seniority, the rug pulled from under their feet. Left alone with the speechless woman, Jesus merely says he does not condemn her either, and tells her to go, and not to do it again. Still in shock, she goes. She has a lot to think about; for what, exactly, *are* the rules by which this man lives?

Jesus' next client is a blind beggar, a spunky individual whose condition provides a context for another sabbath encounter between Jesus and the Pharisees.[32] Jesus puts mud on the man's eyes and tells him to go and wash in a particular pool; he goes, without question, and returns, sighted. He then tells his story with the straightforward simplicity of one explaining the obvious to a child; except that those to whom he explains it are the offended Pharisees. Undeterred, he insists that he couldn't see, that now he can see, that Jesus made him see, and that Jesus must be from God; and expresses incredulity at their attempts to find some other way of looking at it. His simple faith in the obvious contrasts sharply with the acerbic reaction of the Pharisees, whose rigid assumptions about the relationship between a people and its God are under assault. The Pharisees know that religion is about righteousness, that righteousness is about obedience to the law, and that the law states that the sabbath is about abstaining from work in order to observe the appropriate rituals in the synagogue – and not about powerful and socially disruptive encounters with God. Powerful encounters with God were not dreamt of within their religious philosophy – as perhaps often they are not in ours. Furious that they cannot prevent Jesus from apparently producing these unseemly encounters with God, and unassailable in their conviction that this man's blindness comes from sin, they expel him from the synagogue for his obduracy. He nonetheless tells Jesus he believes, and worships him, showing that he, with his simple faith, is quite open to receiving a truth which they, with their carefully controlled way of relating to God, can only reject. And so who is it here, John asks, who is blind?

Finally, let us go back to a story told by Luke.[33] A lawyer stands up and asks Jesus what he has to do to receive eternal life. Jesus gives an apparently conventional answer, referring him to the law and asking him what it says there. The lawyer happily recites the law, which says that you shall love the Lord your God with all your heart, and with all your soul, and with all your strength, and with all your mind; and your neighbour as yourself. Quite right, says Jesus, that's all you need to do. But the lawyer, hoping to catch Jesus out, asks who his neighbour is. This is an ingenuous question, for the lawyers had defined very precisely who your neighbour was, according to the criteria we have already looked at. Your neighbour was another righteous Jew. Jesus answers, as so often, not by discussing the law but by telling a story. A robber lay in the road. A priest and a Levite walked past, leaving him wounded and unassisted. A Samaritan, however, bound his wounds and took him to an inn. "Who was his neighbour?" Jesus asks. The lawyer, defeated, can only mutter that it was "the one who showed mercy on him" – the Samaritan, an unrighteous non-Jew, one with whom it was forbidden to associate. "Go and do likewise", said Jesus. Another set of assumptions overturned, and another set of carefully positioned parameters redefined.

Conclusion

So why was Jesus breaking all the rules and rearranging the parameters of these people's lives, be they rich or poor, good or bad, self-important or perfectly ordinary? It is clear that he wasn't exactly upholding the values and norms of the society into which he had been born; he wasn't trying to repair or restructure the wall, to go back to the image with which we started. The only explanation is that Jesus was trying to build something quite new.

Far from affirming the validity of the human society into which he was born, and far from bringing medicine to soothe its ills, Jesus had come to announce its demise. He came to proclaim the inauguration of a new kingdom, a kingdom not temporal but eternal, and not earthly but heavenly; a kingdom ruled not by the powers and principalities of a fallen order, but by the word of God, the word which creates and destroys and creates again. He came to offer entry into this new world; but entry would be possible only for those who were prepared to leave the false practices and promises of the earthly order behind, and to build their lives on a new foundation. And in order for them to do that, it had to be made abundantly clear in what ways those practices and promises were false. That was what was going on in the encounters we have looked at. Jesus was not a Levitical priest, concerned to remove the mildewed stones from the social building, throw them on the rubbish dump and replace them with the fresh-hewn ones of people who met the three criteria of being Jewish, male and righteous in the eyes of the law. His task was far more radical than that. His task was to be himself the foundation stone of an entirely new building, a building standing solidly on the soil of this world, but with its upper storeys reaching into the skies of eternity. It is an image first found in a psalm, repeated by the prophets, adopted by Jesus, and picked up by his disciple Peter and quoted at the beginning of this chapter.[34] Jesus regarded each of the people he spoke to as a potentially living stone, rejected by the exclusive norms of a hierarchical society, but precious in God's sight, and chosen to be part of a beautiful new building, a building whose bricks will be as unpredictable and as varied as the individuals who chose to respond to his invitation to live their lives a different way.

So I propose that Jesus took on the culture not as an end in itself, but primarily in order to reach out to the individual within it; that this is a task which must be repeated in every generation; and that herein lies the key to the continuing power of the gospel in subsequent ages. It is certain that had Jesus conformed to the culture-specific expectations of what salvation would consist of, we would have no gospel today, for our culture is different, and our social and religious structures bear little relationship to those of first-century Israel. But he didn't. He offered something new. With a blistering critique of the society of his day he brought truth, exposing the values and practices that were keeping individuals from God. It is the truth that sets people free: and so it was truth that he poured all over the rigid social and religious parameters of the culture into which he was born, truth which he offered as a new foundation for the lives of those he met, and untruth which he exposed as being the cause of their separation from God. As he spoke to individuals, he exploded, as Ruth did for me, the faulty foundations on which they were building their lives, and issued a challenge for a new way of thinking and living. And so it was that he reconnected people with God, offering them freedom of a kind they had never before experienced.

Now if this is the right way of looking at what Jesus was doing in his criticism of the culture and his interaction with the individual, it has profound implications for us. For we too are enmeshed in a culture, although of a very different kind; and we too must learn to look critically at the assumptions of that culture as they impinge on individuals, in order to speak truth into falsehood and bring light into darkness. That will be the subject of Part 3 of this book; but meanwhile let us complete our discussion of the life of Jesus by asking ourselves how his teaching supported his critique of the culture and his ministry to the individual.

Notes

1 Suicide is now reported to be the third greatest cause of death among men aged 25 to 34 in the UK. *The Week*, 20 January 2001, p.17.

2 Matthew and Luke both give the genealogical history of Jesus. John the Baptist was named in defiance of the tradition which would have called him Zechariah, after his father (Luke 1:59–63). Apparently no fewer than 25% of women in Galilee at the time of Jesus were named Mary – an enormous contrast with our practice of choosing names from any field of life or even of our own invention. See Tal Ilan, "In the footsteps of Jesus", in I R Kitzberger, *Transformative Encounters*.

3 J D Crossan remarks that the supreme value for the twentieth-century American imagination is individualism, whereas for the first-century Mediterranean it was

groupism, based on kinship and gender. See his *Jesus: A Revolutionary Biography*, ch.3.

4 See M Goldsmith, *Jesus and his Relationships*, p.79.

5 The early history of Samaria is given in 2 Kings 17:24–41. See also Leon Morris, *The Gospel According to John*, pp.255–56 and 267–78. For the importance of racial and religious purity, see Deuteronomy 14:2. Distrust and on occasion violence was characteristic of the relations between Jews and Samaritans.

6 For tax and the use of pagan images on Roman coinage, see F F Bruce, "Render to Caesar", in E Bammel and C F D Moule (eds), *Jesus and the Politics of his Day*. Riots followed Pilate's introduction of Roman standards into Jerusalem at dead of night, and use of money from the temple treasury to finance an aqueduct; see C J Roetzel, *The World that Shaped the New Testament*, ch.1, "The political setting". The Roman occupation had itself begun with Pompey's unforgiveable violation of the Holy of Holies in the temple in 63 BC. For the Syro-Phoenician woman, see Mark 7:24–26; for Jesus' refusal to speak to her, see Matthew 15:23–24. Sepphoris is not mentioned in the New Testament; Tiberias only when John mentions "some boats from Tiberias" (John 6:23) and calls the lake of Galilee the "Sea of Tiberias" in 6:1 and 21:1.

7 For tax collectors, see S Blanch, *Encounters with Jesus*, p.38–39, and H Marsh, *The Rebel King*, pp.81–82.

8 See J D M Derrett, *Jesus's Audience*, pp.61–62; and B F Meyer, *The Aims of Jesus*, pp.159–60. See also Exodus 23:7.

9 For people of the land, see C J Roetzel, *The World that Shaped the New Testament*, pp.44–45. For the underclass, see J D Crossan, *Jesus: A Revolutionary Biography*, ch.1. For non-observance of the law due to poverty, see M J Borg, *Jesus: A New Vision*, ch.4, "The social world of Jesus".

10 The laws concerning purity and the distinction between clean and unclean are laid down in Leviticus 11–15; the "holiness code" in Leviticus 17–26 sets out the rules for maintaining relationship with God. Crossan defines "ritually unclean" as meaning "socially inappropriate", and links the emphasis on bodily boundary protection to the ever-present danger of absorption by a more powerful culture; see J D Crossan, *Jesus: A Revolutionary Biography*, ch.4, "In the beginning is the body". For the stones of a house, see Leviticus 14:37–53; for leprosy in people, see Leviticus 13; For childbirth and contact with dead bodies, see Leviticus 11–12; for discharges, see Leviticus 15.

11 For the synagogue prayer, see M J Borg, *Jesus: A New Vision*, ch.6. For the status of women at the time, see also P Yancey, *The Jesus I Never Knew*, p.152; R J Cassidy, *Jesus, Politics and Society*, ch.3, "The social stance of Jesus"; J D M Derrett, *Jesus's Audience*, ch.1, "The social scene". For the feeding of the 4,000, see Matthew 15:38. For the rules of social intercourse, see B Milne, *The Message of John*, p.83. For the bleeding Pharisees, see P Yancey, *The Jesus I Never Knew*, p.130. A call for realism is given by Amy-Jill Levine in her article "Lilies of the field and wandering Jews" in I R Kitzberger (ed.), *Transformative Encounters: Jesus and Women Reviewed*.

12 Herod's massacre of the innocents passed without comment from his Roman masters. For the status of children in Egypt and Palestine, see J D Crossan, *Jesus: A Revolutionary Biography*, ch.3, "A kingdom of nuisances and nobodies"; and in the Greek empire, J O'Faolain and L Martines, *Not in God's Image*, p.19.

13 See Luke 17:15–16 (the Samaritan leper); John 4 (the woman at the well); Matthew 8 (the centurion's servant; S Blanch points out that centurions were usually recruited from one part of the empire and sent to serve in another;

he suggests that this man is therefore likely to have been a native of Egypt or Greece or Syria, *Encounters with Jesus*, p.210). For the calling of Matthew, see Matthew 9:9; for Zacchaeus, see Luke 19. For the hospitality of Simon the leper, see Mark 14; the importance of table fellowship as the locus of the concrete social expression of the ritual and moral distinctions between clean and unclean, righteous and sinners, is discussed by B F Meyer, *The Aims of Jesus*, pp.159–60.

14 See Luke 7 (anointing), John 8 (woman caught in adultery), Luke 6:15 (Simon the Zealot), Luke 23:39–43 (criminal), Mark 1:41 (leper), Mark 5:25–34 (woman with bleeding). For the demoniac, see Mark 5:1–20; Blanch identifies the place in which this occurred as Gergasa, on the Greek side of the Sea of Galilee, *Encounters with Jesus*, ch.5. The female disciple is Mary Magdalene; see Luke 8:2. Mary, Susanna and Joanna are said here by Luke to have supported Jesus financially and to have travelled with him; Mary Magdalene, Mary the mother of James and Joses, Salome and many other women are said by Mark to have travelled with him to Jerusalem (15:40–41).

15 See Mark 10:2–9 (divorce); John 4:26 (Jesus reveals his identity to the Samaritan woman); Mark 14:3–9 (anointing by Mary of Bethany); Mark 16:9 (first appearance to Mary Magdalene); Matthew18:1–7 and Luke 18:15–17 (importance of children). For a general discussion of Jesus' relationships, see G Theissen and A Merz, *The Historical Jesus*, ch.8, "Jesus and his social relationships".

16 See B F Meyer, *The Aims of Jesus*, p.160; and P Yancey, *The Jesus I Never Knew*, p.152. Yancey quotes Walter Wink in saying that Jesus violated the mores of his time in every single encounter with women recorded in the four gospels.

17 See his protest to those who thought him guilty of political revolution: "Am I leading a rebellion, that you have come out with swords and clubs to capture me?" Mark 14:48 (NIV). For his remarks on the law, see Matthew 5:17.

18 Quotation from J D Crossan, *Jesus: A Revolutionary Biography*, pp.195–96; W Brueggemann, *The Prophetic Imagination*, p.28.

19 See Luke 18 (the rich young ruler), Mark 5 (Jairus), Luke 8:1–3 (wealthy women). Joanna would have been based in Tiberias, Herod's capital city. Magdala was a flourishing port town connected with the trade routes of the east and specialising in the export of salt fish. See Marianne Sawacki, "Magdalenes and Tiberiennes – city women in the entourage of Jesus", in I R Kitzinger (ed.), *Transformative Encounters*.

20 See Luke 7 (Simon the Pharisee), Luke 14 (another Pharisee), John 3, 7:50–51, 19:38–40 (Nicodemus and Joseph of Arimathea), Luke 23:50–53 (Joseph). An executed prisoner's body was normally kept in the custody of the Sanhedrin without mourning and burial rites for one year after death, and only then released for burial. See M Sawacki, "Magdalenes and Tiberiennes", in I R Kitzberger (ed.), *Transformative Encounters*. For the centurion, see Luke 7; for the official, see John 4.

21 John 13:34 (love one another); Luke 7 (the raising of the son of the widow of Nain); Luke 8 (daughter of Jairus); John 11 (Lazarus); John 19:26–27 (care of his mother).

22 Matthew 10:34–38 (sword); Luke 14:26 (hate family); Luke 9:61–62 (saying goodbye); Mark 3:31–35 (family).

23 Luke 18:18–30 (rich young ruler); Luke 6:20 (the inheritance of the poor); Matthew 25:34–46 (care for the destitute); Luke 12:32 and Matthew 6:19–21 (treasure in heaven); Luke 6:29 (giving your shirt); Luke 19 (Zacchaeus); Matthew 25:34–46 (giving to the poor);

26:10–13 (ointment); Luke 8:2–3 (wealthy followers); Luke 23:50–53 (purchase of the tomb). For the contradictions in Jesus' attitude to the financial status of those with whom he mixed, see C Bartholomew and T Moritz (eds), *Christ and Consumerism*, ch.4.

24 Luke 4:18–19.

25 R J Cassidy remarks that Jesus offers no analysis of why the poor were poor, that he never charges the rich with being responsible for their poverty, and that he has no apparent programme for overcoming poverty. See *Jesus, Politics and Society*, ch.2, "The social stance of Jesus".

26 Matthew 19 (rich young ruler); Matthew 8 (scribe, bereaved man). For the importance attached to wealth, which was seen as a blessing from God, see M J Borg on the values of Jewish society in *Jesus: A New Vision*, ch.5.

27 Matthew 19:27–30.

28 The first meeting with Nicodemus is described in John 3. His subsequent loyalty to Jesus is described in John 7:50 and 19:39. For Jesus' teaching about light and darkness, see John 1:4–5.

29 John 4.

30 John 5.

31 John 8. For the law, see Deuteronomy 22:22–23. Note that death is prescribed for both parties, whereas only the woman is brought to Jesus here. It seems that the penalty was rarely carried out. See Leon Morris, *The Gospel According to John*, p.887. Morris also points out that adultery was not an offence for which Roman law sanctioned execution.

32 John 9.

33 Luke 10.

34 Leviticus 14:37–54; Psalm 118:22; Isaiah 28:16. The image is used by Jesus in Matthew 21:42–43 and Mark 12:10–12.

CHAPTER THREE:

JESUS' TEACHINGS: A NEW VISION

*If anything, his teachings were more radical than
his actions, for his teachings played out the implications of the harsh challenge and radical transformation at which his actions hinted.*

Walter Brueggemann[1]

The world is a funny place. It takes us a lifetime to make
sense of it. We begin as babies, with unfocussed eyes, whose
first task is to learn to separate self from mother, and then
one thing from another. We learn the elementary laws of the
universe – that our hands are attached to our bodies, that
when we can no longer see an object it nonetheless continues
to exist, that the black and white marks on a page can be
made to correspond to spoken words. Gradually we build up
a set of expectations of how the world will behave and how
we can interact with it. It is a fascinating process. I have
watched my children stare transfixed at their feet, discovering
they can move them at will; I have faced their demands to
mend broken ladybirds, and seen the inexplicable wonders of
computers taken completely for granted. I have seen them, bit
by bit, acquire the conceptual framework which will help
them make sense of life, a mental map which will help them
find their way around reality as they experience it. It is a

process common to us all. By the time we reach adulthood, we have developed an intricate and largely subconscious world view by which we measure and test everything that happens to us. It carries within it a wealth of interpretive information: things look smaller when they are further away; this is right and that is wrong; particular facial expressions carry particular meanings; happiness will be found in the following ways; and so on. Armed with this worldview, we sally forth. Each new bit of data which life flings at us is carefully considered, and then either rejected as dissonant, or incorporated into the framework which we have developed. Without such a framework we would be as helpless as the babies we once were; it provides us with the equipment we need to survive in a complex world. We are all, whether we know it or not, philosophers.

Jesus had the task of teaching people who had developed such a mental framework. Developed over centuries, the Jewish worldview was firm and clear. And yet for many people it wasn't working. For them there was a painful mismatch between the inherited philosophy of their fathers and the harsh reality of daily experience. Pharisees, Sadducees, Essenes and Zealots struggled, in their different ways, to find a solution; but the majority laboured on with the familiar framework of agreed beliefs and practices, often preserving it only at the cost of admitting their own exclusion from it. It was a worldview for which Jesus had little sympathy. The challenge he mounted both to the conventional way of thinking and to the various radical solutions adopted by the reform movements was apparent in his behaviour and reinforced in his challenges to individuals. But it was in his teaching that it was spelt out most clearly. For if in his behaviour he overturned a world, in his teaching he built another one. And he built it not in the logical ways of religious philosophers and secular teachers, but in the piecemeal way in which it had been built up in the first place by each indi-

vidual: by offering not a carefully expounded rational manifesto but rather a series of pictures, metaphors, and challenges which, taken together, undermined and dismantled one
framework and encouraged the hearer to use the pieces to
build a new one. Jesus' teaching differed from any teaching
we are likely to have known, in that it was addressed not so
much to the conscious mind as to the imagination. And it is
in the imagination that the seeds of change are sown.

The parables

Approximately one third of the sayings of Jesus recorded in
the gospels of Matthew, Mark and Luke have come down to
us in the form of parables. These parables carry varying
degrees of interpretation, but it is in Luke that they appear to
stand closest to the form in which they were first spoken, and
so it is to Luke that we will mostly turn in this chapter.

Jesus' parables are so surprising that biblical scholars are
still struggling to interpret them two millennia after they were
first uttered. In itself the form was not new; a parable is really
just a story with a message, and Jesus' parables are related to
both Jewish and Greek tradition.[2] But Jesus extended their
scope far beyond anything which had been seen before, and
in so doing made the form peculiarly his own. Sometimes
taking the form of a short comparison, and often developed
into a   long and enigmatic story, the parable is a peculiar
form of teaching which has the effect not so much of answering questions as asking them, not so much of offering a solution as demanding that the hearer redefine the problem. A
parable, unlike the more logical forms of teaching we are
used to, stands not at the end of a mental process but at its
beginning. In the mouth of Jesus a parable, traditionally
presented as a helpful picture from the ordinary, familiar
world, in fact has the habit of suddenly becoming the vehicle
for a whole new way of looking at things – story it may be,

but a story which has an alarming tendency to carry within it a revolution, to demand a decision. A parable, to describe a metaphor with a metaphor, is a dart thrown with unerring accuracy at the centre of a badly made mental jigsaw, scattering the pieces and challenging the owner to begin the task of reassembling them in a way that will prove less susceptible to damage. Many attempts have been made to soften the blow, to smooth the edges and find a way of dealing with the implications of Jesus' parables in a way which is not too destructive of the carefully constructed philosophy of the hearer. Perhaps the interpretation which has been the most readily embraced in our time is the one which sees each parable as the pictorial illustration of a single moral point.[3] But the parables cannot be so confined, and their essential demand always springs back: the demand to recognise that we have too much dissonant data, to open our imaginations to the task of starting again, and to embrace the task of constructing our reality a different way.

The parables as metaphor

When Jesus first began to teach, the message he gave was a simple one: "Repent, for the kingdom of heaven has come near."[4] And it was around this notion of the kingdom of heaven that most of his parables were centred. This is one example of the many short comparisons Jesus drew between the kingdom of heaven and everyday events and objects:

> He said therefore, "What is the kingdom of God like? And to what should I compare it? It is like a mustard seed that a man took and sowed in the garden; it grew and became a tree, and the birds of the air made nests in its branches." And again he said, "To what should I compare the kingdom of God? It is like yeast that a woman took and mixed in with three measures of flour until all of it was leavened."[5]

In this parable Jesus offers a double comparison to help his hearers understand about the kingdom of heaven. The comparisons are straightforward: the kingdom is like a mustard seed, and it is like yeast. The property of the mustard seed and the yeast that is being evoked here is the capacity to grow from something small to something large. The meaning therefore is that the kingdom also will grow.

But if we allow ourselves to think about it, there is much more to this parable than meets the eye. First, there is the context. Jesus was speaking in a synagogue, and synagogues are places where the sacred scriptures were studied and learned by heart, along with the oral tradition which stood as a commentary on them; the language spoken in the synagogue was the language of law and theology. Jesus, by contrast, uses the language of the garden and the kitchen, inviting his audience to relate their faith not to the application of the law but to the mundanities of what men and, even more unusually, women do in their daily lives. This in itself was a challenge – the equivalent, perhaps, of arriving at a civic reception wearing shorts and a T-shirt. But if the way he chose to explain this theological concept was unusual, it was as nothing compared with what it was that he was trying to say about it. The kingdom of God will grow, he said. But they knew that the kingdom of God was fixed. Of course it doesn't grow, they must have thought; its inhabitants are predetermined, and they can even be counted. The kingdom of heaven isn't for flocks of incoming starlings; it's for observant, probably male, Jews. And the number of observant, male Jews is finite, traceable by ancestry, recorded by census, and known to every member of every community.

And so we see that this parable, apparently simple and straightforward, in fact must have mounted an enormous challenge to the way of thinking of those who heard it – a challenge so great, in fact, that they would not have been able to even begin the process of interpretation unless they were prepared first of all to set aside some of the assumptions which they had held all their lives. This parable is more than a helpful comparison. Like its fellows, this parable is nothing less than a weapon of warfare, trained on the glass edifice of a passionately held but imperfectly formed worldview.[6]

One of the best known definitions of the parable is that given by C H Dodd: "The parable is a metaphor or simile drawn from nature or common life, arresting the hearer by its vividness or strangeness, and leaving the mind in sufficient doubt about its precise application to tease it into active thought".[7] It is in viewing a parable as metaphor that I think we find the most fruitful way of thinking about it, and this is a way which has been emphasised by the most recent studies.[8] But for it to be meaningful we need to be clear what a metaphor is and how it works. A metaphor is a particular kind of comparison in which the characteristics of one thing are implicitly attributed to another, thereby compelling the hearer to think about that second thing in a new way. When a metaphor becomes familiar it no longer has this effect – we talk about the leg of a table, for instance, without batting an eyelid. But a new metaphor can be revolutionary in its impact, because it puts together two things that previously had no connection, and in so doing opens up a whole new avenue of imagination and thought.[9] Each of Jesus' parables does this, and so each can be said to function metaphorically.

The parables have been embedded in our collective consciousness now for 2,000 years, and often they have no more freshness to us than the dead metaphor of the table leg. But seen in context, they offer a radical challenge to the world into which they were spoken, for they burst into a prose world of settled reality with all the disjointing force of poetry. When Jesus uses a picture or a story as a metaphor for the kingdom of God, he isn't offering theology, conducted by experts for experts, but metaphor, which belongs to the world not of the mind but of the imagination. The poor, the ignorant and the young are excluded from theology; but not from poetry. Even children can do poetry; "I don't like this rusty weather", said one of my children in a sandstorm at the age of four, demonstrating a perfect command of the use of metaphor. It is poetry which Jesus offers in the parables; and the job of a poet is to build a new world, a world which makes sense of the inner realities of our lives – and to invite us to enter into it.[10]

The parables: stories in action

Many of Jesus' parables offer a short story in illustration of a single point. The story seems uncontroversial, and is drawn from the everyday experience of his hearers. A man is building a tower. He has to draw up an estimate of the cost before he calls in the builders, otherwise he'll run out of money halfway through. Or a king is going into battle. He has to assess the strength of the enemy before committing his men, and if it is greater than his own he is wise to try the negotiating table instead. So much is obvious. But then Jesus gives the other half of the comparison, which seems bewilderingly overstated: it's the same for you when deciding whether to commit yourself to me; you need to do your sums first, for it will tie up all your resources – and only then decide.[11] The implications this time are extraordinary – it was common enough for individuals to join themselves for a limited period as students to a travelling rabbi; why, they must have wondered, do the stakes need to be so high with this one?

Another example of an initially straightforward story is found in the parable of the wicked tenants.[12] Jesus tells the tale of a distant landlord who sent his agent to collect the rent from his tenant farmers; they beat him up and refused to pay. He sent another agent, but the same thing happened. So he sent his son, only to be brought the news that he too had been killed, in the hope that the absence of an heir would eventually leave the farm in the ownership of the tenants.

This was a familiar scenario in this land of exploitative land-lords and rebellious peasants; and so Jesus' hearers nod their heads in recognition as the story unfolds. But then comes the ending: the landlord, Jesus says, made the long and no doubt dangerous journey back to the farm, in order to evict the wicked tenants. A stunned silence ensues while everybody present digests this unexpected twist to the story. "Heaven forbid!" exclaim those who had seen their own situation in that of the tenant farmers, and looked forward to hearing a Zealot-friendly conclusion from this charismatic leader who was promising a new kingdom. Then Jesus quotes from scripture: "The stone that the builders rejected has become the cornerstone . . . and it will crush anyone on whom it falls". And it dawns upon the scribes and Pharisees that not only is the kingdom of God being redefined by being expressed in the coarse language of this unsavoury story; but that it is their heads which lie on the chopping block, not those of the notoriously rebellious peasants.

The parables: incompatibility and confusion

It is characteristic of metaphors that each one stands on its own. Each has a particular job to do; each will appeal to the imagination in a different way, and although metaphors will often work in harmony within a particular poem, no such consistency is required from one poem to another. And in this they are distinguished from the illustrations used in prose writing directed at the mind, where a single comparison is more likely to be used consistently and cumulatively to build up a clear and coherent statement of the matter in hand. We have often assumed that although Jesus' teaching was diffi-cult to grasp, yet somehow the parables, which after all form part of a single written gospel book, must all add up to the same thing, and that they must all be different ways of illus-trating the same thesis. And so the picture has emerged of Jesus as a moral teacher patiently expounding a new ethic, using stories and metaphors to express a simplified but consistent theology to an uneducated audience.[13] For most of us this Jesus is a familiar figure, but scarcely one who hereby shows that he holds the key to the meaning of life, and certainly not one who can be said to destroy and build again whole worlds. But if we look more closely at the parables, if we face up to the inevitable conclusion that they simply don't add up in the coherent way we expect them to, and if we resist the temptation to conclude that we just aren't meant to understand them, but rather try and feel them; perhaps then we will find that in their very incompatibility lies their message.[14]

The best examples of this apparent incompatibility between one parable and another are found by looking at those which deal with money. On one occasion Jesus tells of a dishonest accountant given notice by his rich employer.[15] Aware that he is going to need a new job, this man sets out to make friends for himself by rewriting the bills of his employer's clients for lesser amounts. "And his master commended the dishonest manager because he had acted shrewdly," said Jesus; you do the same. This parable is surprising in itself, first in that no real employer is likely to congratulate his employees on diddling him, and second in that it clashes violently with the value system of its hearers, who know the law regarding matters of financial honesty. It thus invites instant rejection on its own terms. But leaving that aside for a moment, this parable comes into clear conflict with what Jesus said and did on other occasions; Levi and Zacchaeus enter the kingdom precisely because they are willing to turn *away* from their posts as dishonest revenue collectors.[16] And even if we manage to keep our heads and decide that Jesus is advocating the shrewd giving-away of worldly goods to ensure we get a job offer in the eternal economy, we are then brought up short when we reach the parable of the talents, or coins, and find that we are apparently being encouraged to make as much money as possible on the basis that "to all those who have, more will be given; but from those who have nothing, even what they have will be taken away".[17] The parables simply will not work as helpful and systematic illustrations of moral points; they work only as carefully packaged boxes of explosives, innocently presented and devastatingly detonated in any number of different places. In so far as they have a coherent message, it is simply this: that things are not as they seem, and that we must be open to having our tidy vision of reality shattered.[18]

Other parables invite rejection on the grounds that they are incompatible not one with another but with the social and cultural framework within which they are told. The best examples here are those parables which are given in the context of dinner parties. Luke tells the story of what happened when Jesus was invited to a meal at the house of a leading Pharisee.[19] We know that the society of the day was based around certain core values, and that prominent among these were honour and prestige. One of the ways in which these values were expressed was through the practice of hospitality, and this was the primary means by which the social bonds which defined the value of each member of the community in relation to one another and to God were created and maintained.[20] And so Luke tells how Jesus walked into a room full of nervous energy as guests jostled for the most important seats. "Go and sit down at the lowest place," he advised them; it's safer. Then, turning his attention to the priorities of the host, he recommended that next time he invite those who can't invite him back, so that the prestige he accrues from his hospitality will be credited to him not in this world but in the next. And finally, he told the story of a host whose original guests snubbed him by failing to turn up, and who flung open his doors to the poor instead, swearing that the first lot could go and take a running jump. Now none of this fits in even slightly with the acknowledged way of doing things. The guests have been told that their priorities are upside down, the host that his energies are being directed in the wrong place, and finally it has been suggested that those who thought their social status secure enough to turn down the invitation are in fact the very ones who will be excluded. Only two reactions are possible to the extraordinary behaviour of this so very unconventional guest: to move from reeling disbelief to a sincere attempt to understand what it is he is trying to say; or to take offence and dismiss his words as those of a social and religious misfit.

This deliberate overturning of the social status quo is apparent in others of Jesus' parables too. On another occasion he tells the story of a beggar, Lazarus, who enjoys the company of the patriarch Abraham in heaven, whilst the rich man outside whose gates he lay suffers torment in the flames of Hades.[21] To us, accustomed to the language of socialism, this seems quite logical. But to Jesus' original audience, it could not possibly have been so. To them, wealth was a sign of God's blessing, poverty of his displeasure; and the heirs of Abraham were the righteous and upstanding citizens who observe the law, not the pockmarked beggars who lie in the street. This parable is thus an outrageous way of suggesting that the criteria which govern standing in the kingdom of heaven may not in fact be the same as those which prevail on earth. The same message is given when Jesus tells the story of two men at prayer, the righteous Pharisee who thanked God that he was not like thieves, rogues, adulterers and tax collectors; and the dishonest tax collector in a corner, beating his breast and crying, "God be merciful to me, a sinner."[22] The one saved, Jesus says, won't be the one you think. The divine economy is not as pictured by the human economy after all; it stands to it in some kind of ludicrous inverse proportion which will demand a lot of careful thought.

And finally, there are those occasions when Jesus simply won't give a straight answer to a straight question. There is the time, for example, when he tells the story of the servants who wait up one night for their master to come home; he's pleased with them, for they could have slept and allowed thieves to break in.[23] "You also must be ready, for the Son of Man is coming at an unexpected hour," Jesus says to the disciples. Uh? asks Peter, who's the "you"? Us or everyone? But instead of answering the question – for he seems rarely to have been willing to answer questions – Jesus just persists with the parable; almost as if he is saying to Peter that he wants to make him think, to work on his imagination, and not to give rational explanations that he can just slot comfortably into his existing conceptual framework. The same thing happens when a man asks him to help him secure his inheritance from his brother – a reasonable request, one might think, to make of a popular rabbi with great charisma and a strong sense of social justice.[24] But "Who set me to be a judge over you?" enquires Jesus, launching into a story about a rich landowner who thought he needed to build bigger barns to store his bumper crop, but who in fact should have been laying up his treasure in heaven, because his life was required of him that very night. Why could he not just have said no? the man must have thought. Why; because more important than his need for justice was his need to rethink his values, to start again within a different framework and, eventually, perhaps to find that the question he wanted to ask was in fact a quite different one.

The Sermon on the Mount

Most of Jesus' teaching comes in the form of parables given in different ways to different people on different occasions. But sometimes, and particularly by Matthew, it is presented in narrative form. The most famous of these narrative passages is the Sermon on the Mount, apparently delivered on a single occasion to a whole crowd of people.[25] It consists of a series of extraordinary statements followed by a series of impossible demands, and like the parables it has been the subject of centuries of debate. For some commentators, it seems to set up an ideal, an exhortation which is purposely overdone and which only a few will be expected to reach. For others, it knowingly portrays an impossible goal in order to emphasise our need for grace, and the ethical commands it contains are thus to be seen more as an assertion of guilt than as a new imperative. Others have insisted that Jesus meant to be taken at his word, and that the Sermon offers a new ethic which we are enjoined to adopt. And for yet others the Sermon contains an ethic of intention; it is about being rather than doing, and speaks of internal attitudes and dispositions rather than imposing a new law.[26]

I think the best way into the Sermon on the Mount is to begin by imagining the scene. Jesus is travelling through Galilee at the start of his ministry. He has called for repentance and announced that the kingdom of heaven is at hand. He has healed sick people brought to him from all over Syria, and is now followed wherever he goes by a large crowd. The time perhaps has come for a little explanation of what exactly it is that is going on; and the Sermon on the Mount represents that explanation.

It begins with a series of blessings, or "beatitudes", as we have come to know them. For us, "blessing" has become a religious word; but all it meant when Jesus used it was "happy", or "fortunate".[27] These are the people whom Jesus defines as happy, and whom he expects to inherit the kingdom of heaven:

Blessed are the poor in spirit, for theirs is the kingdom of heaven.
Blessed are those who mourn, for they will be comforted.
Blessed are the meek, for they will inherit the earth.
Blessed are those who hunger and thirst for righteousness, for they will be filled.

Blessed are the merciful, for they will receive mercy.

Blessed are the pure in heart, for they will see God.

Blessed are the peacemakers, for they will be called children of God.

Blessed are those who are persecuted for righteousness' sake, for theirs is the kingdom of heaven.

Now this raises a number of problems. First of all, it must have seemed simply incomprehensible. They, like we, knew what made them happy, and it surely didn't include poverty, depression, powerlessness, injustice, working without reward or recognition for the benefit of others, persecution, slander and rejection. Second, here we are once again a million miles from the usual view of the criteria for pleasing God: salvation, they knew, was about observance and status and educated middleclass piety; it wasn't for the poor and the persecuted. And then third, even if we leave all that aside for a moment and concentrate on unpacking these rather dense statements, we find that it is far from clear what exactly Jesus meant by each of the terms he used. Who, for example, are the pure in heart? Even after 2,000 years there is no common agreement. The early church thought that they were those who were free from the voice of the enemy and the lies of the world. The Eastern church Fathers held that purity of heart was about freedom from passions and impure thoughts. Luther said it was about thinking God's thoughts, not your own. Post-Reformation critics believed it to be about simplicity and integrity. Kierkegaard saw it as meaning to will one thing, which was to see God.[28] Given that the only person who *doesn't* seem to have an opinion about what Jesus meant is Matthew, it would seem that any interpretation is possible; and even today, each commentator has his or her own.

I think there is only one possible way of reconciling this extraordinary discrepancy between what we expect Jesus to say about happiness and what he did actually say, and the equally extraordinary lack of clarity about what he meant by each of the terms he used: and that is to assume that it is deliberate. More than that, I think we have to conclude that here we find the whole point. Jesus wanted to startle. The clash is intentional. Simple observation of the world tells us, as it told them, that the rich, not the poor, are the fortunate ones; that those who laugh, and not those who mourn, are to be envied; and that the powerful, not the meek, are the lucky ones. As a description of the way things are, the beatitudes simply won't do. They don't make sense. But let's assume for a moment that Jesus was not trying to make sense. Perhaps he wasn't trying to explain things at all. Perhaps this too is a challenge not to our minds but to our imaginations, and perhaps it contains not description or prescription so much as suggestion, the radical suggestion that there is another way of thinking about life. Perhaps, in fact, this is not a legal or ethical text at all, but rather a statement of vision, a challenge to leave our inherited values and enter a new world, the topsy-turvy world of the parables, a world where we will indeed receive blessings – not the ones we are used to, but ones which will connect us with God, and never leave us.

Vision of a new reality

Everything Jesus said and did pointed to a new reality. He came not with a manifesto of political reform, but with a new concept of kingdom. He came not with a new ethic, but with a new vision. The Sermon on the Mount makes sense only if we see it as a poetic text, as the prophetic imagining of an alternative world; for the kingdom of God is within before it is without, and must be looked for as inner reality before it can take shape as outer reality.[29]

What might this mean in practice? What exactly might this new world look like? What is it that must happen within these fishermen and peasants, and what is the nature of the invitation that is opened to them by the parables and the beatitudes?

First of all, it is an invitation to face up to the harsh realities of life. These were people who were *not* fortunate; despite the power and pomp of the Roman empire of which they were a part, and despite the assurances of the priests that all was well, and would be well, for those who kept the law, the actual facts were that they were quite literally poor, mournful, hungry and persecuted, that they could not meet the demands of tax and tithe, and that increasing numbers of them were living on the margin both socially and religiously. The only vision of happiness that these people had was out of reach, in the hands of those who set out to achieve it by the acquisition of worldly power and wealth. Those in political office, landowners and traders were rich. Tax collectors were unscrupulous in lining their own pockets. The chief priests were amongst the most powerful and wealthy of all segments of the community. The Roman governors were the victors in an international and personal power struggle, and had neither understanding nor compassion for the people they ruled – while the people prayed for an adequate harvest, and orphans and widows gathered discarded ears of wheat one by one, the civil authorities were building a gleaming new imperial city just down the road from Nazareth. These were the facts of life, and it was no use pretending otherwise. Jesus offers no solution, in practical terms; but in spiritual terms he suggests that people start by facing up to the realities of life as it is, principal among which is this: it hurts. Life is not a bed of roses; it brings grief, isolation, injustice, and lack of recognition. And this is a message for us too, for little has changed; for most people today, reality is a painful struggle to find meaning and relationship, a struggle sustained by the illusion that we are on the right track, that happiness is always round the corner, and that somehow we can earn it or buy it. But

Jesus knows that denying pain does not make it go away, and that facing up to the facts is the first step in healing.

Secondly, Jesus invites us to see that this prevailing reality does not come from God – that it is not a desirable reality, but one which is antithetical to the kingdom and one day will be overturned along with all its advocates. He is announcing a different order, with a different value system and a different set of rewards – *for all the wrong people*.[30] The announcement must have come as a bombshell to every single person who heard it – to the zealous revolutionaries who wanted to make the kingdom of the chosen people a political reality, to the scribes and Pharisees who wanted to create the kingdom through religious and moral reform, to the priests and Roman officials who wanted things to stay just as they were, and, last but not least, to the ordinary people who knew their place to be at the bottom of every conceivable pile.

And then thirdly, Jesus invites his hearers to enter this new world, to live knowing themselves not to be life's losers, but life's winners; to allow the new reality to transform their inner lives, to throw away the old mental map and the old pair of spectacles and the old, shattered jigsaw puzzle, and to step outside the parameters of the bubble, ready to start all over again like the children they once were, and embark on the task of building up new identities and viewing life's problems a different way. For the inner circle of disciples to whom he primarily spoke, this was an invitation to change the course of history; for the crowds who followed him, it was an invitation to throw back their shoulders and think about themselves in a new way as the true heirs of the kingdom, as the invited guests at the banquet of honour, as the sick to whom new life had been given. In a sense it was not just Jesus' teaching which was parabolic; Jesus himself was a parable, in everything he said and did. The parables and the beatitudes are the spoken equivalent of enacted parables – the eating with outcasts, the healing of the blind and the lame, later on the overturning of the trading tables in the temple.[31] Simple explanation was rarely what Jesus was about.

And finally, this is an invitation to live a different way, with a new identity and different values, in a world which can take shape only as it begins to take shape within each individual. And so Jesus's sermon does not stop with the beatitudes; it goes on. Living in the new world means allowing yourself to be salt and light to flavour and illuminate the darkness of the outer world you find yourself in. It means letting light into your own darkness just by opening your eyes and seeing in a different way. It does not mean that life will be easier, or, as he puts it in yet another parable, that your house will not be battered by storms; but it does mean that the house will stand firm, because it is built on a new, more solid, reality. And finally, it means doing your best to live as if the outer world were already your inner one, and the kingdom has already come – doing conflicts, relationships, money, and prayer all a different way, in a way which flows not from the 248 commands, 365 prohibitions and 1,521 amendments of the Pharisees, but from the liquid reality of a new relationship with God. This is what Jesus meant by the kingdom. And in it I too have found life, as I have faced up to the inevitable pain which circumstances have brought since the early days of my conversations with Ruth.

Conclusion

We live now in a world of fragmentation, a fragmentation which we find reflected in our art, our music and our poetry. Our world is no longer the officially tranquil, well-lit world painted by Raphael, where fashionably dressed madonnas hold docile goldfinches and project serene smiles, but the fragmented and disjointed world of modern art, of cubism, surrealism and abstract expressionism. We have already reverted to our childhood incoherency, and we, like Jesus' first audience, need a new way of looking at things, a way that will make sense of the pain which surrounds us as it did them. This was the way concealed in the jolts and the surprises of the parables and the beatitudes. For the whole meaning of Jesus's life and above all death was that God is found not in the absence of pain but precisely through pain. The whole message of the cross is that death precedes resurrection and that pain precedes joy. Even Jesus, in his humanity, cried out to have the pain taken away; but God knows that the joy of new life can be found only through the agony of childbirth. That is the way the world is. So Jesus is asking these first disciples to face up to the fact that the happiness of the world is ultimately an illusion, and that its value system is hollow. In giving it up they will give up something which seems solid, and yet which has a nasty habit of turning to dust just as their fingers reach out to grasp it. He is asking them to embrace different values instead, and asking them to believe that it is here, and in the eternal relationship with God which they will find as they do so, that true happiness lies. This is the word which speaks a new world, for, as Brueggemann remarks, "The energy of this blessing word comes in the reality that God has alternative futures, that he is free to bestow them, and that those futures are not derived from or determined by the present".[32]

"Let anyone with ears to hear listen", cried Jesus.[33]

The invitation remains open.

Notes

1 *The Prophetic Imagination*, p.103.
2 For a discussion of Jesus' parables in the light of the comparisons of the Old Testament, see C Westermann, *The Parables of Jesus in the Light of the Old Testament*. For parallels in the rabbinic tradition and classical fable, see B H Young, *Jesus and his Jewish Parables:*

Rediscovering the Roots of Jesus' Teaching, and his later work *The Parables: Jewish Interpretation and Christian tradition*.

3 An interpretation first put forward by A Julicher in 1888–89 as a correction to the previously universal allegorical interpretation of the parables. The shortcomings of Julicher's approach are eloquently exposed by D Buttrick, *Preaching the New and the Now*, ch.5, "Parables of the new order". A helpful outline of the critical history is given in G Theissen and A Merz, *The Historical Jesus*, ch.11, "Jesus as poet: the parables of Jesus". See also J Donahue, *The Gospel in Parable*, ch.1, "How does a parable mean?" Meanings which have been found in the parables over the years include allegorical, moral, eschatological, social, homilectical and metaphorical ones.

4 Matthew 4:17.

5 Luke 13:18–21, with the original parallelism of "man" and "woman" restored.

6 A phrase used by J Jeremias, *The Parables of Jesus*, p.21.

7 *The Parables of the Kingdom*, p.16

8 For a discussion of the parable as metaphor and a survey of the recent literature, see J R Donahue, *The Gospel in Parable*, and D Wenham, *The Parables of Jesus: Pictures of Revolution*.

9 See J R Donahue, *The Gospel in Parable*; "From a literary perspective . . . parables are metaphoric in combining in one assertion two orders of reality and in using the language of concrete imagery to suggest an analogy or comparison with the thing signified", p.12–13. For a general discussion of metaphor, see S Ullmann, *Language and Style*, ch.9, "The nature of imagery".

10 W Brueggemann links prophecy, poetry and preaching the gospel in *Finally Comes the Poet: Daring Speech for Proclamation*; he describes preaching as "a poetic

construal of an alternative world", p.6. For the parables in particular as poetry, see D Buttrick, *Preaching the New and the Now*, ch.5, "Parables of the new order" and ch.7, "Preaching a new vision".

11 Luke 14:28–33.

12 Luke 20:9–19.

13 The warning against this approach was first sounded by C H Dodd, *The Parables of the Kingdom*, ch.1 "The nature and purpose of the gospel parables", and J Jeremias, *The Parables of Jesus*, ch.1 "The problem"; but it persists nonetheless.

14 Some commentators have suggested that the "incomprehensibility" theme is one we owe not to Jesus but to the gospel writers themselves. See Matthew's setting of the parable of the sower, Matthew 13, discussed by C H Dodd, *The Parables of the Kingdom*, ch.1 "The nature and purpose of the gospel parables". B H Young holds that in view of the use of the parable in the rabbinic tradition it is inconceivable that Jesus was intending to confuse rather than illuminate his hearers; see *The Parables: Jewish Interpretation and Christian Tradition*, p.37. Jesus' perspective is perhaps best summed up in his own repeated cry of "Let anyone with ears listen!" Matthew 11:15, 13:9, 13:43, Luke 8:8, 14:35, Mark 4:9, 4:23, 8:18.

15 Luke 16:1–9.

16 Luke 19 for Zacchaeus, Luke 5 for Levi (Matthew).

17 Luke 19:11–27. Dodd identifies the man who buries his one coin and makes nothing as the pious Jew who seeks personal security in meticulous observance of the law, at the cost of making the religion of Israel barren, *The Parables of the Kingdom*, ch.2 "The setting in life".

18 A view expressed by J D Crossan and discussed in J R Donahue, *The Gospel in Parable*, p.16–17. Donahue also draws attention to the work of P Ricoeur, who sees in the

parables a sign that religious language dislocates our project of making a whole of our lives.

19 Luke 14.

20 See J D M Derrett, *Jesus' Audience: The Social and Psychological Environment in which he Worked*, ch.1, "The social scene".

21 Luke 16:19–31.

22 Luke 18:9–14.

23 Luke 12:35–48.

24 Luke 12:13–21.

25 Matthew 5–7. Matthew has often been regarded as the teacher's gospel; Jesus' teaching is presented in five successive blocks. See P S Minear, *Matthew: The Teacher's Gospel*. For a discussion of the occasion or occasions on which this teaching was given, see J Stott, *Christian Counter-Culture: The Message of the Sermon on the Mount*, pp.21–24.

26 As an ideal: the so-called "monastic interpretation", first advanced in the *Didache*, a text of the first or second century.

As a new ethic: this is the view of Luther. For a recent reformulation, see G Theissen and A Merz, *The Historical Jesus*, ch.12, "Jesus as teacher: the ethic of Jesus". As a new ethic: the best modern exponent of this approach is J Stott, *Christian Counter-Culture: The Message of the Sermon on the Mount*. Few have attempted to live by it in a literal sense; Tolstoy tried and failed.

As an attitude: a position developed in recent years by scholars such as W Hermann and E F Scott. For an overview of the critical history, see D C Allison, *The Sermon on the Mount: Inspiring the Moral Imagination*, pp.1–26.

27 The Greek word *makarios* expresses good fortune which brings joy; see D C Allison, *The Sermon on the Mount*, p.43. J Stott points out that it is to be given an objective

(status) rather than a subjective (feelings) meaning; see *Christian Counter-Culture*, p.33.

28 For a discussion of the various interpretations of this and other beatitudes, see D C Allison, *The Sermon on the Mount*, pp.44–57.

29 Luke 17:20–21. See W Brueggemann's comments on the Sermon on the Mount in *The Prophetic Imagination*, pp.103–07.

30 A point eloquently made by T Wright in his BBC series on Jesus and in the associated book, *The Original Jesus: The Life and Vision of a Revolutionary*, p.50.

31 J Jeremias calls them "parabolic actions", *The Parables of Jesus*.

32 *The Prophetic Imagination*, p.106.

33 Luke 14:34–34.

PART TWO:

WHAT WORKS AND WHAT DOESN'T

CHAPTER FOUR:

THE GOSPEL IN HISTORY

The gospel is now 2,000 years old, and it has wended its way through many different centuries, societies and cultures. It is a tribute to its power that it has persistently grown in influence: a higher proportion of people in the world are now Christian than at any time in history.[1] The gospel stands beyond nationality and culture; it is universal in a way that few other religions or philosophies are. And yet its fortunes have waxed and waned over the centuries, and at times it has been preached more effectively and received more enthusiastically than at others. Today the church is growing in many parts of the world, but few people in the West now think of Jesus as a revolutionary or the gospel as life-changing, and the number of those wishing to belong to the church has declined sharply over the last few decades.[2] We face something of a crisis.

It will by now be clear that I think that if we are to resolve this crisis we must get back in touch with the dynamic nature of the message which Jesus first brought. The big question, of course, is how; and this is the question which I want to address in the second part of this book. I think that the key lies in understanding the nature of the relationship between the gospel itself and the culture into which it is spoken.

The gospel, which just means "good news", comes into a

culture rather like the interruption of a fact into a story.[3] A culture is like a story, and its task is to make sense of what it means to be human. The story has its own inner rules, its own plot, its own characters, its own world. But somehow the story is disjointed. Too many of the people within it are marginalised, the heroes and heroines aren't really convincing, the narrator's voice not entirely reliable, the ending so often not a happy one. Everyone in the story is trying hard to make it work; but at bottom it just isn't a very good story, and they know it. Because of this, every so often a society will change the story. And so at different times in history the story has been told a different way: the Roman story is very different, for example, from the medieval story, and that again from our own story.

Jesus was born into a particular culture, into the telling of a particular story, at a time when the story was becoming increasingly unsatisfactory to the people who lived within it. Into that culture he brought the "gospel", which we may understand as an announcement which exposed the weaknesses of the story and offered an alternative resolution. This announcement was so disruptive to the culture that after three short years of public ministry Jesus was executed as a dangerous revolutionary. But from that point onwards there has always been a tension between gospel and culture, and I would like to suggest that it is in this tension that we find the key to the effectiveness or otherwise of the church in any given period. I suggest that vibrant periods in the life of the church have come when the truth has been spoken perceptively into a particular culture; and that conversely, atrophy has come when the gospel has been allowed to degenerate into formulae and practices which fail to connect with the real issues of the day, and which express themselves in the common currency of the time. That, in other words, when the fact is spoken into the story all goes well; but when fact and story become indistinguishable then people are effectively denied access to the life-changing message which Jesus brought.[4]

But more specifically even than that, it seems to me that changes in the fortunes of the church have always come at times of change in society; it is when the story changes that the church has the task of adapting its mission and learning (or failing) to speak the fact of the gospel into a new cultural situation. And there is a common consensus that as we face a new millennium we find ourselves standing at such a point of change: the old story, which we have called "modernism", is being exchanged for a new story, which at present we call "postmodernism". If the church cannot learn to speak creatively into the postmodern story it will be left behind by the tides of change. And I suggest that it is as we look at the lessons of history that we can best begin to understand the task facing us today.

The Roman empire: speaking the gospel into the culture

When we think of the Roman empire, certain images crowd into our minds. We think of theatres and laurel crowns, senate and emperors, roads and forums, olives and wine, villas, palaces and statues. We think of the security of the Roman army, of the luxury of Roman baths, of the sophistication of Roman literature. We can still stroll through the quiet sunlit streets of Pompeii and stand amongst the peaceful ruins of marbled temples. But we also know that Christians were thrown to the lions, that emperors murdered their wives, that pagans pressed constantly and violently against the borders. What was it really like to live in the Roman empire 2,000 years ago?

By the end of the first century the Roman empire stretched from Britain to North Africa, and from Spain to Syria. It had 6 million citizens, and maybe 50 million subjects, who enjoyed a common language and currency, a uniform legal system and an international road network.[5] Peace within its borders was assured by the presence of a large army, and there were greater opportunities for travel and trade than ever before. Since the time of Augustus, emperors had been venerated as gods, and a state-supported imperial cult was observed all over the empire. Professional priests offered regular sacrifices to the many gods of the Roman pantheon, ensuring their continued goodwill towards the security of the empire, and whilst philosophers debated the existence or otherwise of the divine, individual spiritual needs were met by the various Eastern mystery religions which offered a more sensual and personal approach to faith.[6] It seems, however, that whilst people were happy to participate in these cults and religions, they did not find in them any ethical dimension. And so the Roman empire in the first century was a terrifyingly insecure and brutal place to be. The pages of the contemporary writer Tacitus reveal an astonishing world of intrigue, poisoning, murder, suicide, persecution and torture. A careless remark at dinner could lead to prosecution, people suspected of sedition could be publicly massacred and their rotting bodies dumped in the Tiber whilst their relatives were forbidden to intervene or even look upset, children could be raped and executed for their father's crimes, and ordinary citizens spied on at the games and punished if their expressions were not sufficiently enthusiastic. People committed suicide at the drop of a hat rather than face torture, denial of burial and the confiscation of assets, and those who hesitated to kill their enemies outright commonly resorted to the use of spells, curses, incantations and philtres – for which they too could of course be prosecuted.[7]

Into the midst of this chaos came Christianity. At first it excited little official attention. Paul and his fellow evangelists travelled across the empire, speaking in synagogues and establishing small groups of Christians in many of the major towns. Always they spoke the same message, announcing the fact of Christ into the story world of the culture, speaking against the futility of idol worship, proclaiming the existence of the one true God, and explaining the moral implications of the gospel.[8] Everywhere they went, people found that their words penetrated the jungle of their insecurity and offered them life, and by the end of the century there were groups of Christians all over the eastern empire. Of course it wasn't a straightforward process: study of the New Testament shows that the gospel had to be expressed in language its hearers could understand, and focussed into the parts of their story which took them furthest from God; it couldn't be announced in the language of Jewish thought forms. So in Athens Paul quotes from the Greek poets and points to the altar of the unknown god; in Lystra he heals a cripple and invites his hearers to consider the power of God the Creator; in the synagogue of Pisidian Antioch he points to Jesus as the fulfilment of the scriptures; and in Ephesus he runs lunchtime classes in the school of philosophy.[9] The same differences of approach are found in the gospels; John in particular writes in the language and thought forms of the Hellenistic culture.[10] But always the facts announced are the same: that there is one God, that Jesus who died and rose again is his Son, and that reconciliation with God is to be found through him alone.

It is not hard to see that the gospel, as Paul and his colleagues presented it in the context of the Roman empire, was profoundly countercultural. Christians could not, and would not, offer sacrifice to the emperor and other gods; they debated long and hard over whether they could eat meat which had been offered to idols; they were reluctant to attend gladiatorial shows, games, and plays where people were sacrificed and the imperial cult promulgated; and they felt that occupations which involved teaching about, or taking oaths to, pagan gods were not compatible with their faith.[11] Furthermore, the gospel changes people, and the Christians developed ethical standards which differentiated them from the majority. To help them do this, Paul wrote long letters to the new churches. He urged the Christians in Corinth, whose city was the centre of worship of the love goddess Aphrodite, to turn away from the sexual immorality for which their community was notorious. He explained to the Christians in Rome, living in a world preoccupied with money, power, and bloodthirsty entertainments, how to allow the Holy Spirit to transform their hearts and minds. He wrote to the Colossians, surrounded by the Eastern mystery cults and the teachings of astrologers, correcting their misunderstandings about the spirit world and encouraging them to rely only on Christ. As the Christian communities grew, it became increasingly obvious that the gospel offered a new way of living. In a world of scheming and self-protection, the Christians showed commitment and care; in a society obsessed with hierarchy, they offered equality of membership to all; in a culture riddled with shame, they offered forgiveness and reconciliation; to people who knew only the emptiness of the imperial cult or the sensuality and secrecy of the mystery religions, they offered a worldview which not only involved the whole of life but also promised life after death. And everywhere, they prayed for the sick and released people from spiritual oppression.[12]

Much of this did not go down very well with those who did not wish to embrace it. Paul and his colleagues were thrown out of synagogues and forced to flee rioters in many of the cities they visited. As the faith spread more widely, Christians came to be regarded as atheists whose refusal to worship the gods endangered the security of the empire, and their commitment to one another and to meeting together aroused suspicion of cannibalism, incest and sedition. Emperors, whom we know from Tacitus to have been ready to persecute anyone for anything, occasionally turned their attention to the Christians, and at such times it was highly dangerous to be a leader in the church. Most notoriously, Nero mounted a kind of gladiatorial fireworks display with Christians as the fireworks, wrapped in skins, mauled by dogs and finally set on fire.[13] Despite these disincentives, and partly indeed because of the fortitude shown by the Christians in the face of death, the gospel was embraced all over the empire; it has been estimated that by 300 AD 10 per cent of the population – by then 6 million out of a total 60 million – had decided that it was as Christians that they would make the most sense of life as they experienced it.[14] The gospel had penetrated the culture.

Constantine and the beginning of Christendom: the fusion of gospel and culture

But the culture was already doomed. Internal division and external pressures combined to begin the process famously known as the decline and fall of the Roman empire. Would-be emperors fought for power and struggled against waves of invading barbarians, the cohesion of the empire and its culture was under threat, and the general atmosphere was one of impending catastrophe. Then one night in the year 312 AD, the emperor Constantine had a dream in which he was told to mark the sign of the cross on the shields of his soldiers. He did so, and the next day defeated his rival Maxentius against overwhelming odds. The following year he published an edict in which he granted religious liberty to "Christians and all others"; and the fusion of gospel and culture began.[15]

Constantine took his new responsibilities as Christian emperor seriously. He began a programme of ambitious church-building, and took steps to ensure that doctrinal orthodoxy was established and enforced.[16] He interested himself in the appointments of bishops. The church was encouraged to develop a hierarchical administrative structure which reflected that of the empire, and which indeed, as the empire weakened, began to replace it. The ancient practice of public munificence was transmuted into the giving of alms, and Christians were encouraged to leave money and land to the church. In line with their increasing civic duties, bishops were paid the same as provincial governors, and clergy were exempted from tax.[17] As the church grew in wealth and status it became socially and professionally advantageous to be a Christian, and people flocked to join. Numbers of Christians increased from 6 million at the beginning of the fourth century to 30 million at the end of it.[18] Augustine and Ambrose condemned insincere conversions, and Tertullian complained that the church had been turned from a manifestation of the Holy Spirit into a conclave of bishops. But the changes were irreversible, and the church found itself facing something of an identity crisis. Even without its mounting political and social responsibilities and the increasing amount of energy it was devoting to doctrinal disputes, the church lacked the resources to teach and pastor so many new converts adequately, and inevitably they brought the assumptions of their secular lives with them, thus contributing to the gradual secularisation of the Christian community. The Christian standards of behaviour patiently taught to his new converts by Paul were often forgotten, and the Roman tradition of persecution flourished in the new Christian context: there was street fighting and violence between Christians and pagans all over the empire as sacrifices and idol worship were banned; the death penalty was imposed for celebrating Easter on the wrong day in Egypt; and competing temples and shrines were smashed. Dissenting bishops had their hands and tongues cut off and eyes torn out; in 366 AD rival mobs fought in Rome over the election of a bishop, leaving 137 people dead on the floor; and in 449 a doctrinal council held in Ephesus was reduced to chaos by rioting theologians.[19] Often paganism was merely reclothed in Christian garb: the pagan calendar of festivals was carefully replaced with Christian equivalents, and holy sites were identified to take the place of the much venerated classical shrines. In 380 the emperor Theodosius proclaimed Christianity the official religion of the empire; but by that time there was little discernible difference between a Christian and his pagan counterpart.[20]

So instead of the gospel being spoken into the culture, it became clear that the culture was swamping the gospel. As paganism was gradually stamped out, Christianity ceased to be about the subversive statement of a gospel fact into an alien culture, and became instead an established religion permeating, and permeated by, the social structures at every level.

The ascetic movement and the recovery of a countercultural faith

Whilst the church settled down to work out its role in society, individual Christians began to worry about what they saw as the capitulation of the gospel to the culture. This, in the words of the fifth-century writer Cassian, is how they responded:

> With the passing away of the apostles, the multitude of believers began to lose their fervour and especially as crowds began to flock to faith in Christ from foreign nations of all sorts ... so the primitive rigour of the faith became attenuated, both among the people and its leaders. As their fervour cooled, many combined their confession of Christ with wealth; but those who kept the fervour of the apostles, recalling that former perfection, withdrew from their cities and from the society of those who thought this laxness of living permissible for themselves and for the Church, to spots on the edges of towns, or more remote places, and there practised privately and in their own groups the things which they remembered the apostles had instituted for the whole body of the Church.[21]

And so the ascetic movement was born. Whilst theologians continued to thrash out doctrine, bishops to build aqueducts and exercise other municipal authority, and the majority of Christians to acquire wealth and social status, a small number of individuals began to seek a return to the dynamic and committed Christian life of the first century. Convinced that such a life could no longer be pursued in the context of an increasingly secularised church, they left their urban homes and took up dramatically alternative lifestyles, founding Christian communities or shunning human society altogether for a life of prayer and fasting in the Egyptian desert.[22] Many were colourful and eccentric characters who were not afraid to be radical. The best known was Anthony, whose reputation as a desert hermit survives to this day. Son of a farmer, he gave away his lands, left his community and, despite suffering horrendous hallucinations, persisted in living alone in the desert on bread and water. Sleeping on the ground, never washing his feet, with a wardrobe consisting only of a hair shirt, a sheepskin and a girdle, his singleminded devotion to a life of prayer earned him a worldwide reputation for holiness.[23] Another figure who took his faith to extremes was Symeon the Stylite; long before the age of media harassment he was so sought after for his spiritual counsel that he was reduced to living on the top of a column to escape the unwelcome attention of the crowds; people flocked from far and wide to speak with him, and whole communities of bedouins apparently went home converted to the Christian faith as a result of the encounter.[24]

By the year 375 the eastern deserts were populated by hermits or monks (the word "monk" simply means "alone"). Many found the solitary life hard going; gradually they began to form into loose associations, and the monastic movement was born. A monk named Pachomius wrote down some simple guidelines to assist groups of others to develop a common life based on prayer, study, shared meals, obedience to a superior and working at a trade.[25] Before long, monasteries and convents were springing up outside every town and village of any size. Basil of Caesarea integrated monastic communities more closely with the church, encouraging them to provide poor relief, health care, and education for the general community. Monasteries were founded in Italy, France, and in the Celtic north; and in the sixth century Benedict wrote the first extended Rule, making provision for eight daily services of prayer and worship in addition to private study and the pursuit of manual labour.[26] It is a mark of the influence of the monastic movement that these services still form the basis of the worship of the Catholic, Anglican and Episcopalian churches today. Once again the gospel and the culture had become sharply distinguished from one another.

The ascetic movement represented a serious and spontaneous attempt by thousands of individual Christians to find a new way of articulating their faith in a culture which was beginning to lose sight of the radical implications of the gospel. It stimulated the faith of many, and served to carry the torch through to the next generation. Ultimately, however, it would fail to provide a satisfactory long term solution to the tension between gospel and culture; for as asceticism became monasticism it would gradually be reabsorbed into the institution of the church.[27]

The Middle Ages: creation of a Christian culture

Meanwhile, back in the culture, the story was still changing. The barbarian invasions intensified. In the course of the fifth century Rome was sacked twice, and for the next 500 years wars raged across the continent. This is the period traditionally known as the Dark Ages, and it was characterised by political and social chaos. It was in the monasteries that the Christian faith was nurtured during this time, and their importance grew enormously. They provided a focus in the local community for a life of prayer and devotion to God; they acted as centres of learning and education in a war-torn world, and they offered pastoral and medical care and hospitality. Meanwhile missionaries were sent out to preach the gospel to the new settlers, landowners were encouraged to found the first parish churches, and the concept of Christian kingship developed. Gradually religious and political stability returned, and by 1050 the church had emerged as the dominant institution of society.[28] Church and culture became one, and Europe became known as Christendom. The process begun by Constantine was complete; at last society itself was Christian, and every member of it able to live as a Christian with the full support of a free and universal church.

In practice, however, they didn't. In the great monasteries and convents, mystics like Bernard of Clairvaux, visionaries like Hildegard of Bingen, theologians like Thomas Aquinas, and contemplatives like Benedict developed the rich spirituality of the age. But amongst the ordinary people things were very different. Most were illiterate; they had no access to the Bible, they attended incomprehensible church services in Latin, and were taught by parish priests whose training consisted, if they were lucky, of memorising the Lord's Prayer, the creed, and the Hail Mary. For the average medieval villager the Christian faith was about taking part in processions and ceremonies and listening to stories of saints.[29] Old magical practices were often retained; in eleventh-century France the consecrated host was used both as a love philtre and as a remedy for the infestation of cabbages by caterpillars.[30] Christian discipleship was no more advanced than it had been in the fourth century; the manuals written to help priests hear annual confessions reveal a wide variety of common practices ranging from fornication with animals through witchcraft, abortion and alcoholism to dozens of different forms of violence.[31] The lion-defying confidence of the early Christians in their salvation had given way to a universal fear of hell fuelled by the graphic paintings of eternal torment which decorated the inner walls of churches and the many popular descriptions of hell which were part of the common culture.[32] Rich patrons built churches and hoped for the best, but for ordinary people there was little comfort; for as one writer explained in the twelfth century, "Lay men are allowed to have a wife, to cultivate the earth, to judge and promote lawsuits, to lay their offerings on the altars, to pay tithes. *If* they do this they will be able to be saved, *on condition* that they avoid evil by well-doing".[33] Many did not even try; the Italian poet Dante laments the growth of material and political greed between the twelfth and thirteenth centuries in the city state of Florence, painting a picture of ostentatious wealth, callous ambition and widespread immorality.[34] One authority has suggested that the ecclesiastical culture from which the written texts come to us masks the reality of a society mostly unconverted and pagan.[35] Mission virtually ceased; the early desire to share the good news of salvation through Christ with people who had not heard it now found expression in a desire to wrest the Holy Land back from its Arab conquerors by force, and a series of crusades were mounted in which the infidels were encouraged to embrace the gospel by being given the unappealing choice between conversion and defenestration.[36] That the crusaders saw themselves as pilgrims who happened to be armed, desiring to serve God whom they thought of more in terms of a feudal overlord than as a Father, is an indication of how far cultural assumptions can lead the most loyal of Christians into actions which in another age would be regarded as highly inappropriate. Even the monasteries were subject to a creeping secularisation. Often founded by lay rulers who demanded a continued voice in their running, they were endowed with lands and properties which they managed commercially, peopled with members of local families with whom they retained close links, and were expected to provide poor relief and hospitality as well as praying for the community. Many monks were there under coercion, and elaborate liturgies were devised to guard against the loss of natural enthusiasm for the spiritual life. The local monastery, in short, had become less a centre of devotion to God and more a complex business whose affairs stretched into every aspect of community life. It had become part of the cultural landscape.[37]

Meanwhile the church was becoming increasingly embroiled in politics. Popes and cardinals occupied positions of wealth and influence, and the church owned vast tracts of land and imposed a heavy tax on every peasant in Europe. Corruption, both moral and financial, was endemic. The ideal of a Christian society seemed doomed to failure, and Dante wrote an empassioned treatise arguing for a permanent separation between church and state. Once again it seemed that the gospel had been lost under a vast edifice of human accretions, and that its greatest strength, its ability to transcend culture, had again become its greatest weakness, its inclination to be overwhelmed by culture.

Francis and Dominic: speaking the gospel in new ways

In the year 1206 it occurred to the heir to a successful textiles business that a radical restatement of the gospel was needed. Like Anthony, we have heard of him: his name was Francis.[38] We have learned to think of him as a gentle man who loved birds and founded an order of friars. But behind the popular image was a man with the singleminded determination to sweep aside centuries of church culture and preach the gospel to an increasingly materialistic society by taking literally Jesus' command to sell all you have and give to the poor. Disowned by his father after using some of the family assets to repair a local church, Francis set off to lead a life of poverty, wandering from town to town and calling people to a renewed relationship with Christ. In 1210 he obtained the Pope's blessing, drew up a Rule of life based on the parables of Jesus, and with his followers set out on a radical renewal of the Christian mission. For the first time in centuries, "conversion" came to mean a deliberate and inner acceptance of the gospel, and not enrolment in a religious order. Francis allowed anyone to join him, providing only that he, or she, was willing to give his or her possessions to the poor.[39] Within 100 years there were 1,400 Franciscan communities scattered all over the known world, and the Franciscans continued to be at the forefront of international mission for centuries. Francis himself travelled to Egypt to present the gospel to the Sultan, in a lone attempt to convert the Saracens by words rather than force. He was unsuccessful; but the enormous response to the Franciscan movement in the Christian West offers an astonishing testimony to the readiness of people to accept the gospel when it is focussed clearly into a failing story.

Francis chose to speak the gospel into the new medieval urban environment with its problems of materialism and exploitation, and he spoke it in a compelling biblical language of renunciation and love. At the same time, his contemporary Dominic chose to speak it to the heretics of southern France and Spain, amongst whom the comfortable lives of the churchmen sent to correct their errors had cut no ice at all.[40] He too saw that rejection of the church's preoccupation with wealth and status was necessary, and like Francis he and his companions adopted a life of poverty. But Dominic's obsession was with truth, and he founded an order of friars dedicated to studying and preaching the gospel.

Whilst the church developed tactics of armed force and then inquisitorial repression in the attempt to stamp out the unorthodox beliefs of the Albigensian heretics in south-western France, Dominic persisted with his strategy of explanation. He recruited men who were prepared to devote themselves to study, and Dominicans soon began to occupy key posts in the universities. They put the excitement back into scholarship, and made the academic life serve the greater aim of equipping individuals to grasp and express the truth of the gospel in order to go and convert the world.[41] They too have continued to be a worldwide missionary movement, seeking to speak the truth of the gospel in a relevant way into many different cultures.

Renaissance and Reformation: culture and counterculture

It has been said that when Christianity takes itself seriously, it must either renounce or master the world.[42] As the Middle Ages became the Renaissance, it must be said that renunciation went increasingly out of fashion. It wasn't so much that the church became assimilated to the culture as that it *became* the culture. Church and world fused in a glory of artistic patronage, political power and luxurious living. But while popes and princes vied for supremacy, the medieval peasant struggled on, forced to finance this new culture but firmly excluded from its benefits. The rift between church and people became ever wider, and understanding of the gospel dwindled to its lowest ebb.

Rather than plunge into the intricacies of politics and patronage, perhaps it is easier to think of two men, one representing the best of the culture, the other the reproposal of the gospel. They never met. But their lives embody the ferocious and unprecedented clash between gospel and culture which we have come to know as the Reformation. Michelangelo was born in 1475. Painter, sculptor, architect and poet, he worked for the most powerful figures of the age in both Rome and his native Florence. Christian, as were all his contemporaries, he carved beautiful statues of the dead Christ, of Moses, of David, and responded repeatedly to commissions to decorate the chapels and rooms of the

Vatican with biblical scenes as successive popes sought to consolidate their power and status by outdoing their secular rivals in displays of wealth and patronage. In 1506 Julius II began the rebuilding of St Peter's, to be the largest (and most expensive) church in the world, and commissioned Michelangelo to carve a 40 piece tomb for himself to go in it. In 1513 Leo X (whose attitude to being elected pope is summarised in his statement that as God had willed it, he would enjoy it) employed him to decorate the Sistine chapel ceiling.[43]

The Sistine chapel ceiling was, and remains, one of the greatest achievements of human endeavour. The problem was that it, like so much else, had to be paid for. Some of the money came from the private wealth of the ruling families from whom these ambitious popes were drawn. But much of it came from the uneducated and half-starved peasants of Europe, who paid it in tithes, offered it for masses for the salvation of their souls and those of their families, confessed their sins and bought penances (likened by one historian to paying a fixed penalty for a parking ticket), and purchased "indulgences" with it.[44] And it was this latter practice in particular which was to appal our second protagonist, Martin Luther. Born in 1483, seven years after Michelangelo, into a German family of peasant stock, and ordained priest the year after Julius had called for the rebuilding of St Peter's in Rome, Luther watched his parishioners part with money they hadn't got to buy these indulgences – promises that sins could be forgiven, and time in purgatory after death therefore reduced, by the payment of cash sums to the church. The cash was useful; some went into the pockets of the indulgence sellers themselves, as we know from Chaucer's *Pardoner's Tale*; some went to the local bishop to pay off the debts he had run up in order to purchase his bishopric, as was the case in Luther's own diocese; and the rest went to Rome – for, amongst other things, the building of St Peter's.[45] "Did Christ

say, 'Let him who has a cloak sell it and buy an indulgence'?"
demanded Luther; and so the Reformation began. The issue
with which Luther grappled was that of salvation itself; could
it be secured, as the church had taught, by good works and
proper observance of rite and ritual – or did it not depend
rather on grace, to be received freely, through faith alone, as
a result of the death of Christ on the cross?

Michelangelo, still working away in Rome, was a child of
his age, and his work is imbued with the cry which defines
the Renaissance itself, the cry to return to the sources, and to
develop the human mind by a recovery of classical art and
scholarship. Further north, the same cry led Erasmus to
publish the New Testament in the original Greek, rather than
the approved Latin translation; and as Luther studied the text
he found that it offered little support for many of the
doctrines and practices of the church. With the invention of
the printing press and the spread of literacy, others found this
too, and the cry for reform grew stronger. Luther insisted that
the life of the church should be the life in Christ of the individual; that each individual may come directly and freely to
God in repentance and faith, and that the church in its
attempts to mediate between man and God had attempted to
chain and control the gospel itself. Within a few years indulgences and relics were a thing of the past, cloisters stood
empty, the Bible was being read by ordinary people in their
own language, and the power of the church was broken.
Luther was excommunicated on the grounds that his teaching
provoked "rebellion, division, war, murder, robbery, arson
and the collapse of Christendom",[46] and Michelangelo was
recalled to Rome and asked to decorate the altar wall of the
Sistine chapel with the traditional medieval theme of wrath
and judgement. The painting contains clear allusions to the
pre-Reformation themes of salvation by works and of the
efficacy of the intercession of Mary and the saints; gone is the
beauty of classical form and the celebration of the human

body, and once again the mood is dark and threatening. But it was too late. The corruption and control of the Renaissance church had been destroyed, its partnership with the culture exposed, and reformed churches sprang up all over Europe, preaching a renewed gospel of individual repentance and faith.

The Age of Reason

It is at this point that the modern era really begins. In the sixteenth and seventeenth centuries an enormous shift in thinking occurred. Fuelled by the Renaissance engagement with classical science, a new experimental approach to knowledge developed which paved the way for a complete change in people's understanding of the universe and their place within it.[47] It took the form of a scientific revolution. Its best known representative was Galileo, a mathematician who spent his life developing instruments which would enable him to base theories of the way the world works on accurate empirical data. This, in an intellectual environment which relied exclusively on text and tradition for the foundation of knowledge, was subversive enough; but in 1632 Galileo came up with proof that the earth goes round the sun, and not the other way round as was traditionally believed.[48] Fully grasping the implications of his methods, and unable to countenance what it regarded as an arrogant and heretical assault on the teaching of the church, the Holy Office of the Inquisition summoned Galileo to Rome to stand trial for heresy, forced him to recant, and placed him under lifelong house arrest.[49]

But the experimental approach was here to stay. The man who fixed it ineradicably on the map of human thought was Isaac Newton, born in the year of Galileo's death and consumed with the same independent desire to understand the physical universe. Galileo had dropped objects of differing weight from the top of the leaning tower of his native Pisa to see what happened; equally famously, Newton sat in a Lincolnshire orchard during an outbreak of plague, watching apples fall from trees and wondering why. He came up with three laws of motion, principles of universal application which could be used to explain both the motion of bodies on earth and also the movements of the planets round the sun; and founded the science of mechanics.[50]

The impact of the new scientific outlook was enormous. A living universe of mysterious forces had suddenly turned into one of predictable events governed by known laws; the world had become a machine, and human reason – not doctrinal obedience – was the new way to understand it.[51] Philosophers rushed into action, anxious to apply these new insights to their understanding of the human condition. A new confidence in human reason developed, and the eighteenth century would become known as the Age of Reason, or the Enlightenment.[52] The gospel fact was lost in the cultural story once again – God was still God, but his job description was sharply redefined to exclude anything which could not be measured, proved and understood. His new role is summed up in the title of a popular book of the time: *Christianity Not Mysterious*.[53]

One way or another, the church proved utterly inadequate to the task of evaluating these cultural changes. The Vatican rejected the new scientific outlook altogether as being (ostensibly) incompatible with Christian belief and (realistically) immensely threatening to its own power. It stuck to this ostrich-like strategy well into the nineteenth century, condemning Darwin's theory of evolution with the same repressive determination which it had used against Galileo and would use again when faced with the challenges of liberation theology. In England, where much of the new philosophy was born, the response of the church was more accommodating: its fortunes were ineradicably bound up with those of the state, and anything other than gentlemanlike conformity to the spirit of the age would have been severely disruptive to the welfare of both. And so the ministry of the church was essentially redefined as that of upholding "a moderate, rational and moral religion"; responsibility, rather than spirituality, came to characterise Anglicanism in the eighteenth century, and the church which developed was that rather unflatteringly depicted by Trollope half a century later.[54] Once again the secularised religion had lost touch with the needs of the people. Whilst philosophers and theologians debated and the clergy scrambled for livings, the ordinary people rioted against social conditions which left them badly paid and poorly fed. And all the church had to offer them was a secularised ideology which not only ignored their material needs but denied the emotional and spiritual aspects of their lives as well.

The solution was revival. First in Germany with the Pietists and the Moravians, then in Britain with George Whitefield and the Wesleys, finally in America with Jonathan Edwards and the First Great Awakening, the eighteenth century saw a resurgence of spirituality which stood in sharp contrast to the rationalism of the age. All these movements, called evangelical, were founded on the recovery of a personal response to a simple gospel of salvation through repentance and faith.[55] All were led by charismatic personalities who were not afraid to defy the established church, and all were characterised by mass turnings to Christ. In England Whitefield and Wesley soon found themselves banned from preaching their "enthusiastic" message in churches; they turned undeterred to open air preaching. Travelling all over the country on horseback, they addressed gatherings of thousands – to the dismay of the bishops, one of whom remarked that "the pretending to extraordinary revelations and gifts of the Holy Ghost is a horrid thing".[56] The eventual outcome in England was the Methodist Church, and one of the consequences was the social reform programme spearheaded by Wilberforce and others.[57] The impetus of the evangelical revivals sent missionaries all over the known world, and the gospel began to spread at a rate not seen since the first century. In many parts of the world that growth continues today.[58]

Conclusion

The gospel comes into a culture rather like the interruption of a fact into a story. As we trace the ebb and flow of its fortunes through history, we find a consistent pattern: starting with Jesus himself, the fact of the gospel is carried by people who use it to puncture the story rather as a pin punctures a balloon. These people have not been the influential members of society, the narrators of the story. Rather they have been ordinary individuals who have received the clarity of vision to identify the ways in which fact and story have become intertwined, and who have turned out to possess the determination to live and preach the gospel counterculturally. And because the culture is always different, they have had to live and preach the gospel in different ways. For the Roman Christians this meant disengagement from everything which called for the taking of religious oaths and the observance of secular cults, and at the same time learning to live out the commandment of love in a violent and plague ridden society. For the ascetics it meant withdrawing altogether from a world in which the church had seen its responsibilities of spiritual oversight mould with those of civil administration, and learning to pursue an independent relationship with God in the desert. For Francis it meant giving up his inheritance in an increasingly wealth and power conscious society and learning to act out the gospel through a life of poverty and service. For Dominic, on the other hand, it meant the pursuit of study in order to draw the heretical communities in south-western France and northern Spain back to an understanding of the truth – in an age when heretics and infidels were accustomed to receiving the gospel forcibly at the hands of the Inquisition or the crusaders. For Luther it meant risking career, reputation and life itself in order to mount a direct assault on the corruption of the Renaissance church, by relentlessly and publicly contrasting the truths of the New Testament with the oppressive doctrines and practices of the establishment, by waging a propaganda war all over northern Europe, by the skilful drawing in of political leaders, and not least by the subversive preaching of freedom to the peasant population. For Wesley it meant leaving the comfort of his Oxford college and the middle-class world of religio-philosophical debate which had come to dominate the church, and travelling all over the country on horseback to preach a non-intellectual gospel of salvation through faith to a working population effectively ignored by those whose job it was to teach and pastor them.

All these people proclaimed the gospel, and always it was the same gospel of repentance and faith; but in different cultures those simple facts of repentance and faith have needed to be proclaimed and lived out in different ways. Francis would not have had much impact preaching poverty to the peasants of the Reformation. Dominic's learning was not what was needed in the intellectual church of eighteenth-century England. Wesley's hyperactive lifestyle would not have been effective in the hustle and bustle of the late Roman empire, and I doubt whether Luther would get further than his own family doctor today. It is the same fact which is always on offer; but it must be offered in culturally relevant ways.

The obvious question remains: What then of our own culture? What is our own story about? What are the false assumptions which have become woven into the plot of our own lives as we cross the threshold of the third Christian millennium? We are the heirs to everything that has been told in these pages; but the story is being recast yet again, and now we too have the task of identifying the ways in which it is preventing us from understanding the life-changing fact of salvation. That is a hard thing to do; it is much easier, with the benefit of hindsight, to see what went right and what went wrong in history than it is to come to an objective view of a new story for which as yet we have no defining name, other than that it comes after what went before: postmodernism. And yet if we do not succeed in understanding this new culture and speaking relevantly into it, whole generations will be deprived of the life which Jesus died to bring them, and the focus of the Christian faith will remain elsewhere.

Notes

1 See P Johnstone, *The Church is Bigger Than You Think*. Johnstone estimates that, taken individually, almost 40% of the world's population is now Christian (pp.67–68); and that, taken nationally, nearly half the world's peoples have a majority of their population that would claim to be Christian (pp.106–07).

2 Peter Brierley (www.christian-research.org.uk) reports a decline of 31% in the number of those attending church each week in England between 1979 and 1998, and predicts that by 2020 fewer than 5% of the population will be churchgoers, decreasing to 2% by 2040 (*The Future of the Church: Religious Trends no.5).* Whilst weekly attendance doesn't provide a complete picture - 8 million out of a population of about 60 million say they attend church at least sometimes – it is significant that their average age is rising – Brierley suggests that by 2040 65% of churchgoers will be over the age of 65.

3 Over the last 20 years much has been written about the relationship between "gospel" and "culture" in contemporary society. A history of this movement and its main

exponents is to be found on the website www.gospel-culture.org.uk. The clearest definitions of "gospel" and "culture" are perhaps those given by L Newbigin, *Foolishness to the Greeks: The Gospel and Western Culture*, pp.3–4: culture is "the sum total of ways of living developed by a group of human beings and handed on from generation to generation"; gospel is "the announcement that in the series of events that have their centre in the life, ministry, death and resurrection of Jesus Christ something has happened that alters the total human situation and must therefore call into question every human culture".

4 One of the first to write about the enduring problem of the relationship between gospel and culture was Richard Niebuhr, *Christ and Culture*, 1952. Short historical overviews have been given by various writers, but as far as I know we do not as yet have any thorough study of the relationship between gospel and culture in different historical periods.

5 A census of citizens taken under Claudius is recorded by Tacitus in his *Annals of Imperial Rome*, p.245. A recent estimate put the total number of inhabitants at 45 million at the beginning of the first century. See P Johnstone, *The Church is Bigger Than You Think*, p.43.

6 For the imperial cult, see R Horsley, *Paul and Empire: Religion and Power in Roman Imperial Society*. For the mystery religions, see W H C Frend, *The Early Church*, ch.1; A H M Jones, *Constantine and the Conversion of Europe*, ch.3; and J T Sanders, *Charisma, Converts, Competitors*, pp.116–19. An evocative insight into the mix of religions is given in Lord Litton's novel *Last Days of Pompeii* (1834). For the philosophical approach, see the works of Cicero and Lucretius, both writing in the first century BC.

7 All these are reported in Tacitus' *Annals of Imperial*

Rome.

8 The best study of the spread of the gospel in the early centuries is Michael Green's *Evangelism in the Early Church*; see especially ch.5, "Evangelising the Gentiles". For the missionary journeys of Paul, see F F Bruce, *Paul, Apostle of the Free Spirit*.

9 Acts 17 (Athens), 14 (Lystra), 13 (Antioch), 19 (Ephesus). For a discussion of these episodes, see F F Bruce, *Paul, Apostle of the Free Spirit*. For Paul's presentation in Athens, see also M Green, *Evangelism in the Early Church*, pp.153–55.

10 See L Newbigin, *Foolishness to the Greeks*, p.6.

11 See M Green, *Evangelism in the Early Church*, ch.2. A H M Jones comments that religion was regarded as a department of government, and that paganism pervaded all public gatherings; *Constantine and the Conversion of Europe*, ch.3.

12 They were especially noted for their care of the sick during the plagues which swept the empire during the second and third centuries. See R Stark, *The Rise of Christianity*, ch.4, "Epidemics, networks and conversion", and R MacMullen, *Christianising the Roman Empire*, ch.4. Stark also has an excellent chapter, "The role of women in Christian growth", in which he points to the countercultural attitude to women prevailing in the early church.

13 For Nero see *Tacitus, Annals of Imperial Rome*, pp.365–66. For the various periods of persecution under Nero, Marcus Aurelius, Valerian and Diocletian, see W H C Frend, *The Early Church*, ch.6, 9, 11.

14 Statistics from R Stark, *The Rise of Christianity*, pp.6–7. Stark points out that fewer than a thousand of these Christians actually suffered martyrdom.

15 Accounts of Constantine's dream have come down to us in the works of Eusebius and Lactantius. See A H M

Jones, *Constantine and the Conversion of Europe*, ch.6. A good summary of the impact of Constantine on the church is given in C Howse (ed.), *AD: 2,000 Years of Christianity*, pp.32–33. Another excellent general historical survey is O Chadwick, *A History of Christianity*; see pp.58–61. Both these works are readable, illustrated and readily available.

16 He went to Africa to deal with the Donatists and called an international conference at Nicaea to deal with the Arians. See N H Baynes, *Constantine the Great and the Christian Church*.

17 All these changes are documented by R MacMullen, *Christianising the Roman Empire*, and R Markus, *The End of Ancient Christianity*.

18 Estimated by R MacMullen, *Christianising the Roman Empire*, p.86.

19 For the election, see O Chadwick, *A History of Christianity*, p.60; for the council, see W H C Frend, *The Early Church*, ch.21.

20 See P F Beatrice, *Introduzione ai Padri della Chiesa*, p.232.

21 Quoted by R Markus, *The End of Ancient Christianity*, p.166.

22 The earliest Christian communities seem to have been for women; Antony was able to entrust his sister to a community of virgins. See K Ware, "Eastern Christendom", in *The Oxford History of Christianity* (ed. J McManners). The first known Christian hermit was Paul of Thebes, who retired to a cave in 250.

23 We know a lot about Antony (251–356) from the Life written by his contemporary Athanasius. For this and the ascetic movement generally, see W H C Frend, *The Early Church*, ch.17, "Asceticism and the monastic movement in the fourth century"; and the classic work of D J Chitty, *The Desert A City*.

24 A good flavour of the ascetic life is given by O Chadwick, *Western Asceticism: Selected Translations*, which includes a number of sayings of the Fathers. For Symeon (390–459) and the "pillar saints", see the chapter on monasticism in D Schaff, *History of the Christian Church III*. Symeon's impact on the bedouins is recounted by R MacMullen, *Christianising the Roman Empire*, pp.1–3. See also the entries in *The Penguin Dictionary of Saints*.

25 Pachomius lived from 290 to 345, and founded his communities in the Nile valley. See D J Chitty, *The Desert A City*, ch.2; and W H C Frend, *The Early Church*, ch.17.

26 A good summary of the development of monasticism in the West is given by M A Smith, "Christian ascetics and monks", in *The History of Christianity*, ed. T Dowley. For further details, see C H Lawrence, *Medieval Monasticism*.

27 The extreme lifestyles of the ascetics were not easily reconcileable with the lifestyle of Jesus himself; too great a burden was placed on the individual; and it was hard to avoid the implication that there were two ways of living the Christian life: one committed, one less so.

28 In his study of church and culture in the Middle Ages, Richard Southern points out that "the dominating ideal in the rebuilding [of society] was that the unitary authority of the Empire should be replaced by the unitary authority of the papacy", *Church and Society in the Middle Ages*, p.24. For an overview of the whole period, see D Hay, *The Medieval Centuries*, Part I, "From empire to Christendom".

29 For a general sketch of the period, see C Morris, "Christian civilisation (1050–1400)" in *The Oxford History of Christianity*. The best work on the interaction of faith and culture in the Middle Ages is A Gurevic, *Medieval Popular Culture*. He describes a mix of folklore

and faith and points to the impossibility of eliminating traditional habits of thought amongst an essentially pagan and illiterate people.

30 See D Nineham, *Christianity Medieval and Modern*, ch.11.

31 The best general work on this penitential literature is J Delumeau, *Sin and Fear*. See ch.6.

32 For an account of popular medieval beliefs about life after death, see A Morgan, *Dante and the Medieval Other World*.

33 Gratian, quoted by D Nineham, *Christianity Medieval and Modern*, p.211. Italics mine.

34 *The Divine Comedy*, Dante's picture of the hereafter and its inhabitants, is available in a number of English editions.

35 J Le Goff, *Time, Work and Culture in the Middle Ages*.

36 There were also strong economic factors at work in the crusades. See H E Mayer, *The Crusades*.

37 See R Southern, *The Making of the Middle Ages*, pp.150–62; and D Lawrence, *Medieval Monasticism*, ch.7 "The cloister and the world".

38 An account of the life and mission of Francis is given by R Southern, *Western Society and the Church in the Middle Ages*, pp.272–99. For a more detailed study, and for earlier movements with similar aims, see R B Brooke, *The Coming of the Friars*.

39 Francis himself was never a priest, though many later Franciscans were. Even after ordination became common, there were separate lay orders for both men and women.

40 See R B Brooke, *The Coming of the Friars*, chs.4–5.

41 R Southern, *Western Society and the Church in the Middle Ages*, p.298. Southern treats the Dominicans alongside the Franciscans (see ref. above).

42 R H Bainton, *The Medieval Church*, p.42.

43 For a general introduction to the Renaissance, see P

Burke, *Culture and Society in Renaissance Italy* and D Hay, *The Italian Renaissance in its Historical Background*. Leo's remark is quoted by J Lortz, *How the Reformation Came*, p.92.

44 O Chadwick, *A History of Christianity*, p.158.

45 For indulgences, see R H Bainton, *Here I Stand: A Life of Martin Luther*, ch.4.

46 The verdict of the authorities at the diet of Worms in 1521, quoted by Bainton p.147. Luther was lucky – many of the would-be reformers of this period were burnt at the stake – Savanarola in Italy, Hus in Germany, Tyndale and Cranmer in England, among others.

47 It has been suggested that the emphasis of the reformed churches on individual thought also played a significant part in the development of the new science. The major theological thinker of the Reformation was John Calvin, who believed that God is to be understood in part through the study of the created world; this also acted as an encouragement for the development of empirical science. See A E McGrath, *Science and Religion*, p.10–11.

48 The theory had first been propounded by Copernicus who, fearing reprisals from the church, reluctantly published it only in 1543, the year of his death; it was developed by Brahe and then Kepler before receiving final proof in 1632 in Galileo's treatise "Dialogue concerning the two chief world systems". See A E McGrath, *Science and Religion*, pp.6–15.

49 His story has been movingly told by Dava Sobel in *Galileo's Daughter*, using the surviving correspondence between Galileo and his daughter.

50 See A E McGrath, *Science and Religion*, pp.16–21.

51 For the change from an organic to a mechanistic world-view, see C Merchant, *The Death of Nature – Women, Ecology and the Scientific Revolution*.

52 The passage from the new mechanistic worldview to the

Age of Reason is charted by W Barrett in *Death of the Soul: From Descartes to the Computer*. For outlines of the major scientific and philosophical movements of the period, see R Stewart, *Ideas that Shaped Our World*. The major philosophers were Descartes and Locke in the 17th century, Voltaire and Rousseau in the 18th. For a discussion of the Age of Reason, see G R Cragg, *The Church and the Age of Reason*, ch.15. For the implications of the Age of Reason, see D J Bosch, *Believing in the Future*, ch.2, "The legacy of the Enlightenment".

53 By John Toland, published in 1696, a popularisation of the philosophy of John Locke. See G R Cragg, *The Church and the Age of Reason*, p.78.

54 H D Rack, *Reasonable Enthusiast: John Wesley and the Rise of Methodism*, "Society and religion in the early 18th century", p.31. In England "ecclesiastical life was so intimately intertwined with the structure of politics that few who occupied places of power were willing to alter a system wherein the very defects proved convenient"; in Germany the church was "now not regarded as an institution sustained by a certain faith and expressing that faith in an appropriate corporate life, but as a useful agency of public policy, designed to inculcate such valuable attitudes as integrity, loyalty, submission, and obedience" – G R Cragg, *The Church and the Age of Reason*, pp.14, 97. The novels of Trollope offer a caricature of the church which retains more than a grain of truth even today.

55 The term "evangelical" in reference to churches was coined during the 18th century to denote those movements "which maintain that the essence of 'the Gospel' consists in the doctrine of salvation by faith in the atoning death of Christ, and denies that either good works or the sacraments have any saving efficacy" – OED.

56 Bishop Butler of Bristol. See the readable, if somewhat

hagiographical, biography of Wesley by Basil Miller, p.72. The standard study of the rise of Methodism is H D Rack, *Reasonable Enthusiast*, cited above.

57 In the 18th century Wilberforce and the Clapham Sect fought for the abolition of slavery and for educational and prison reform; in the following century Shaftesbury, Gladstone and others passed further social reform laws covering conditions in factories and mines, as well as political and further educational reforms.

58 International missionary work had been carried out by Franciscans, Dominicans and Jesuits during the 16th century in particular. But the father of modern mission is taken to be William Carey, who founded the Baptist Missionary Society in 1792. The Church Missionary Society followed in 1799, the British and Foreign Bible Society in 1804. The first World Missionary Conference took place in Edinburgh in 1910. For a brief history of mission and an outline of current developments, see P Johnstone, *The Church is Bigger Than You Think*.

CHAPTER FIVE:

THE GOSPEL TODAY: ASSESSING A CULTURE

If you want a definition of water, don't ask a fish.
Chinese proverb[1]

It is difficult to understand anything when you are personally immersed in it. It is more difficult when your whole experience of life has been shaped by it. It is virtually impossible when your very concept of who you are depends upon it. And yet this is the situation in which we find ourselves when we try to come to an objective understanding of our own culture. Like the fish in water, we are by definition the least qualified people to embark upon this task. But, unlike the fish, we do have various tools at our disposal. International air travel permits us to step outside our culture and into other quite different ones, more or less at the drop of a hat. And it has been my experience on doing this that the familiar assumptions which explain reality as you have experienced it in the first culture suddenly and alarmingly reveal themselves to have no validity whatsoever in the second. And that this happens most unnervingly not upon your arrival but upon your return: you step off the plane into the same airport, and drive home to the same house from which you came, and yet it all looks different, as if viewed through new spectacles with a radically different prescription. It is said that intellectual propositions often have a hidden source in personal experiences. For a Christian this is perhaps how it should be, for our faith is not a philosophy but a relationship with God himself. And it is therefore with my own experience of the dislocation of reality, and my reflections upon it, that I would like to start this chapter.

Out in Africa: reality changes shape

Sub-Saharan Africa is an increasingly common tourist destination. It is a land of sunsets and safaris, a magical world where lions stalk through shimmering landscapes and hippos laze in wide, slow-moving rivers. It is a place of adventure, offering the opportunity of escape from the stress of modern living into an ancestral world of natural beauty, seen from the safety of a four-wheel drive and through a comfortable haze of tented comfort. I first went there in 1999. Except that I didn't go on safari, I went to Chibwika. And in Chibwika I met the people.

Chibwika is a community of small settlements loosely scattered amongst the tangled woods of north-western Zambia, in a remote corner of land defined by its borders with the war-torn lands of Congo and Angola. The Foreign Office advises British nationals not to go there, but it was nonetheless there that I found myself, a member of a small SOMA team sent to support the ministry of the Anglican Church under the local leadership of Bishop Bernard Malango.[2] To get there we travelled backwards in time for two days, exchanging the hi-tech efficiency of bustling Heathrow for the more modest comforts of Lusaka Airport, and those in turn for the single-storey building of Kitwe, glued to a dusty landscape of red soil and high-rise termite mounds. After a night in Kitwe we journeyed for another day in two battered pickup trucks along a potholed tarmac road which became progressively narrower until eventually it turned into a single dust track wandering through gradually encroaching bush. Fifty kilometres beyond the last electricity pole, and after a pause to change a punctured wheel, we finally turned off the dust track and bumped down a wide strip cleared by hand through virgin forest in readiness for our arrival. It had taken 87 men, working on 25 metres each, eleven days. We bumped to a halt well after dark beside a blazing fire and one small, roofless, mud brick building.

At this point the party began. Dark figures emerged from the trees, picked out in the light of our headlamps; smiling white teeth shone in the firelight, and a dance of singing welcome erupted into the night air as they pressed around us to the rhythmic accompaniment of drums. For the next few days we slept on the rough floor of the brick hut and found ourselves thrust into a different world, struggling to understand the pressures faced by our hosts and the beliefs by which they tried to manage those pressures. We watched boys collecting firewood, girls fetching water from the single semi-stagnant puddle beneath a tired banana tree, women cooking their white paste cassava. We met Chief Chibwika himself, the donor of this land on which he hoped to see a new church, a school, a clinic, and a farm; and learned how he travels on foot between the villages for which he is responsible, appointing headmen and ensuring that law and order prevails amongst his million, maybe two million, people. We met the 80 or so new Christians nurtured by Thomson Chingembu, a local man trained as a catechist to serve his community but living, like the rest of them, with no income, no clean water supply, no easy access to education or health care, and owning little more than the clothes he stood up in; and we watched their joy as they sang whirling gospel songs of their own composition. It was our task to help these people think about what it might mean to be a Christian community, to encourage them, and to assess the ways in which we could best support them once we got home. And so we slept in the brick hut, preached the gospel, prayed for children with rickets, fevers and worms, and listened to tales of a different world. And then we experienced something of that world ourselves, as we entered with them through prayer into an oppressive realm of unfriendly spiritual forces, of ancestors to be placated and spirits to be acknowledged, of frighteningly ineffective traditional medicine, and of nightmares, bondage and spirit possession. As we prayed we felt spirits leave and peace flow through individuals as they turned to Christ; and we left with the promise that we would raise money towards their dream of a borehole and a road surface.

And then we moved on; an unnerving journey through the Congo past steel-eyed border guards to another, more prosperous, community where we blew bubbles for enthralled children, ate a feast of chicken with our fingers, and listened and taught and prayed for four days in a specially erected wood and brush shelter beside the white clay pits where bricks for the first permanent church building were being laid out to dry. Children sat motionless for hours as we talked, watched over by a man with a large stick, and in the evenings toads hopped along the inside of the straw walls of the wash huts where we learned to balance on one leg on a piece of soggy wood stranded in the middle of a patch of mud whilst attempting to wash the other foot in a tin bath of near boiling water. Often I watched a kite circling overhead, song pulsing out to meet it as it forked and flexed its tail above the banana groves, and found myself reflecting that this was a world of values and practices for which I had neither language nor even adequate thought patterns – a world in which language has no numbers and medicine is a spiritual matter, in which rats scurry past your head as you sleep, and in which women at water holes can't understand why you don't speak Bemba. It is a world where the stars look different and the sun goes round the wrong way, where Thomas Hardy's ore-stained reddlemen still sell oxide in the market, where people have leprosy, and evil spirits address you – in English – through illiterate speakers of tribal languages. And eventually I found it to be a world where pictures burst inside my swirling head and the landscape began to roar words from God, so many words pulsing out from the red sun and the wood-burnt morning and evening mist and the trees and the dust and the singing people, so many words and so little space to take them in and think about them that they all fell over one another for months afterwards. And I learned that it is a world where fear is thinly veiled behind the smiles: the powers of darkness, the need for money, the fragile skin on the waters below which disaster lurks, the menace of the untamed and uncontrolled, the civil wars on the borders, the haunting presence of AIDS.[3]

On the last day of our stay we rose early for the long journey back through the dark and violent Congo to our base at Kitwe, from which we would catch the first of our three planes home. And so I found myself standing on the rocky hillside outside the house in which we had slept, watching the sun come up over the distant horizon. I say watched, but perhaps experienced would be a better word, for it was a moment of perception rather than simply of vision: the enormous breadth of the dusty landscape, the round redness of the glowing sun as it emerged slowly above the wooded land stretched out before us, the mist flowing through the valleys, the river rumbling below and the dark leaves of the tree beside us. And as I stood with my companions on the hillside I was filled with awe; awe at the stupendous beauty and power of the landscape and above all at the one who made it, the one who rules over it, the one who can be found in and through it and in the lives of the people who know they need him. In going to Africa I found myself catapulted out of the false security of the Western world into the stark reality of life and death, in a place where the scale of things is simply vast, and the activities of man so small, like the plumes of scattered smoke rising here and there above the trees. It seemed that God was there, in the air, that we could touch him, feel him, breathe him. I knew that in Africa there are no props, and there is no false security, but only dependence on God: God who creates, God who is, God who acts; God who spoke and God who continues to speak. And I was reminded of the familiar words:

> In the beginning was the Word, and the Word was with God, and the Word was God. He was in the beginning with God. All things came into being through him, and without him not one thing came into being. What has come into being in him was life, and the life was the light of all people. The light shines in the darkness, and the darkness did not overcome it.
>
> John 1:1–5

And as we watched the sun rise, we knew that the darkness could never overcome it. There it was, hanging round and red, from nowhere; we saw it come, and it took precisely three minutes. Three minutes to send light into darkness, three minutes to light up a world, to light it red with the red of the cross, red over a world God made and yet which has no light to see him by, red over a world of other spirits and needy people and the yawning chasm of fear which lurks behind the beauty of it all. And again the thought rushed into my dazed mind: How do we live, in our world of material comfort? We wake in the darkness, we turn on the light, get into the shower, and drive off in the car. We live in man's environment; in Africa they live in God's environment. Ours is more comfortable; but theirs is more real. And it was at that moment, when the round red sun rose above the horizon in the half light and shone from behind the tree over the dark woods and misty valleys, that I understood the urgency of God's desire to bring light and life to his people, be they poor and black or rich and white. And it struck me how desperately we too need to escape, from the false certainties of an illusory material world into the eternal realities of a spiritual one – a world which dominates every moment in rural Africa, but with which we have almost totally lost touch.

Back in England: a new pair of glasses

As I returned to England and the curious cluttered comfort of fitted carpets and supermarkets, I began to wonder what exactly was the challenge which Zambia offers to us, if we try to look at our own culture through the values of theirs? The countries of sub-Saharan Africa are notoriously enmeshed in social, economic and political problems which I cannot even begin to evaluate here, and its peoples live not in the romantic world of sunset safaris but in a real one of oppression and debt. But as I found myself welcomed into the homes and lives of the ordinary people first of Zambia and then, a year later, of northern Tanzania, I began to wonder how our take-for-granted world might look through their eyes.

I think that one obvious language which they speak and we do not is the language of community. The people we met in the remote rural areas we visited know what it is to belong to one another. They live a life in which both pain and joy are articulated and shared, in which children are the children of the whole community, in which labour is divided equally amongst people of all ages, and in which a framework of tradition governs relationships and practices. It is a world we have lost, a world which for us is to be found only in the pages of novels from time gone by, and a world which speaks volumes into our fragile culture of fragmentation, independence, and stifled dissatisfaction. In Zambia the gospel somehow makes sense; this is the same world of mutual interdependence, and of reliance on the things that God provides rather than those which man has created, which we find in the pages of both the Old and the New Testaments. It is a world in which you meet women at wells and face their questions about who you are and where you come from; a world in which you shake hands with lepers and accept hospitality from strangers, in which food is cooked over a communal fire and eaten from a common bowl, and the people share with you all they have; and a world in which widows and orphans are cared for by the community, even to breaking point. And it was a world in which we too learned to depend on each other, a small group of strangers flung together and finding that God was there in our relationships with a power and intensity that is rarely possible at home.

The second language spoken in Zambia and almost entirely foreign to us is the language of dependence on God. The people we met know their need of God; they live a precarious life of vulnerability and weakness, disease and death, a life where the spirit world is as much part of daily experience as the material. And as we drank boiled water from the almost stagnant pool which was their only supply, as we listened to them sing the words of the gospel into the embers of a dying fire, and as we retired to sleep on mud floors with rats running round us and goats yowling outside, we too learned again, in this land of joy and of pain, of laughter and of fear, what it is to know that we depend upon God.

And so I returned to England with Jesus's challenge ringing in my ears: the challenge to look at the world not through the spectacles of the prevailing assumptions about where well-being is to be found, but through the spectacles worn by God himself. I came to two immediate conclusions.

The first was that Jesus would challenge the materialism of our whole worldview. By that I do not mean simply our desire to accumulate possessions, but rather our concept that our human needs will best be met within the material world, by the elimination of poverty, by the pursuit of a certain standard of living, and by an increasing reliance on technology and human ingenuity. The truth is that, desirable though all these things may be, ultimately none of them will satisfy. We kid ourselves. We live our lives nestled deep in a bubble of illusion, and when the bubble bursts, as it does for each one of us in one way or another, sooner or later, we are left defence-less and miserable, because we have replaced the realities of the spiritual world with the false comfort of the material one. And so to go to Africa is instructive. We cannot ignore the basic needs they have for safe water and adequate health care, and we cannot ignore the spiritual, political and moral dark-ness in which their lives are so often entrammelled. Africa is a land of hardship, violence, oppression and want, and to claim anything else would be naive. But at the same time I could not but feel envious of a life lived uncluttered in the starkness of dependence on one another and on God, and an existence untrammelled by Sainsbury's reward cards and the ever-present roar of traffic as people who do not know one another honk furiously in their daily attempts to shave as many seconds as possible off the time it takes to get to work. Our affluence carries an illusion: the illusion that in a wealthy, technological society we do not need God. Stripped of the affluence, in many African countries they know that they do.

My second conclusion was that Jesus would challenge the religious assumptions not just of our society but of our churches. They are assumptions which come out of the expe-rience of 300 years of a rationalistic and materialistic culture, in the course of which our values have become tinged with secular beliefs which we have held uncritically – even when we have found them to provide a curiously ineffective base for ministry. We have consoled ourselves by blaming the materialistic worldview of modern society for the decline of interest in the gospel. But perhaps the fault lies not with soci-ety but with the church. Maybe it is not the culture, but our inability to speak the truth into the culture, that has made us ineffective. After all, the Roman empire, with its rigid power structure, its widespread sexual immorality, and its many gods and religions, could scarcely be said to be obviously culturally sympathetic to the gospel – and yet it was during those centuries that the gospel spread at a greater rate worldwide than has been seen in any subsequent period. The gospel is given to bring healing to a culture; often it seems that we allow it to become infected by the culture.[4]

Understanding a culture

The word "culture" is notoriously difficult to define. In this book so far I have tried to express what culture is by using pictures. Culture is a bubble, a wall, a mental framework, a story. But perhaps it is time to be more precise.

> Culture is the way of life of a particular people living together in one place.
> Culture is an integrated system of beliefs, of values, and of institutions which binds a society together and gives it a sense of identity, dignity, security and continuity.
> Culture is the effort to provide a coherent set of answers to the existentialist situations that confront all human beings in the passage of their lives.[5]

Culture is a shared thought world, put into practice in such a way that it forms a society. Thoughts come only in words, and so it follows that the vocabulary of a culture reveals its values. For example, our Western culture offers a vast range of words to describe consumer goods and technological processes, whereas the Maasai people of East Africa have an equally astonishing number to describe the various attributes of cattle. So language provides a guide to culture – and the development of a large stock of new words such as we are seeing at the moment is one of the major symptoms of rapid cultural change.[6] For words both reflect and create the reality which they represent.

The intellectual foundations of our Western culture

All human thinking has to start from somewhere. Indeed, I think we can go further than that, and say that every human culture is ultimately based on a single foundational proposition. From the time of Constantine, the cultural framework of Western society had been formed by the concept of revelation. The source of all knowledge was God, and the foundational statement was the one with which we began this book: "In the beginning was the Word." But in the seventeenth century all that changed. We saw in Chapter 4 that the rise of empirical science provoked a crisis of confidence in the concept of revelation as the source of knowledge, and a search began for a more reliable foundation. The thinking on which our present, modern culture is built takes its starting point from a single sentence written by one man in the year 1637. The sentence was "I think, therefore I am", and its author was the French philosopher René Descartes. Descartes was trying to answer the fundamental question "How do we know things?", and he concluded that the only reliable source of knowledge was human reason. All human thinking in the West since then has been based on this assumption, and great advances have been made in our understanding of the world we live in as a result. The industrial revolution, the development of modern medicine, the rise of technology and the great political, social and economic institutions of our time all spring ultimately from the systematic and rational quest for understanding based on the application of human reason.

The result has been the gradual construction of a new worldview. This worldview we call modernism or secular modernity. It is not a philosophy alone, but rather the building of a whole economic, industrial and political infrastructure on a foundation of rationality.[7] It is a view which places the highest value on the logical, practical, visible, measurable and quantifiable. It has swept the globe, causing turmoil in those cultures whose foundational propositions are incompatible with the statement of Descartes – most particularly, in Islamic cultures.[8] It has brought great advances in our ability to control the world we live in, and in the material and economic prosperity of those societies which have succesfully embraced it. We enjoy a higher standard of living than any society ever before, and according to our own values we should be happier than ever before. And yet somehow this does not seem to be the case.[9] Indeed, if we were to take laughter as a simple index of happiness, we would be forced to conclude that the average inhabitant of Chibwika seems considerably happier than the average inhabitant of Leicester or London.

Painting pictures with square brushes: the nature of modernity

The spectacular achievements of science and technology carry enormous potential for good. I am sitting in a centrally heated house before an extraordinarily sophisticated laptop computer which enables me not only to write but also to research and to communicate with others; I can see perfectly, and well beyond the eight inches within the natural focus of my eyes; and I am married to a man whose life was once saved by spending three weeks attached to an astonishing array of life-preserving machines in an intensive care unit. In Chibwika they have none of these things; they toil, suffer and die.

But we abuse our material achievements if we look to them to meet the inner needs of our souls. The problem with modernism is not that it is bad but that it is incomplete. It has brought us many blessings. And yet it has been said that we are the only people in the whole of history to have supposed that a mechanistic and individualistic understanding of life offers the way to become fulfilled and whole persons – for that is precisely what we *have* supposed.[10] The problem with modernism is that it leaves things out. In stating that the foundational value of society is human reason, it follows that everything which is not susceptible to human reason is marginalised. When we value the material over the spiritual, we also value thinking over feeling, analysis over creativity, fact over intuition, and technology over art. "How" becomes more important than "why", knowledge more important than belief, structures more important than relationships, and money more important than everything.[11] Religion retreats into the private realm and becomes a purely personal matter, and progress becomes the ultimate goal. In modernism, fundamental human needs that cannot be, and were not meant to be, addressed with the tool of rational thought remain unidentified and unmet. And so reality loses its relational and spiritual dimensions.

The result is that reality in the modern world has become, as sociologist Max Weber remarked a long time ago, "dreary, flat and utilitarian, leaving a great void in the souls of men which they seek to fill by furious activity and through various devices and substitutes".[12] In this brave new world worth is measured by income, and fulfilment sought in role, status and possessions, or just in the busyness of a full diary. In our ceaseless search for meaning we have learnt to live by the ticking of the clock, rushing to cram everything in as though our lives depended on it. Tokyo boasts a restaurant which charges by the minute, and books have titles like *How to Have a 48-Hour Day* or even, in a terrifying assault on the timeless world of the child, *One-Minute Bedtime Stories*. The wonders of modern technology are harnessed to help us in our quest; we keep in touch on ever-updated mobile phones, opt for painfree and timetabled Caesareans so as to avoid the unplanned indignity of childbirth, and surround ourselves with more material comforts than ever before. And all this we do as individuals.

The consequences are dire.

> 'God is dead', people say. 'The modern world has come of age and outgrown the tutelage of faith'. But its prodigal descent has been swift. Modern cities make people closer yet more alienated at once; powerful modern weapons bring their makers to the point of impotence and destruction simultaneously; modern media promise facts but deliver fantasies; modern education introduces schooling but fosters subliteracy; modern technologies of communication encourage people to speak more and say less and to hear more and listen less; modern lifestyles offer do-it-yourself freedom but slavishly follow fads and end often in addictions; modern conveniences, being disposable and ephemeral, bring people closer to happiness but further from joy; modern styles of communication make people hungry for intimacy and authenticity but more fearful than ever of being prey to phoniness, manipulation, and power games.
>
> Os Guinness[13]

And it gets worse than that. As secular modernity celebrates its many achievements, God is banished to *Songs of Praise* and man is redefined as essentially good. Meanwhile 167 million people are killed by ideologically or politically motivated tyranny in a single century.[14] "The Lord knows the thoughts of man; he knows that they are futile," observed David, the greatest spiritual writer of all time. Secular modernity cannot deliver the goods.[15]

The vacuum within

There is within the human spirit an irrepressible yearning, an awareness that this world is not all there is, that existence has dimensions beyond the material, that parts of our makeup cannot be rationally defined and objectively catered for. And so, deep down, we know that in our modern society we are not connected to something we need to be connected with if we are to be fully alive. Deprived of the language to express these things, we have grown used to seeking inadequate answers within the parameters of the material. Traditionally, we expressed the yearnings of the spirit in the language of art, poetry, music and prayer. But in a modern world we find we have no time for poetry, our artists reflect the emptiness of our hearts in an array of soup cans, urinals and empty plinths, music is used to dull rather than arouse consciousness, and prayer is seen as little more than wishful thinking.

In other cultures these dimensions of humanity have not been lost; on our first evening in Zambia I watched Bishop Bernard Malango express his welcome in a slow, flowing movement in which he likened himself to a tortoise, shell on the outside, but inside dancing with joy, and realised that here was a whole other language, a language vastly different from the self-importance of the measurable with which we so often cloak ourselves and our affairs. "I think, therefore I am", we mutter to ourselves as we pursue our careers, our rights and our individual freedoms, whilst simultaneously watching the fabric of society gradually break down before the wave of superficiality, drug dependency, family fragmentation and loss of community which follows the tide of individualism. "I am, because we are", the Kenyan liturgy states.[16] In the West we have long since abandoned being for doing and having. Our lives are full, and yet we feel a deep sense of unfulfilment. Spiritual writer Henri Nouwen suggests that one way to express the spiritual crisis of our time is to say that most of us have an address but cannot be found there.[17]

Drinking salt water: the rise of postmodernism

This state of affairs is plainly intolerable. As it has become ever clearer that the promises given by autonomous thinking have failed to provide the security and happiness we were looking for, it has begun to occur to us that we need a different approach. The new approach as yet has no name; it is more a mood than a method, and it is as yet unclear whether it marks a radical change in our thinking or whether it is best understood as a new phase within modernity itself. Whatever it is, we have chosen to refer to it as postmodernity.[18]

What postmodernity does is rebel against rationality. Postmodernity knows that even physics isn't as physical as it used to be. It knows that Einstein worked by intuition, that light is both particles and waves (but not at the same time), and that Stephen Hawking realises he can explain how but not why. It knows that the flapping wings of butterflies cause chaos in the winds of the opposite hemisphere, and that something as solid as an elephant is mostly empty space within dancing atoms, and could be squashed quite successfully into the size of a mouse (albeit a rather heavy one).[19] Postmodernity no longer says, "I think, therefore I am", for all this thinking has turned out to be, in terms of personal fulfilment, rather fruitless and restrictive; and whilst the world of work remains structured essentially on modernist lines, in our personal lives we now prefer a more DIY approach in which truth is created rather than discovered, and in which we build our own values and identities from the variety of choices and experiences available to us. "I feel, therefore I am" is perhaps a more accurate slogan for our postmodern world.[20]

It would be a contradiction in terms to offer an analysis of postmodernity, for its whole purpose is to find a language which does not analyse. Perhaps it is sufficient to slice through the cake in two places, and to look at what we find there.

1. Consumption replaces production

Until recently, the identity of each individual was defined by his or her role in society. My father spent his working life as a civil servant. My father-in-law spent his as a manager in the

Gas Board. My great aunt, who did not marry, worked for an electrical company called Belling and Lee. My mother-in-law, who did, had a rather reluctant career as a housewife. Society was built of farms, factories, companies and institutions, and the key values were production and maintenance. The aim of the modern society was to produce enough food and goods to meet the material needs of the population, and for each individual to find his or her role within the structure of this collective enterprise. I offer a caricature, of course. But let me match it with another. My contemporaries at university went off into a much more transient world of short-term career moves through management consultancies, media organisations, advertising firms and web companies. They went out into a culture based not on production and maintenance, but on choice and consumption. This is the new landscape of our souls. The materialist goals of modernism have been reached, and a whole new world of options is unfolding before us. We now determine who we are and where we seek the answers to life's questions in a different and more fluid way.

In this new world everything is possible, and most of it is for sale. The fastest growing form of communication is advertising; and advertisers sell not products but identities, lifestyles, and dreams. We are buying not a product but an image, not cosmetics or trainers but concepts of self.[21] As we buy, we build a tailor-made world of our own choosing. And it isn't just things that we buy. We buy leisure: package holidays, theme park tickets, laser game shows. We buy relationships: psychotherapy, professional carers, massage. We buy bodies: plastic surgery, beauty treatments, health clubs. We buy experiences: bungee jumping, aromatherapy, rides in little creme egg cars through the chocolate wonderworld of Cadburyland. As a society we have accepted the message that happiness and fulfilment are there to be grasped. Postmodernism is consumption.[22]

And so we buy. I have heard mothers encourage recalcitrant toddlers with the promise of an afternoon's shopping. I have watched the endless queue of cars heading into the city centre on Saturdays, full of people who want to purchase the inner glow of met needs, and come home instead with plastic goods bought on credit. And I have gazed with new eyes on my way back from Tanzania at the luxury of Amsterdam Airport, where toilets flush and perfume themselves after each use, and every luggage trolley bears the glittering slogan "See, buy, fly!" – astonishing when you have been using an insect-ridden hole in the ground, when transport has been, if you are lucky, a method of getting from A to B, and your best endeavours to buy presents for your children have yielded nothing more exciting than two bits of material and a wooden pen. The sophistication of our consumer society is simply unbelievable, viewed through any other eyes but our own. "Do you not find", asked Thomas, a banker in Mbulu, Tanzania, as a chicken strutted through his simple living room, "that in the West people have so much more than they need that they do not know they need God?". As I ate the dumplings cooked over a charcoal burner outside, and watched his daughter hanging the socks she had unobtrusively rewashed for me after my knuckle-busting failure to get them clean, I was forced to agree with him. The postmodern world invites us to slake our thirst by drinking deeply from the golden goblet of consumerism. We drink; only to find that we are drinking salt water.

2. Image replaces word

Until recently, knowledge was based on facts, and facts came in words. Facts still come in words, but they now come with such astonishing frequency that we cannot take them in. We live in a world of information overload, and the only way we can cope with the text messages and the bleeps and the pagers and the emails and the commercials and the radio and the

internet and the junk mail is to switch off and adopt an attitude of continuous partial attention.[23] Words are losing their
power, and as we move into the culture of the screen we are
learning to think not with our minds but with our eyes.
Knowledge now comes in images, and the visual has replaced
the verbal as the major form of communication. I have found
it fascinating to feel the challenge of the internet to my habit-
ual ways of thinking. It is, I find, impossible to use it in any
way which is compatible with the old linear patterns of
rational thought. Every time I follow a link, a new screenful
of information bursts into my mind. These links do not operate in straight lines but in sideways jumps, and I experience a
constant interruption to my train of thought, and the increasing stress of trying to remember where I came from so that I
can get back there – until I realise that the machine won't do
it that way, and that I have no choice but to work with it on
its own terms of successive and disconnected images. It has
been remarked that these processes of electronic communication are inevitably changing not only our patterns of thought
and perception, but also our concept of the nature of reality
itself.[24] *In the beginning was the image.* The image went, and
was replaced by another image. With it went truth, so that
truth now exists only in the present, and in the image in
which it is temporarily incarnated. Did Neil Armstrong and
Buzz Aldrin really land on the moon? my son asked me the
other day. Of course they did, I replied, I remember actually
watching them do it, on a fuzzy black and white television
screen well before breakfast. But, he said, how do we know
the Americans didn't fake it? It's just an image.

If postmodernism is the culture of the image, perhaps its
best representation so far has been the Dome built in
Greenwich, London, to celebrate the millennium and intro-
duce the brave new world that lies ahead of us; and it is here,
in the place of my birth and still the historical centre from
which time and the globe are measured, that I would like to

complete the cultural journey that took me down the meridian and backwards through culture to Zambia.

The Dome was intended as the apogee of 2,000 years of human achievement, a summary of progress so far. I found it intriguing: a vast, teflon-coated circus tent with yellow poles, filled with noise and air and people, screens and zones and fast-food outlets, colours and confusion, yet with little self-contained oases of absorption scattered within it. It seemed as good an incarnation of the spirit of the age as you could wish to find: money, technology, noise, and a bombardment of sensory information from all directions, information that was mostly superficial, and which penetrated by virtue of its jostling competitiveness only into the outer layer of the mind. There wasn't time to see everything in a day; but as we wandered round the various zones it became clear that this was quite different from anything we had experienced before. The Journey zone would once have been called a museum of transport; but as you were carried relentlessly up and along its silver walkways and staircases you were receiving not through your mind but through your central nervous system; and not information but a deluge of ever-changing impressions, voices, images. The Rest zone was an empty shell of whitewashed brick, curved like a rustic kiln or the white-baked form of a southern Italian trullo, a space where people intruded in the moving, rustling black of their polyfibre jackets onto the contemplative calm of a rounded ceiling suffused with the changing colours of the rainbow and washed with an amorphous millennium music, stretching without shape or melody into the promised timelessness of the future. The Mind zone, sponsored by Marconi, was peculiarly empty, with cavernous spaces and almost nothing in them, except for the striking statement that if everyone on earth simultaneously made 200,000 phone calls, they would create the same number of connections as exist in a single human cerebral cortex. The Faith zone implicitly relegated faith to a bygone era of low-tech irrelevance; here the facts of the life and ministry of Jesus were displayed, with an acknowledgement of his contribution to human civilisation: he taught, and began a tradition of Christian schools, and he healed, and became the inspiration for Christian hospitals. After a clutter of other religions we emerged into the statement of postmodern faith: a weird, empty white room called "night rain", lit with soft blue light, with a ceiling shaped like the inside of a snail's shell, there for you to fill with the contents of your meditation; a DIY spirituality with a technological ambience of light and sound.

Everywhere we went, the content was minimal, and the sense impressions everything. I couldn't face the Talk zone, a wall of speech bursting out in a million recorded voices every time you walked past it, suggesting a nightmare of mobile phones and insistent, pervasive information searching through the air like a swat-away hum of hungry mosquitoes homing in on their hapless human targets. The Work zone cast modernism as an array of toy hamsters scuttling round wheels, from which you were ushered into a postmodern interactive room of noise and demands – test your reaction times, your mental maths, your computer skills, your capacity for teamwork, your hand-eye coordination. The Learning zone moved you from yesterday's school lockers into a twee film about sycamores expanding with your horizons from the seed of learning, releasing you finally into a starlit orchard of artificial trees and career-inspiration computer screens. My favourite moment came in the Play zone: a circle of carpet, a screen on the wall, a sensor and you. As you moved on the carpet the sensor translated your movements into light and sound, and then refracted it through mirrors into a kaleidoscope image on the wall in front of you. I circled and turned and swayed; images and music played in harmony all around me, and everything except the fleeting present moment faded into the shadows.

The Dome, suggested a friend from the postmodern world of international consumer consultancy, is a statement of the need to reintegrate the right brain approach into the stifled linear thinking of modernism. He is probably right; but what it actually created was a museum of sense impressions and fleeting images, a statement of the supremacy of the imagination in a culture which has no significant thoughts with which to fill the mind. We emerged with a sensation of the vastness of human achievement, and without so much as a sentence to express it in. And sensation is perhaps the key word of postmodernism. Postmodernism offers experience, impression, superficiality and insubstantiality. It is a media age, an age of the transient, of feelings dressed up as thought, and science experienced as magic. It offers choice and opportunity, but it also masks a profound vacuum. The children retreated exhausted to the comforting familiarity of an outdoor adventure playground, and I gazed at the shining windows of Canary Wharf and noticed how much cleaner the river was than it used to be. And yet I couldn't help feeling that somehow postmodernism has thrown the baby out with the bathwater.

The happiness we try to buy is no more substantial than the crock of gold at the foot of the rainbow.

Notes

1 Quoted by L Newbigin, *Foolishness to the Greeks*, ch.2, and by many others since.

2 SOMA stands for Sharing of Ministries Abroad. Its UK mission statement is "We work for the transformation of individuals and churches and the healing of communities and their lands through the renewing power of the Holy Spirit". See www.somauk.org.

3 Thomas Hardy's 1878 novel *The Return of the Native* has as one of its characters a reddleman, an itinerant

seller of red oxide, whose skin and clothes are stained with the red of his product.

4 For a comparison between the conditions of the Roman empire and our own times, see H A Snyder, *Radical Renewal*, ch.2.

5 See T S Eliot, "Notes towards the definition of culture", p.298; J Stott and R T Coote, *Down to Earth: Studies in Christianity and Culture*, p.313; Donald Bell, quoted in D Carson, *Telling the Truth*, p.19. See also T Eagleton, *The Idea of Culture*.

6 The relationship between culture and vocabulary is discussed by L Osborn, *Restoring the Vision*, ch.1; and R Zacharias, But *Deliver Us from Evil*, p.18.

7 The development of Descartes' thought into a coherent philosophy took place in the 18th century, in an intellectual movement commonly referred to as the Enlightenment. The 19th century saw the construction of a new social reality on the basis of Enlightenment thinking. And yet modernity is not a philosophy, but the embodiment and transmission of that philosophy in institutional carriers. "Modernity cannot be understood simply as a fallout of Enlightenment ideas. It is a composite reality that encapsulates the economic, technological, social and philosophical conditions of the modern world" – A Walker, *Telling the Story: Gospel, Mission and Culture*, p.105. There have been countless recent analyses of the development and nature of modernity; a good summary is given in the introductory essay in the collection *Faith and Modernity* (ed. P Sampson). For the Enlightenment, see G R Cragg, *The Church and the Age of Reason*, ch.15. A briefer discussion is given in R Stewart, *Ideas that Shaped our World*, p.72–73 under the heading "The Enlightenment – reason challenges tradition". A generally accepted definition of modernism is the period 1789–1889 (T C Oden, *Two Worlds*, p.32).

8 See V Samuel, "Modernity, mission and non-Western societies", in *Faith and Modernity*, ed. P Sampson *et al.* R Zacharias quotes Tillich's analysis of three types of culture: heteronomous (directed by authority outside the individual, e.g. Islam), theonomous (a balance of authority from without and intuition from within, e.g. Hinduism) and autonomous (every individual is self-determining and independent of authority, e.g. modern Western culture). He remarks that Western and Eastern cultures are built on diametrically opposed foundational beliefs concerning what brings life meaning, and highlights the fundamental incompatibility between Islam and secular modernity which has since thrust itself onto the world stage. See *But Deliver Us from Evil*, pp.82–88.

9 Robert Putnam reported that the incidence of depression amongst Americans is ten times what it was two generations ago – *The Week,* 9 December 2000. Antidepressant prescriptions in the UK have gone up from 9 million in 1991 to 22 million in 2002 – *Sunday Times*, 19 January 2003.

10 J Drane, *The McDonaldization of the Church*, p.20.

11 A recent survey by the advertising agency McCann Erickson showed that when asked what makes for happiness, British teenagers put money above friends and love. Quoted by G Cray, *The Gospel and Tomorrow's Culture*, p.5. Elaine Storkey remarks that economic factors now take priority over religious and moral ones in deciding issues – see "Change and decay in British society" in *The Gospel in the Modern World*, ed. D Eden and M Wells.

12 Quoted by A Walker, *Telling the Story*, p.115.

13 Os Guinness, "Mission modernity" in *Faith and Modernity* ed. P Sampson, p.333.

14 Statistic given by J M Houston, "Modernity and spirituality", in *Faith and Modernity* ed. P Sampson *et al.*, p.183.

15 Psalm 94:11 (NIV). A brilliant analysis of the implica-

tions and consequences of the modern worldview is given by C Colson and N Pearcey, *How Now Shall We Live?*

16 Quoted by J Mbiti, "The Bible in African culture", in *Paths of African Theology* ed. R Gibellini, p.36. See also his summary statement: "I am because we are; and since we are, therefore I am" – J F Mbiti, *African Religions and Philosophy*, pp.2–3. A person exists primarily as a part of a whole commnity, and not as an individual. V Donovan summarises the Maasai identity in the phrase "I am known, therefore I am", *Christianity Rediscovered*, p.189.

17 *Making all Things New*, p.16.

18 For a discussion of the relationship between modernity and postmodernity, see the introductory essay in *Faith and Modernity* ed. P Sampson *et al.*

19 Einstein: "The supreme task of the physicist is the search for those highly universal laws from which a picture of the world can be obtained by pure deduction. There is no logical path leading to these laws. They are only to be reached by intuition, based on something like an intellectual love"; quoted by L Newbigin, *The Gospel in a Pluralist Society*, p.31. Hawking: "Although science may solve the problem of how the universe began it cannot answer the question: Why does the universe bother to exist? I don't know the answer to that" – interview in *Cam* magazine, Easter 2000. For quantum physics, see P Davies, *God and the New Physics*, ch.9, "The quantum factor". For the butterfly and chaos theory, see A Peacocke, *God and Science*, p.8. For the elephant, see M Mayne, *This Sunrise of Wonder*, p.115.

20 For the postmodern redefinition of truth, see O Guinness, *Time for Truth: Living Free in a World of Lies, Hype and Spin*, p.12.

21 Os Guinness offers the term "designer personalities" to express the way in which we forge our own identities

from an array of surface attributes; *Time for Truth*, ch.2. Charles Revlon remarks, "In the laboratory I make cosmetics, in the store I sell dreams"; quoted by G Cray, *The Gospel and Tomorrow's Culture*, p.4. Susie Orbach comments in *The Sunday Times* that "nothing would excite a young person more than the ability to buy, buy, buy and being famous. Contributing to society is not what it is about any more. Image is everything" (20 January 2002).

22 M Moynagh suggests we have moved from an agricultural economy to a manufacturing economy and now to an "experience economy"; see *Changing World, Changing Church*, p.8. Helpful discussions of postmodernity and consumption are given by J Drane, *The McDonaldization of the Church*, and P Sampson, "The rise of postmodernity" in *Faith and Modernity*. For postmodernity and consumerism, see the excellent article by Alan Storkey, "Postmodernism is consumption", in *Christ and Consumerism*, ed. C Bartholomew and T Moritz.

23 A letter by Doug Varey to the *Daily Telegraph* in June 2002 pointed out that whereas the Ten Commandments required 300 words and the American Declaration of Independence 1,300 words, the European Union regulations governing the export of duck eggs require a phenomenal 26,900 words. Microsoft researcher Linda Stone has concluded that an attitude of continuous partial attention is the only solution to such a world – *The Week* 10 February 2001.

24 "Electronic images draw us into a seduction of simulation where there is no longer any relation between pictures and things, no transcendental or grounded reality, but only a world of self-referential images" – the view of the French sociologist Jean Baudrillard, cited by A Walker, *Telling the Story*, p.76. A similarly profound shift in the landscape of human knowledge occurred with the move

from an oral to a written culture first in ancient Greece, where Plato deplored the negative effects it would have on the power of thought, and then in the Middle Ages, where oral transmission yielded first to handwritten texts and ultimately to the printed book.

CHAPTER SIX:

THE TASK OF THE CHURCH: DANGER AND OPPORTUNITY

I know your works, your toil and your patient endurance. I know that you cannot tolerate evildoers; you have tested those who claim to be apostles but are not, and have found them to be false. I also know that you are enduring patiently and bearing up for the sake of my name, and that you have not grown weary. But I have this against you, that you have abandoned the love you had at first. Remember then from what you have fallen; repent, and do the works you did at first.

Revelation 2:2–5

In 1555 the first European missionaries arrived in Japan, anxious to present the gospel to a people who had never heard it. They met with a puzzled response: "There came one who appeared to have human form at first glance, but might as well be a long-nosed goblin, or a long-necked demon . . . Careful enquiry revealed that the creature was called a 'Padre' ".[1] In a way little has changed: our own culture often regards Christians, and especially ministers, with similar curiosity, as figures from a bygone age who have somehow failed to adapt to a changing environment; and street surveys show that by and large the church is regarded, albeit affectionately, as irrelevant, old-fashioned, and boring.[2] We, like the missionaries to Japan, have something of an image problem.

However you choose to measure it, the church in the West is in decline.[3] As a postmodern culture springs exuberantly from what was long ago dubbed the "iron cage of rationality", an enormous variety of alternative spiritual practices and secular opportunities has arisen to fill the yearning in people's souls.[4] And so it is that while according to the 2001 census, 72 per cent of the UK population continue to define themselves as Christian, scarcely more than 8 per cent wish to go to church, and perhaps even fewer have a clear understanding of what a Christian is.[5] Within the church we respond to this situation in a variety of ways, but most commonly perhaps we resign ourselves to the inevitability of failure. Like any failing company, we adopt a variety of solutions – downsizing our staff and budgets, diversifying our ministry into areas traditionally left to other agencies, advertising for new members, initiating internal reforms. But in effect we plan for decline. In our heart of hearts we no longer expect anyone to be interested in the gospel.

Despite all this, it is becoming clear even within our Western culture that when appropriately communicated, the gospel has lost none of its power and appeal. Decline may be general, but it is far from universal; in many places the church is growing and people are finding a new and life-changing faith. In the UK during the 1990s, a period of overall decline, 22 per cent of churches actually grew by 10 per cent or more.[6] Societies change, but human nature and the human condition do not, and the gospel is as relevant to people's needs now as it ever has been. And yet it remains the case that if the overall trend continues, the church will cease to exist in these islands at some time in the current century. This is how the authors of the worldwide survey Operation World summarise the spiritual health of the UK:

A national awakening is needed. There has been one every century in the last 800 years – the last was in 1859–69. The Judeo-Christian heritage has been so eroded by post-modernist worldviews that public opinion is no longer Christian. Christians have been marginalized in the media, public life, government legislation and school curricula. Religious pluralization has sapped the confidence of many Christians to testify boldly . . . The steep decline in numbers of the Methodists, Anglicans, United Reformed, Brethren and other denominations continues . . . Pray that Christians might become passionate for God's honour, burdened to pray for revival and be freed from a deadening negativism and materialism that pervades the life of the churches.[7]

So how will it look 100 years from now? We have seen that a culture is like an endlessly changing story, and that our task is to interrupt the story with the facts. We have seen that sometimes the church has done this perceptively and accurately, and that sometimes it has been swept aside by the narrative and lost its voice. Which way will it be for us? Will a remnant church look back in 100 years' time, sigh, and say the tide came in but they flunked it; or will a healthy Christian community smile with relief in the knowledge that we leapt onto our boards and rode the waves, adapting to the changing currents and reaching out to the stranded?

The danger of giving in to the culture: dinosaurs and chameleons

In our task of speaking the good news into our world we face two equal and opposite dangers. The first danger is that we cling too tightly to the past, failing to adapt to a changing society, and teaching the Christian faith unintelligibly because we express it in a way that no longer makes any connection with the thought world of the hearers – in other words, that we become dinosaurs. The second danger is that we do make changes, but that we make the wrong ones, listening to the voice of the culture and blending with it as children of our time – in other words, that we become chameleons. And as any child will tell us, neither dinosaurs nor chameleons make good messengers.

1. The dinosaur of Christendom

Imagine yourself living in a thirteenth-century English village. You are, as is every inhabitant of the village, a Roman Catholic. Your family lives, like most of the others, by subsistence farming. Each Sunday you attend the parish church, and you are ministered to by the priest who, apart from the squire who owns the land and who appointed him, is the only person who can read and write. You confess your sins annually in accordance with the decree of the Pope, and you live your life within the moral parameters laid down by the teaching of the church and the laws of the land. You live, in other words, in that delicate interweaving of power between Christian and secular authorities which is called Christendom.

The remnants of Christendom persist in many areas of rural England, where the village church remains part of the fabric of society, even though its role is much reduced. Sometimes it continues to be effective in its work and witness; I think of a particular valley in north-east Leicestershire where the churches stand at the heart of the local community, reaching out in appropriate ways to cater for the needs of those who live there. But for the urban majority of this country Christendom is long gone, the professional pastor is an anachronism and the church an institution of yesteryear, good at adding to the pageantry of state occasions and offering a comforting reminder of our national heritage, but of no relevance at all in the swirling currents of a secular society. In Christendom the task of the church is to help the community live by the gospel it has heard and received; its role is that of chaplain, providing a Christian framework for the moral and spiritual challenges which life inevitably throws up. The theologians of the medieval period spoke out repeatedly on issues public and private, warning against exortionate interest rates, extravagant lifestyles, personal and corporate corruption, and immorality of all kinds. They aimed to keep a Christian society faithful to the teachings of the church, and to help people live as God intended; and on the whole they did it well.

We, however, are not in Christendom, and we must not forget that nearly everyone below the age of 50 was raised outside the church, has not heard the gospel in any form which makes sense to them, and has very little understanding of what the church is *for*. The Christian church can have a significant future – but only if we recognise that it will not be the kind of future that 16 centuries of official Christianity have conditioned us to expect.[8] We must not fall into the trap of seeking to persuade a post-Christian society to stick to the values of the faith it has lost; our task is now to remind its members that the good news is once more available to them. We are called to be not chaplains but messengers. There is something very peculiar about a church which carefully offers its views on everything from immigration to stem-cell research, but fails to communicate the good news of Jesus to a people who have not heard it. Misunderstanding is liable to result, as this comment by a journalist shows: "The Church of England has become the church of social commentators, confining its opinions to secular topics such as poverty or unemployment because it is too embarrassed to talk about God".[9] We must learn to speak to the audience that is actually there.

2. The dinosaur of tradition

While I was in Zambia I was sent to take a church service in a poor area of the copper town of Kitwe. I was warmly welcomed as "Father Alison" (Zambia does not ordain women) and immediately initiated into a backwards culture shock rather more severe than the one I'd experienced on my arrival in Chibwika a week earlier. For as I faced a congregation of 100 adults and 50 barefooted children, I found myself the central figure in what seemed like a surreal religious ritual from another age. Altarboys in long red gowns and white ruffled collars swung censers, a lay reader rang bells, and I picked my way through the English side of a Bemba *Alternative Service Book* while the supple African movements of a musical people were turned into the rigid stand-and-sit responses of the Victorian age. As we sang hymns in Bemba and I administered imported wafers and wine to the confirmed, and offered papal-style blessings to the unconfirmed, I wondered what on earth we thought we were doing.

There is a great force within the church for keeping things as they have always been. Indeed, the core of our calling is to preserve and transmit the unchanging good news of Jesus from generation to generation. We are used to doing this through the conventions of the institutional church, and they have served us well. In times of change the church has stood firm, and the result is that each Sunday Christians all over the world are able to rise and declare their faith according to the historic formularies preserved in the liturgies of all the major denominations. And yet even as we do this, we run an enormous risk – the risk that we will confuse our conventions with the tradition they are designed to protect. At its best, convention is the guardian of tradition, the vehicle by which it is safely conveyed to the next generation. At its worst, it is a servant which usurps the role of its master, preventing the growth and development which are necessary for life. To put it simply, if we continue to transport the gospel in a golden coach of outdated modes and practices – however beautiful the coach – we effectively consign it to a museum: for it is the coach that people will notice and not the gospel itself.[10]

And so we need to be careful that our conventions do not become as meaningless in England as they are inappropriate in Africa. We must be aware that our ministers are in fact wearing Roman togas and Victorian dog collars, that we are meeting in stone buildings paid for by the taxation of medieval peasants and sitting on peculiarly uncomfortable pews installed hundreds of years later to stop the faithful from standing and walking about during services. We must realise that in a society which celebrates eating and drinking we are queueing up in hushed silence to partake (if appropriately confirmed) of symbolic wafers and sips of wine. And we must wonder at our continued capacity, in an age of musical innovation, to sing from books which my son affectionately refers to as *Hymns Ancient and Old*. We are supposed to offer a countercultural message of salvation, and yet by clinging to our conventions we can appear more culturally bound than the people we are trying to reach. As John Henry Newman once remarked, the church must change if it is to stay the same.[11] It was, after all, founded as a movement and not as an institution.

3. *The dinosaur of safe refuge*

The world is changing rapidly. Since the 1960s we have seen a technological and sociological revolution which has fundamentally altered the nature of Western society. Many of the changes have been liberating; but others have brought increased fear and uncertainty. The crime rate has gone up, the nuclear family has all but disappeared, and AIDS and terrorism have reared their heads. Social mobility cuts us off from those to whom we are close and plunges us into an ever more impersonal world; the average Londoner now encounters more people in one week than his pre-industrial counterpart did in a lifetime. The media has transformed itself from the mirror of society into its elite, child abuse and occult practices seem to be on the increase, and drugs are available at the school gate. Many people, and perhaps especially within the churches, have found the increased gulf between their own lifestyles and beliefs and those of the changing world both bewildering and threatening. Taking refuge in Jesus' promise that we would be *in* the world but not *of* it, and the assurance in the letter to the Hebrews that our true citizenship lies in heaven, many of us have battened down the hatches and sought to keep ourselves and our children at a safe distance from the corrosive values of a dangerous and fast-moving society. "They will know we are Christians by our love" – most of which, remarks a cynical preacher, will be exchanged in-house.[12]

Perhaps Lesslie Newbigin was right when he observed 20 years ago that there are now two moods in the church: timidity and anxiety. Timidity causes us to keep away from a world we cannot change, clinging to our beetle drives (where are the beetles? I once wondered) and barn dances (why do Christians like those? I mused). We seek employment with Christian organisations where we hope to escape the dubious ethics and often difficult relationships of the secular world, and we surround ourselves with churchgoing friends. Anxiety, on the other hand, means that insofar as we do engage with the world out there, our contribution is mostly a worried attempt to restrain it; afraid for our children, we strive to uphold the moral standards of a sliding culture by campaigning against abortion or disapproving of stories about wizards. The result is that we keep our moral and spiritual integrity, but our witness is lost. If we build walls round ourselves in order to preserve our Christian identity, we are no more visible and accessible to outsiders than, say, the Jewish communities which meet in the nation's synagogues. And if we speak a message which appears to be moral rather than spiritual, we alienate the very people we are meant to reach.[13] Jesus urged us to relate to the world like light in the darkness, like salt in the food, and like yeast in the loaf; instead, we have set up private clubs for those whose leisure interest is religion.[14]

4. The chameleon of internal reform

It is clear from all this that the church needs to drag itself wholeheartedly into the twenty-first century. We will not remain faithful to our task in a changing context if we cling like dinosaurs to the old ways of doing things. This is a lesson which every successful retailer has learned: retrained staff with new uniforms, working in an enhanced and refitted shopping environment, continue to attract customers and make profits in an increasingly competitive market. If Woolworths looked and behaved as it did 50 years ago, no one would go there.

Many within the churches have reasoned that we must do the same. The intentions are laudable and many of the effects beneficial. The quest for ecumenical understanding and cooperation has deepened. The Church of England has rewritten its liturgy and passed measures to ordain women, and the Baptists have formulated a strategy for church growth. Church buildings have been modernised, emphasis is being placed on team ministry, and clergy assessment and training programmes have been set up. Dioceses and other Christian agencies are recruiting specialised staff to develop ministry to specific sectors of the community, and the media is being harnessed to encourage people to re-examine their views of church.

We must, however, be careful that we are not, like the chameleon, merely changing our colour in culturally determined ways, following the norms of the culture rather than living in the light of the gospel. One worrying indicator that perhaps this is happening lies in the fact that whilst we have been striving so urgently to adapt, the rate of decline in our membership has only increased.[15] Perhaps it is not surprising. Preoccupation with reform has made the church increasingly inward looking. It seems that churches which grow are not those which spend years rewriting the liturgy, but those which don't use it – parrot-like repetition of the same words week in and week out sits ill with the image-based, channel-flicking outlook of the young.[16] New rules and guidelines pour from diocesan offices in quantities which rival the literary output of OFSTED, but they are mostly to do with church order and not with the gospel. And so it is that while parishes are issued with discussion papers for the admission of children to communion, no one has noticed that children have stopped coming to church. While five-year contracts are introduced for the clergy, nobody seems aware that churches grow only if their ministers stay for ten years. While rules are drawn up governing where clergy may or may not live on retirement, no active steps are taken to find able and godly recruits to replace them.[17] Increasingly there is a distinction between "the diocese", with its central policymakers and ever increasing ministerial and administrative staff, and "the parishes", whose main responsibility seems to be not to present the gospel to the real people who actually live in the houses, but to pay for this wider and more nebulous ministry. In its desperate attempt to update itself, the church has fallen in with the solution of many other organisations to the challenges of postmodernism: centralisation.

Centralisation brings many advantages – better use of resources, and elimination of the worst features of the organisation in question at grass roots level. And yet as we see it increasingly practised by government, few of us like it. The reason is that centralisation brings control, and control inhibits personal inititative and local diversity. For Woolworths it ensures uniformity of quality and good practice; but in spiritual terms it spells death. Jesus brought freedom and dignity to every person he encountered, entrusting many with ministry and giving them the spiritual gifts they needed to carry it out. Paul did the same, founding churches, allowing them to grow in different ways under local leadership, and insisting on the full participation in ministry of all believers. And yet all too often the institutional church persists with the culturally conditioned belief that increased central control is the appropriate response to declining interest in the gospel.[18] It is as unlikely to work in churches as it is in schools and hospitals, for we are dealing not with consumer goods but with relationships, and experience suggests that motivation and creativity, both preconditions for growth, flourish in atmospheres of empowerment and affirmation rather than in ones of control.[19] We must not forget that the flames of our faith are fanned by the Holy Spirit, which blows like the wind, equips and empowers in unpredictable ways using unlikely people, and cannot be confined within the orderly structures of anxious overseers. If we respond to crisis by tightening the reins of control, we will merely ensure that those spiritual and ministry gifts which are not amenable to human structures are stifled, and prevent radical, innovative thinkers who could bridge the gap to the next generation from functioning effectively. What works for Woolworths will not work for the church.[20]

5. The chameleon of social action

I once had the task of explaining the gospel to a small community in a remote part of Tanzania. The people to whom I spoke had to walk five kilometres to the nearest water source, and their maize had failed for the third year running. They lived in low houses of sticks and straw, ate one meal a day, owned one set of clothes, and made their tools over a charcoal fire using goatskin bellows. They had heard the gospel only once before. Trembling at our own cushioned existence, we told them Jesus said that he had come to bring good news to the poor, sight to the blind, release to the captives, and freedom to the oppressed.[21] We apologised for the inequity of our respective situations, and told them that this morning we could say little more than that God loved them and wanted to be with them, that we would like to pray for them and that he wished them to draw close to him. Their response was astonishing; we were forgotten, and they began to pray in a way that bore witness to the beginnings of the inner transformation of a group of desperately deprived people.

We are not usually as powerless to help as I felt then. Some years ago I visited a team ministry in a new town in Hertfordshire, England. The clergy of the town were united in their concern for those on the margins, and they were devoting themselves day by day to running drop-in centres for the elderly, and mother and toddler clubs for the many single parents stuck at home; they were visiting the sick, and trying to make some provision for the disaffected youth. They were offering what we so desperately wished we could offer in Tanzania: faithful support for the least privileged members of society. They did so unstintingly and sacrificially, in the belief that we are called to share Jesus' concern for the poor and the marginalised, and that in doing so we are expressing the gospel more effectively than by merely speaking it. The only problem was, their churches were empty.

Many people believe that in a faithless age Christians are called to offer what has become known as the social gospel – that, taking as our model the story of the Good Samaritan, we should speak God's love in the contemporary language of social action. This means that we seek to deepen our under-standing of such matters as urban regeneration, social depri-vation, the changing rural economy, and issues of family life and human sexuality. We care for asylum seekers and try to be sensitive to those with AIDS. We work in partnership with local government and other agencies, and we enjoy good rela-tionships with the community. And yet, judged in terms of introducing people to a life-changing relationship with God, this involvement often bears little visible fruit. The social gospel, declares one critic from within the church, is nothing more than the proclamation of a this-worldly kingdom of

God as the fulfilment of Western liberalism: not life-changing at all, but merely a reflection of the middle-class secular agenda.[22]

The ministry we offered that day in Tanzania and the ministry offered by the clergy in Hertfordshire represent the two extremes of the church's approach to human need. At one end stand those who think the gospel is best presented by *speaking* it. At the other are those who prefer to *do* it. Jesus himself enacted his gospel, filling Peter's nets with fish, feeding hungry crowds, healing the sick, restoring a destitute widow's son to life; and yet he did not shy away from stating it with a boldness which causes us, in our inclusive society, to shuffle from foot to foot and wonder whether we might not be able to find some less embarrassing way of communicating it. To share the gospel in words alone is rather like having a conversation on the phone instead of face to face; all the non-verbal part of the message is lost, and with it much that is necessary to faith.[23] But to enact the gospel without speaking it is like leading a horse to water without allowing it to drink – for what we have to offer is not just human concern but a life-saving relationship with God. It has been said that the message of the church is a specific word, and that if the church does not get this word said, all the other words it might say are better said by someone else.[24] We have it within us to do both.

6. *The chameleon of pluralism*

We live in a world which is culturally and religiously plural-ist. We place a high value on tolerance, and we therefore earnestly desire to respect and affirm every person of every race and faith. Nowhere is this so more than in Leicester, where Hindus, Muslims, Jains, Sikhs, Buddhists and Jews live peacefully alongside Christians, agnostics and atheists, accounting together for more than a third of the city's popu-lation. All the major world faiths are taught in our schools, the city council facilitates the celebration of significant dates in every religious calendar, and the leaders of the largest faith groups meet together regularly. The result is that we enjoy a peace and harmony between peoples which we must do our best to safeguard. And yet often it seems that the harder we try to understand and respect the other faith communities, the less we appear to have anything distinctive to offer them.

One of the assumptions of modernism has been that there is a clear distinction between facts and values. Facts are those things which are capable of scientific and rational proof, and values are ideas and norms which cannot be verified in this way.[25] Religion, not being susceptible to proof, is often seen to be about values rather than facts. It follows that religions become perceived as essentially interchangeable, each offering a culturally determined way to make sense of life. To undermine religious values in individuals or in vulnerable communities would clearly be deeply offensive. And so we instinctively focus on whatever common ground we can find, celebrating our differing faiths as part of our cultural diversity. This extends to the teaching of the Christian faith in schools, where children learn about the cultural trappings of Christianity but do not, in general, hear the challenge of the gospel. In Leicestershire the syllabus covers church buildings and symbols, the lives of famous Christians, family values, creation, well-known Bible stories, and traditional festivals – but not Jesus's claim to be the only way to the Father, the need for a personal response, or the work of the Holy Spirit today.[26]

The problem with this approach is that, like the previous one, it owes more to liberal secular assumptions than to the imperatives of the gospel. In demanding tolerance, it actually practises censorship, for everything is to be tolerated except disagreement.[27] But if we really believe not as a value but as a *fact* that the Son of God was born as a human being in a particular place at a particular point in history; that he

brought a particular message with him and invited a particular response; and if we know our own lives to have been
changed by making this response – then surely we wish to do
as Jesus asked, and go out to make disciples of all nations, to
proclaim the good news of salvation to all peoples?[28] In
accepting the assumptions of secular religious pluralism, we
effectively announce that the gospel, like the facilities in the
parks of old South Africa, is for whites only.[29] This is a
baffling thing to explain to the Iranian and Indian Christians
in our midst, to the Chinese who increasingly arrive in our
churches to find out what the Christian faith is all about, to
the children of missionaries who have given their lives to
make Jesus's exclusive offer of eternal life available to the
Yoruba of Nigeria, the Iroquois of Canada, the Auca Indians
of Ecuador. It harmonises beautifully with the postmodern
conviction that there is no such thing as truth. But it
doesn't sit well with Jesus's claim to *be* the truth, or with the
extraordinary event of the first Pentecost, when the
Holy Spirit descended on the disciples and they found themselves proclaiming the gospel in the languages of many
nations from both within and beyond the Roman empire.[30]
The gospel is for everyone, and the chameleon which
modestly wraps itself in a multi-faith banner disguises it as
perhaps never before.

An opportunity to ride the waves of change

The gospel stands to a culture like gold poured into an iron
mould. As the culture changes, our task is to crack open the
old mould, heat the gold in the crucible of our faith, and pour
it into a new one – and then to have the courage to throw the
old mould away. Much of this chapter has been about the
ways in which we are failing to do this, hanging onto the
shapes of yesterday's mould and frantically trying to persuade
people to purchase entry tickets to our foundry museum.

Mostly they aren't interested, and it is clear that if we wish to stay in business we must move with the times. We must learn to speak in the language of the culture, but without surrendering to the assumptions of the culture; and we must live the gospel in a way that is meaningful not just to ourselves but to others also. We must, in short, learn not to be fashionable but to be relevant – for, as Dean Inge remarks, a church which is married to the spirit of its age is always liable to find itself widowed in the next.[31]

I think there is great hope that we can do this. The church is a remarkable institution. Endlessly dying and being reborn, and sustained by the love of Christ who gave his life for it, it has faithfully and fallibly endeavoured for 2,000 years to pass on the good news with which it was entrusted. It is a task which is never complete, not just because generations come and go and new peoples must be reached, but because ways of thinking and being change all the time. It has been said that the gospel must be constantly forwarded to a new address because the recipient is repeatedly changing his place of residence; and perhaps that is as good a way as any of describing the task which once again is ours.[32] We will look at some ways of seizing the opportunity which lies before us in Part 3. But before we do that, I would like to suggest three simple principles for cultural engagement which will underpin our thinking.

1. Language is important: in the beginning was the Word

John wrote his gospel in the terminology of Greek philosophy. The author of the letter to the Hebrews presented the gospel in the language of Jewish tradition. Language is inseparable from thought: words themselves are cultural things, and reflect the values of the society that uses them. I still remember being told that I needed to repent of my sins, and wondering, firstly, what those two words meant, since I had never used either, and secondly, what it had got to do with the question I was asking, which was about the overarching meaning of life. I remember years later explaining to a university lecturer in philosophy that "repent" means "think again", and meeting with a startled response – he'd never seen it that way, he said; he'd thought it was to do with morals, not meaning. As for sin, when they hear the word, many people now assume immediately that the subject under discussion is sex.[33] Similarly, talk of Jesus as our shepherd may still be helpful in the remote pastoral highlands of Sicily, but Jesus as conqueror might be a more comprehensible figure to the skate-boarding, Nintendo-playing children of our inner cities. Nativity scenes with cuddly animals and stories about arks and whales are very nice, but scarcely likely to convince modern secular children that here lies the key to the troubled world they see all around them.[34] We cannot rely on yesterday's articulation of the gospel; we must find ways of speaking it in words that make sense today. But before we can do that, of course, we must make sure that we know what it actually *is*.

Twenty years ago, the members of the British Council of Churches met to discuss their responsibility to present the gospel to those who had not heard it. They decided to begin by defining it. The problem was that only two of them were prepared to hazard a guess.[35] Strange though it might seem, such confusion is common. Why? I think it is partly because we are so undermined by the assumptions of our age that we have lost the confidence to proclaim anything at all as truth, and perhaps even to believe that there is such a thing; but partly it must be to do with the nature of the gospel itself.

The word "gospel" just means "good news". The good news is that Jesus Christ, the Son of God, was born, died, and rose again, and that this changes things. This event is offered as a simple, historical fact – the kind of fact which could be put on the front page of a newspaper. It is how Peter explained it to the crowds in Jerusalem, and it is how Paul presented it to the people of Corinth.[36] The problem is that it doesn't *sound* like good news if it is expressed in culturally inappropriate terminology. It was good news to the Jews to whom it was first announced, because they had been waiting for a Saviour for centuries, and they understood the implications of the statement for them both personally and collectively. They realised that this single event offered a new answer to the age-old dilemma of human life and purpose. But modern Westerners aren't looking for a Saviour, and when they see Christians standing up in town centres wearing sandwich boards and handing out leaflets announcing that Jesus is alive, the likely response is: "er, yes, so?". It may or may not be true; but it certainly isn't relevant.

Perhaps a better way to think about it is to ask, what is the *bad* news? Jesus expressed the gospel in many different ways. This is how he put it to the upwardly mobile Zacchaeus: "The Son of Man came to seek out and to save the lost".[37] And here perhaps he offers us an easier language in which to explain it. Ask most people where the pain and disorientation are in their life, and they will know. We live in a world of false promises, and sooner or later we tend to realise that the crock of gold at the foot of the postmodern rainbow is more elusive than we had thought. Like Zacchaeus, and as Thomas the banker in Mbulu suspected, we find that our material wealth masks a deepening spiritual angst: the reality is that when push comes to shove we have no answers to the fundamental questions of human existence. If we are to reach the lost whom Jesus came to save, we must learn to articulate the good news of the gospel in a way that makes sense to those who are experiencing the bad news of alienation, futility and loss of hope. The good news, like truth itself, is both universal and personal, and it needs to be expressed to each person in words that make sense.

2. Assumptions are important: the Word shines light into darkness

Jesus expressed the gospel to individuals by pinpointing those things which were holding them back from God. He expressed it not according to a single formula, but according to the needs and circumstances of each person to whom he spoke. In every case he brought not condemnation for wrong-doing but release from wrong assumptions. Zacchaeus learned not that his financial dishonesty was wrong (he knew that already), but that his whole strategy for life was based on the misassumption that wealth would bring happiness. The woman with six husbands learned not that her lifestyle was immoral (she didn't doubt it) but that the fulfilment she craved was not to be found in relationships with men. Nicodemus learned that spiritual life was to be found not through religious observance (his firm belief) but by the power of the Holy Spirit. Each one found life only when they discarded their false assumptions about how to find it.

It is one of the arguments of this book that such assumptions are culturally determined, and that we must learn to stick the pin in the right balloon. To state the obvious, we must get to where people are at before we can enable them to go somewhere else. It is no use helping someone look for a £5 note in Piccadilly Circus if in fact they lost it in Trafalgar Square, and it won't make it easier for my son to get home from Calais if I go to meet him in Birmingham. If we want people to understand what the good news means for them, we must learn to identify the commonly shared beliefs which are holding them back. Many of these concern the nature of Christianity itself – that the gospel is about caring for the poor or living a moral life or going to church, or that faith is about values rather than facts and that therefore all faiths are equally (in)valid. Others concern assessments of what matters in life – individual freedom, the right to self-determination, material and physical wellbeing, career success, social recognition, having a good time. Others are about the nature of reality itself – that it is arbitrary, incoherent and meaningless, that truth is relative, experience everything. None of these things is true, and it is our job to say so. The gospel stands to a culture as the master key to a house: the key will open all the doors, but different doors are locked at different times. Martin Luther, who unlocked his own culture magnificently, said that if you preach the gospel in all its aspects with the exception of the issues which relate specifically to your time, then you are not preaching it at all.[38]

Perhaps it is easier to see how this might work if we look at another culture. Missionaries Don and Carol Richardson tell the story of their work amongst the cannibalistic Sawi people of New Guinea. They shared the gospel stories with little effect until one day they got to the betrayal of Jesus by Judas. Sudden cries of appreciation greeted their tale; and it was explained to them that in the Sawi culture treachery was the highest value – a man who could betray those whose trust he had won was the noblest kind of man. The dismayed Richardsons persisted unsuccessfully with their attempts to persuade the Sawi that Jesus was the key to life – until they got caught up in intervillage conflict and discovered that peace between two warring villages was traditionally achieved only by the offering of a "peace child", a real human baby, by one to the other. The Sawi, initially prevented from recognising the good news by their culturally determined appreciation of treachery, were able to identify Jesus with the peace child and to accept the gospel as the natural fulfilment of their own beliefs. The result was that their cannibalistic culture was transformed. [39]

3. Example is important: the Word was made flesh

Much of this chapter has been about the way in which we express ourselves, as a faith community, to the secular world in which we live. It is important to use meaningful language and to challenge wrong assumptions. But, for all that, our faith will remain irrelevant unless it is seen to actually *work*. Jesus offered everyone he met an alternative way of living, a way that would bring a freedom and a fullness of life not accessible by other means.[40] The early church saw itself as the community of those who had embraced this alternative way of living – followers of the Way, as they were known.[41] Followers of the Way did not seek to found an institution or to reform society, but rather to love one another, for that was how Jesus had said that people would recognise their faith.[42] He has often been proved right. Many turned to Christ during the plagues of the early centuries because the Christians were the only ones who dared to offer prayer and nursing care to the sick. The gospel has spread in Latin America because it has been expressed in a way which confers dignity and self-esteem on the oppressed. The Alpha Course has helped many in the West to find faith because it offers the gospel within the context of relationships. If our faith is genuine and our spiritual life informs our relationships with one another and with those amongst whom we live, then we too, like Christ himself, will be words made flesh. It isn't either–or; it's both–and.

I think it follows from all this that we must ask deep questions of ourselves, questions to do not just with what the church *does* but with what it *is*. As we move from a society dominated by institutions to one dominated by individuals and networks, we have an enormous opportunity to rediscover what it means to be, together, followers of the Way. And as we do that, we will become increasingly free to experiment with the way we do things, for our identity will be not in the doing but in the being. Already, experimentation both with forms of worship and with concepts of community suggests that changing the way we express ourselves can be a powerful tool for reaching people who do not find the old ways of doing things meaningful. Where once we sought to help people enter into the spiritual realm by the use of incense, candles, choirs and organs, now we can harness computer technology to the same end. Where once we met as Sunday congregations within traditional communities, now we are reorganising ourselves into cell churches, youth churches and even cyber churches. Where once the church was a medieval building, now it is a bus, or a café, or a barge. Even our metaphors can change – from destination to journey, from refuge to adventure, from organisation to community. We must be open to a future which is uncertain, but exciting – for God has said:

> And now, here's what I'm going to do: I'm going to start all over again.
> I'm taking her back out into the wilderness where we had our first date, and I'll court her.
> I'll give her bouquets of roses. I'll turn Heartbreak Valley into Acres of Hope.
> She'll respond like she did as a young girl, those days when she was fresh out of Egypt.
>
> Hosea 2:14–15[43]

Notes

1 Quoted by M. Mayne, *Learning to Dance*, p.5.
2 The Spring 2002 newsletter of the South American Missionary Society reported that when young people in Madrid were asked to identify the most unnecessary institutions, the majority (66%) named the church. A similar survey in England conducted for the *Restoring Hope in the Church* video found that most people, when asked how they felt about the church, responded with words like "old-fashioned", "boring" and "out of date".

3 The decline is charted by many studies, both national and international, covering most of the major denominations. For statistics see PW Brierley, *The Tide is running out,* 2000 (UK) and *The Future of the Church: Religious Trends no.5 (2005),* and M Regele & M Schultz, *The Death of the Church,* 1995 (USA). Overviews are given by D J Hall, *The End of Christendom,* 1995 (Canada); M Riddell, *Threshold of the future,* 1998 (New Zealand); E Gibbs and I Coffey, *Church next,* 2001 (USA/UK); and, most recently, B Jackson, *Hope for the Church,* 2002 (UK). The *Anglican Mission in America* website (www.theamia.org) reports a 35% decrease in the membership of the American Episcopalian Church over the last 35 years, and J Cornwell, *Breaking faith,* 2001, suggests that within 10 years the number of Catholic priests in the UK will have halved, while internationally attendance in Catholic churches is at an all-time low. Bob Jackson reports that membership of the Church of England in the UK declined by 14% in the 1990s alone (more if you include children); and the Religious Trends Handbook 2001 published by the Christian Research Association indicates that similar declines have affected the Catholic and Methodist churches. Gallup polls commissioned by the Sunday Times in 1997 showed that 80% of the UK population say they believe in God; but only 10% say they go to church. These figures are confirmed by the 2001 census, in which 72% of the population described themselves as Christian, and a further 5% as belonging to other faiths (www.statistics.gov.uk/census2001).

4 Max Weber, cited by D Smith, *Crying in the Wilderness,* p.43. Research by David Hay for the BBC *Soul of Britain* series showed an increased awareness of the presence of God, of answer to prayer, of a pattern in life, of spiritual presences and other factors; cited by B Jackson,

Hope for the Church, p.84.

5 A Mori poll in 2001 reported that when asked to choose "inspirational" figures from a list of famous people, only 1 per cent chose Jesus; the *Mail on Sunday* reported in 2000 that 43 per cent do not know what Easter commemorates, and Gallup as long ago as 1979 that 28 per cent believe in reincarnation (up from 18 per cent ten years earlier).

6 Amongst Anglican churches, 7 per cent grew by at least 60 per cent, and one entire diocese grew by 12 per cent. See Bob Jackson's excellent recent study *Hope for the Church*, p.33. See also P Johnstone and J Mandryk, *Operation World* (www.gmi.org/ow), whose figures indicate a steady growth in the evangelical and charismatic membership of the churches in particular.

7 P Johnstone and J Mandryk, *Operation World*, 21st century edition, p.651.

8 See D J Hall, *The End of Christendom and the Future of Christianity*, p.ix.

9 Melanie Phillips, *Sunday Times*, 2 September 2001. The Church of England website is a case in point. See www.cofe.anglican.org.

10 Expressed more severely by H A Snyder, *Radical Renewal: The Problem of Wineskins Today*, p.23: "It is hard to escape the conclusion that one of the greatest roadblocks to the gospel of Jesus Christ today is the institutional church."

11 Quoted by A E McGrath, *The Future of Christianity*, p.73. Newman (1801–90) initiated a campaign for spiritual renewal which became known as the Oxford Movement (and which as it happens took the form of an increase, rather than a decrease, in ritual within the church).

12 D Buttrick, *Preaching the New and the Now*, p.41. Charles Colson remarks: "Battle weary, we are tempted

to withdraw into the safety of our sanctuaries, to keep busy by plugging into every program offered by our megachurches, hoping to keep ourselves and our children safe from the mounting destruction", *How Now Shall We Live?* p.x. Bible refs: John 17; Hebrews 11:16, 13:14.

13 This is an error for which the evangelical church has been criticised in the US in particular, where political activism on moral issues is charged with having detracted from the church's effectiveness in communicating the gospel. See P Yancey, *What's So Amazing About Grace?*, and D Smith, *Crying in the Wilderness*, which points out that the presence of evangelical Christians in American churches has had little effect on society as a whole.

14 For the two moods in the church, see L Newbigin, *The Gospel in a Pluralist Society*, p.243. For church as club, see L Osborn, *Restoring the Vision: The Gospel and Modern Culture*, p.76.

15 The lengthy debates over women's ordination and the compensatory packages and structures to be set up for those whose faith was offended coincided precisely with the peak years of decline in church attendance during the mid-1990s. See B Jackson, *Hope for the Church*, pp.47–48.

16 A McGrath, *The Future of Christianity*, p.97.

17 B Jackson, *Hope for the Church*, shows that growing churches tend to have ministers who have been in place for between nine and thirteen years; and that the greatest drop in church attendance has been amongst children. The examples come from Leicester Diocese (communion) and Oxford Diocese (retirement). Most of the historic denominations still rely on volunteerism as the main way of recruiting new ministers; one cannot help noticing that Jesus did not recruit in this way.

18 The Roman Catholic Church still orders the books of would-be reformers to be destroyed and removes the

licences of over-adventurous theologians. The Anglican Church is downsizing by removing freehold, amalgamating parishes and licensing centrally trained lay volunteers as those who are permitted to minister alongside the clergy. The evangelical Reform movement seeks to reform belief rather than structures; and yet all too often its admirable aim of upholding doctrinal orthodoxy produces members who seem unnervingly like the Pharisees Jesus so disliked, inflexible and judgemental in a way that Jesus never was. A powerful case for changing the leadership style within the church is made by E Gibbs and I Coffey, *Church Next: Quantum Changes in Christian Ministry*. For a biblical model of ministry, see Ephesians 4, Romans 12 and 1 Corinthians 12.

19 See K Blanchard and T Waghorn, *Mission Possible: Becoming a World-Class Organisation While There's Still Time* – an acclaimed secular management book which draws on Christian principles. John Taylor points out that where Christianity is spreading, it is distinguished by a multiplication of small, locally led congregations (Latin America, Philippines, China), a weakening of central control (Africa) and a preference for loose federations of churches (China, Zaire); *The Oxford History of Christianity*, ed. J McManners, ch.19.

20 Church structures usually exclude prophets, although Paul names them alongside apostles, pastors, teachers and evangelists as ministers appointed by God in the church (1 Corinthians 12:28; Ephesians 4:11); other unruly spiritual gifts like tongues, healing, and spiritual discernment also tend to be kept firmly out of sight in our very English churches.

21 Luke 4:18.

22 L Osborn, *Restoring the Vision*, ch.13, "To Athens with love". Niebuhr long ago suggested that this approach has its source in the liberal tendency to regard Christ as active

within culture, rather than as speaking counterculturally – see *Christ and Culture*, especially ch.3.

23 This approach comes from an earlier culturally influenced misunderstanding of our task, for it depends upon the modernist assumption that faith is a private matter separate from wider social concerns. See L Osborn, *Restoring the Vision*, and articles in P Sampson, *Faith and Modernity*. The dichotomy between the two approaches is explored by L Newbigin, *The Gospel in a Pluralist Society*, ch.11.

24 P Jensen, quoted in L Osborn, *Restoring the Vision: The Gospel and Modern Culture*, p.142. See Jonathan Edwards: "Why should we be afraid to let persons that are in an infinitely miserable condition know the truth, or to bring them into the light for fear it should terrify them? It is light that must convert them, if ever they are converted. The more we bring sinners into the light while they are miserable and the light is terrible to them, the more likely it is that by and by the light will be joyful to them" – quoted by S Hauerwas and W H Willimon, *Resident Aliens*, p.168. The same sentiment was expressed to me by Stanley Hotay, the diocesan missioner of the Diocese of Mount Kilimanjaro in Tanzania, as he shared his concern at the reluctance of Westerners who would dig wells to offer the living water of the gospel to those using them.

25 See L Newbigin, *Foolishness to the Greeks: The Gospel and Western Culture*, ch.1.

26 These are the areas covered by the Leicestershire Agreed Syllabus of 1991 and the Diocesan Agreed Syllabus for use in church schools of 1992. This is what the Diocesan Syllabus recommends for Pentecost at KS1: "It would be inappropriate to read or tell the story as it is written in Acts [ch.2] . . . Explore the children's own experiences of similar feelings, for example, being afraid of what might

happen, overcoming fear, becoming confident perhaps because a parent comes. Related themes . . . are: feelings, special days, friends, talents and gifts."

27 A McGrath points out that the pluralist view boils down to the idea that it is not individual religions which have access to the truth, but the Western liberal pluralist. This means that the Western liberal doctrine of religious pluralism is defined as the only valid standpoint for evaluating individual religions – which is in fact a form of fundamentalism. *Bridge-building: Effective Christian Apologetics*, ch.5.

28 Matthew 24:14, 28:19–20.

29 L Newbigin, *The Gospel in a Pluralist Society*, p.4.

30 Acts 2.

31 Inge's comment is quoted by J Drane, *Faith in a Changing Culture*, p.44.

32 H Thielecke, quoted in Springboard's Paper on mission and evangelism, no. 2: "The culture".

33 "If we say we need to repent of our sins, many people in Postmodernia will conclude that we are uptight about petty matters which people ought to be able to take in their stride. Christ died for our sins, but if our sins are not perceived to be a problem, the gospel will sound like an antidote to a remote disease we don't have"; and "when we use the word *sin*, most Australians think that we are speaking about sex"; D A Carson (ed.), *Telling the Truth: Evangelizing Postmoderns*, pp.185 and 108.

34 For a startling exposé of the way the Bible is taught to children, see H Oppenheimer, *Finding and Following: Talking with Children about God*.

35 See A Walker, *Telling the Story*, p.11.

36 Acts 2; 1 Corinthians 15.

37 Luke 19:10. Kelly defines lostness as the predominant characteristic of young people today: *Get a Grip on the Future Without Losing Your Hold on the Past*, ch.11.

38 Quoted by J Drane, *The McDonaldization of the Church*, p.176.
39 D Richardson, *Peace Child*. Another example of the cultural expression of Christianity is given by Vincent Donovan, who discovered that the Maasai people of East Africa were willing to embrace the gospel if it was presented to a whole community, but not if it was offered to individuals (*Christianity Rediscovered*).
40 "Abundant life", John 10:10.
41 For example, Acts 9:2.
42 John 13:34–35; 15:12–17.
43 Quoted from *The Message*. In May 2002 Martin Cavender of Springboard and Tim Morgan of CMS undertook an 800 mile cycle ride round the cathedrals of England, meeting with local representatives in each for a service of prayer for the life and mission of the national church. The passages from Revelation 2 and Hosea 2 which frame this chapter were the words given to them as they travelled.

CHAPTER SEVEN:

SEIZING THE MOMENT

"I still haven't found what I'm looking for"[1]

While I was living in Florence I went one day to the Galleria dell'Accademia to see Michelangelo's sculpture of David, a smooth laconic lad of classical marble carved in the proportions of the giant he slew. But justly famous though David is, it was not he who caught my attention, but the unfinished carvings of the prisoners once intended for Pope Julius' magnificent tomb. Whereas other sculptors would make detailed clay models which they would then copy carefully in marble, Michelangelo used to say that every block of marble already contained a statue, and that the task of the sculptor was merely to release it. And so he would go to the marble quarries at Carrara, inspect the rough-hewn blocks and choose those in which he could see a hidden statue calling for freedom. Nowhere is the power of his vision more apparent than in the four unfinished statues of the Accademia, where prisoners struggle to release themselves from the marble which binds them, fixed in immobility as they strain with thrashing limbs to throw off the cold constraints of external form, a form which clings so closely that they and it are of one substance. And it occurred to me that in their struggle perhaps we may see our own; for the longing for freedom which bursts from the fragmentary and unfinished figures is one which speaks to our age far more powerfully than the smooth polished calm of the victorious David.

Times are changing. We have come from a world where sculptors copied models, a world where without realising it we allowed the gospel to be reduced from something subversive and life-changing to something which seems boring and conventional. We allowed this to happen because we accepted that the tools on offer to us were the tools we should use – the rational, material, well-meaning tools made in the factories of a modern society. But the factories have gone, and tired of trusting official voices and relying on the conventions of the past, people are increasingly looking for a different approach. The culture which has prevailed in the West over the last couple of hundred years has been a scientific culture focussed on the seen: a culture of rationalism, of reductionism, of systematisation and of certainty. It is now being replaced by a culture which emphasises the unseen: the spiritual, the spontaneous, the experiential and the ambiguous.[2] Many of the characteristics of this postmodern approach to life are not so much new as recovered, the re-emergence of voices still flowing beneath the surface currents of the dominant culture; and we need the courage to embrace them, to reappropriate some of the things we have lost, as we pursue our desire to grow into the wholeness of a living faith. Other features of the changing worldview are like turbulent waters rushing into dangerous whirlpools which bring only destruction. Our task is to distinguish between the two, to accept the challenge to embrace change in the way we experience and express our faith, and at the same time to have the courage to expose the false values of a culture which is becoming increasingly disconnected from God. We must release the statue from the marble; and we must begin with ourselves.

From modernism to postmodernism

The modern era was characterised by great hope. It has been compared to the painstaking construction of a magnificent new building: on a foundation of reason we built a first floor of science, a second floor of technology, and a third floor of prosperity.[3] We believed that with the new tools of modernism we could create a beautiful world of order, harmony and fulfilment; that the rough edges of poverty and conflict could be smoothed away, and that progress would provide the answer to all ills. We believed that by the scientific investigation of the world we would acquire the technological expertise to control nature and generate wealth, and that with the resulting elimination of poverty we would finally achieve our ultimate goal of peace, fulfilment and security, and so add to our beautiful new building a luxurious top floor fitted with every modern comfort. God would be able to take early retirement – if indeed he was not, as the German philosopher Nietzsche famously proclaimed, already dead.

This was a view that the church rather reluctantly learnt to subscribe to. Taken in by the confidence of the new worldview, proved wrong on one thing after another by scientists, squeezed out by psychologists, and with its traditional teachings overturned by new economic and political philosophies, it effectively withdrew from public life, and the gospel became little more than an optional add-on to the materialist outlook of the culture. Christianity became not a life-changing route to reality but a comfortable reiteration of familiar values. The horizons of faith shrank further and further, and many Christians are now distinguished from their non-Christian counterparts primarily by the conservatism of their lifestyle. The gospel has become part of the furniture, a truth which has been trimmed and shorn so that it can be fitted safely into the framework of a material worldview, a habit of thought which poses no threat and offers no solution. "Fish for dinner", I read in blue biro in my service book one Sunday morning; such is the revolutionary nature of the message Jesus came to bring. The general view in the West is that the church has lost its way, and become an irrelevance whose demise has been marked by the ever fewer feet beating a passage to its doors.

Perhaps this would not matter if things had worked out as we expected, but they haven't. It is true that reason enabled the development of science, that science has enabled us to control our world through the use of technology, and that technology has brought great prosperity. But that's as far as it goes; for the top floor of the beautiful new building has rather mysteriously turned out to be not a penthouse suite but a padded cell, a place of nightmares where images of unimagined horror flicker on darkened walls – violent and unprecedented images of war, nuclear bombs, holocausts, political oppression and international terrorism. The modernist dream is over – as Ogden Nash remarked, "Progress might have been all right once, but it has gone on far too long". The modern reduction of truth to a tool of investigation left too much of reality out. The postmodern solution is to reject that definition; truth is now conceived as a multifaceted thing, a matter of personal perspective, something which does not express facts so much as describe values. To be postmodern is to be aware that truth is not as cut and dried as once we thought it was, and that maybe out there somewhere throbs a reality which cannot be measured or controlled, which is bigger and more complete than anything modernism had to offer. To be postmodern is to be looking for answers – but not to have found them. The question is, how can we make them available in a form which is more adequate than the reduced form in which we have grown accustomed to expressing them?

Ministering the truth

I began my adult life with the question: What is truth? Truth, I thought then, must be something you could get hold of, something you could explain, something you could know; it must be an intellectual thing, a thing you could find in books. Eventually I realised that truth was both simpler and infinitely more complex than that. Truth is not facts, propositions, or statements; it isn't something you can shutter, possess and define, something which can be packaged and confined in sentences, something which is just the opposite of false. Truth is much bigger than that: it is the power and the principle which informs life, the universe and everything in it, the surging essence of everything. Truth is in fact a person. And so I think that now I would ask the question a slightly different way; I would ask not what is *truth*, but what is *reality* – for truth is just the representation of reality, and reality is that which is given and guaranteed by God, who is himself the final reality.[4] And reality is not, as I thought, there to be explained or even created: like the statue for Michelangelo, it is there to be discovered. It is discovered not in order to be understood but in order to be lived.

The task of ministering the truth into a particular culture, and so getting back in touch with spiritual reality, is one which has been undertaken many times – most powerfully by Jesus himself, and by many others since. But it is a task that was first of all given to the prophets of the Old Testament, who were called to bring the power of the word of God into the settled certainties of a world which had built itself on a platform of lies. Time and again they spoke out against the worldview of their culture, challenging the official assurance that all was well, exposing the pain and offering a vision of hope, a statement that things could be done a different way. The words they spoke were words of truth. They were also words of power, carrying within them the creative seeds of change; for merely to articulate the truth, the spoken reality of God, is to begin to bring it about. And I think we can have the same confidence. Of ourselves we can change nothing. But as we learn to express truth into what has been described as a world of lies, hype and spin, then we will enable people to experience and articulate their need, and thus create for them the possibilty of entering in a new and more powerful way into relationship with God. In the mysterious pages of the Old Testament we catch a glimpse of how.[5]

Stage one: opening a can of worms

The first task of the Old Testament prophets was to expose the hidden pain and false optimism of the society to whom they spoke. Their words were not always encouraging. Take Jeremiah, for instance. Like us, Jeremiah stood at a pivotal point in history. Like us, he lived at a time of economic prosperity, over which the threatening clouds of international instability were beginning to gather. Over a 40-year period, Jeremiah spoke words of warning into a culture which had strayed far from God; his ministry ended just after the catastrophic year 587 BC, when the kingdom of Judah was invaded and the people taken into exile in Babylon. Jeremiah was sent to burst the bubble of satisfaction within which his society lived, to intrude upon their peace of mind with a clear articulation of what was going wrong, and to deliver a fearsome warning to rulers, priests and people alike. He made three essential points.

Firstly, Jeremiah laments that prosperity has brought complacency.[6] This is a people whom God had brought out of slavery, a homeless people to whom he had given land, a weak people on whom he had bestowed victory. But that was a long time ago; gratitude has a tough time in the midst of affluence, and God now finds himself forgotten in a land of plentiful fruits and desirable consumer goods. Maybe we should listen to Jeremiah, for we too have come very recently from a God-centred poverty to a self-centred prosperity. Only 150 years ago in Leicester whole families were working for up to fifteen hours a day in the stocking trade, and still relying on poor relief to keep body and soul together. Housing was cramped, diet consisted of bread and potatoes, sewage ran in the gutters and collected in stagnant pools between the houses, and education and medicine were far-off dreams. Infant mortality was 25 per cent, epidemics rife. In Bolton in 1842 a government report declared: "Anything like the squalid misery, the slow, mouldering, putrefying death by which the weak and feeble of the working classes are perishing here, it never befell eyes to behold nor imagination to conceive".[7] But for us too that was a long time ago. Since then we've built new houses, put in sewers, set up schools and passed employment acts. We've got electricity and we've founded the National Health Service. We've won two world wars and seen the establishment of peace between all the major Western nations. Both nationally and individually we are now more prosperous than ever before: over the Christmas period in 2001, British consumers were able to spend £35 billion – more than the annual output of Romania and *nine times* the gross domestic product of Zambia in the same year.[8] But whereas in the year 1900 one person in three attended church each week, now it is less than one in twelve.[9] We no longer feel any need for God.

Jeremiah's second point is that moral decay and a culture of exploitation has set in amongst the people as a direct consequence of this loss of gratitude. Oppression of other foreign nationals and of their own poor, violence, adultery and dishonesty have become normal in Judah.[10] Things are not so very different here: in Britain someone breaks the law every six seconds, a violent crime is committed every two minutes, and 150 people are sentenced by the courts for drug offences each day. We have a pornographic industry worth over £100 million annually, and since 1967 we have terminated more lives through abortion (4 million) than we lost soldiers in the First World War. Only half our children are brought up by two parents living together under the same roof, and every day 75 of them are added to child protection registers. Meanwhile the economic exploitation of the poor has assumed global dimensions as rich nations extract punitive interest payments and offer unsustainable wages to poverty-stricken workers in undeveloped countries.[11]

Jeremiah then points out that far from bringing fulfilment, this disconnection from God means that a whole society now suffers from spiritual restlessless and dissatisfaction. Like the woman Jesus would one day meet at the well, the people of Judah have turned away from living water and hewn out cisterns for themselves, cracked cisterns that constantly leak. Rich and sophisticated though they may feel themselves to be, the reality is that they are no different from a restive young camel interlacing her tracks, in her heat sniffing the wind, lustful for anything that passes by, seeking spiritual reality in foreign divinities and "New Age" practices, and relying on gods which have no more solidity than scarecrows in a cucumber field.[12] These may not be images which speak immediately into our city lifestyles, but they describe the same quest for immediate fulfilment which characterises our society. As we move from the modern dream of achieving wealth to the postmodern realisation that wealth is not enough, we are seeing people redouble their efforts to achieve inner satisfaction. By day it is sought in consumerism: the families of Leicester are no longer to be found struggling from bread and potatoes to cholera to rags and exhaustion and an early grave; they are to be found in Dixons on a Saturday afternoon, seeking fulfilment in the acquisition of material goods bought on credit – for we are conditioned by a whole media and advertising industry to believe that we will feel better if we buy something. By night it is sought in drink and sex, and the city centre is transformed into an unnerving environment of competing electric lights and throbbing music from club doorways manned by burly bouncers, where groups of girls and boys roam the streets in search of a place of their own in an adolescent world of uncertainty, the boys drinking and bragging, the girls giggling and suggestively dressed. This is a culture of instant gratification, in which sexual encounter is glorified by film and fantasy as one of the few contemporary means to self-transcendence.[13] The consequences range from the creation of a violent underclass of fatherless youths to offices full of professional women who remain involuntarily childless because they cannot find a partner willing to undertake the commitment of marriage. Sex, designed as the glue which would bind society together, has become the drug which is tearing it apart.

This is the dream we as a society have sold our young people: we have reduced the technicolour of created light to the banality of a black and white rainbow, and in the process we have lost our soul. It has been said that to live in our culture is to suffer from emptiness, to experience personal and social life as a maelstrom, to find one's world and oneself in perpetual disintegration and renewal, trouble and anguish, ambiguity and contradiction – to be part of a universe in which all that is solid melts into air.[14] And as increasingly we realise that we haven't found what we are looking for, our society, like Jeremiah's, is turning to alternative spiritualities in the attempt to meet the needs of our souls. In Leicester we promote Diwali, Ramadan, the Chinese New Year and Hanukkah with equal and politically correct enthusiasm; we have the biggest Jain temple outside India, the Mormons use us as a training ground, and a splendid new mosque complete with four minarets is going up just down the road from where I live, next to a rundown Anglican church which first sold off its vicarage to pay its bills and then saw its minister suffer a nervous breakdown and its premises set on fire. We are a world centre for freemasonry, psychic fairs are held regularly in a hotel round the corner, and practitioners of various New Age and occult therapies advertise their services in the local paper and sell their wares in a shop in the city centre. Our teenagers are more likely to have experimented with ouija than with church, and there are now more registered witches and fortune tellers in Britain than Christian ministers.[15]

And so we are watching a whole society exchange the truth about God for a lie. Knowing there was something missing from a mechanistic universe, our culture has succeeded magnificently in jumping out of the frying pan into the fire. In turning our backs on reality we have come to acknowledge no wider framework than that of our own desires, and now we find ourselves not so much trapped in the constricting forms of a rigid society as suspended in a vacuum of meaninglessness. Our whole world is now built on assumptions of our own creation: assumptions about human need and human fulfilment, and assumptions about reality itself. They are assumptions which even within the church we question no more effectively than many of our ancestors questioned theirs, and yet which our ever more violent and dissatisfied culture testifies to offer a false foundation for human living. It is not that we have not known God; we have. In England our faith goes back to the period of the Roman empire, taking firm hold with the ministry of Augustine of Canterbury in the sixth century, flourishing on our Celtic fringes throughout the Dark Ages which engulfed most of Europe, and seeing many revivals and periods of growth in the centuries since then. And yet now we are a so-called post-Christian society, and most of the population have a clearer grasp of the concept of reincarnation than they do of the basic tenets of the Christian faith.

Jeremiah's is a call to walk away from the false values of a culture, and to take God seriously. Speaking out against the official proclamation that all was well, criticising silent religious leaders, godless politicians and prophets who peddle false hope, he sought to dismantle the fictitious reality they wished so ardently to maintain.[16] Our task is the same. We are living at a time of rapid social change and increasing personal dissatisfaction. We have a political leadership which builds domes to a bright new future, a consumer industry which promises fulfilment in the next purchase, and a mass media which holds up unreachable images of health and wealth as the key to success. Media celebrities and sports personalities have become our icons, and the crossed fingers of the lottery the symbol of our hopes. And yet we, like the people of Judah, are drinking water which can never slake our thirst, from cracked cisterns of our own construction: for beneath the hype and the party lies the simple fact that our culture is, when it comes down to it, a culture of despair. Only when it is acknowledged that the emperor in fact has no clothes on may the task of providing him with some begin.

Stage two: recovering the hope

Jerusalem fell in the year 587 BC, and the people were carried into exile in Babylon. Two generations passed. Many of the exiles assimilated into the Babylonian culture, establishing businesses, buying land and gaining positions as civil servants.[17] Life was comfortable in the prosperous capital of this new world power; and yet they continued to cling to the memory of their identity as the people of God. Fifty years after the exile, God began to speak to them again, this time through a prophet whom we know as Isaiah of Babylon.[18] If it had been Jeremiah's task to expose the folly of a people far from God, it was Isaiah's to help them imagine that things could yet be different. Through Isaiah God began to promise an alternative world, a world not of judgement and disaster, of pain and failure, but a world of new beginnings, a world of the possible – a poetic world of renewed imagination.

Isaiah spoke not in the rational language of prose but in the poetic language of metaphor. He spoke not to teach but to inspire, not to rebuke but to envision. To a people living far from home, surrounded by the gods of another culture and tempted to listen to the voices of an imperial worldview, Isaiah offered poetry. God was not dead, God had not taken early retirement, God had not been emasculated by the glittering culture of a successful superpower. Their God was *the* God, cried Isaiah – the God who created the universe, weighing the mountains, measuring the heavens, scooping the dust of the earth and the waters of the seas in the hollow of his hand. He was the God who governed nations, appointing and dismissing rulers, sustaining and sacking empires. He was the God supreme over all others, the God who sits above the circle of the earth and sees its inhabitants like grasshoppers, the God who stretches out the heavens like a curtain and spreads them like a tent – and not a god made of mulberry wood, carved with care so that it won't fall over, like the so-called gods of a culture which puts its trust in what can be seen and made. Above all, he was a God who cared, a God who had delivered them before and would do so again, a God who would give power to the faint and strength to the weak, a God who would cause those who wait for him to rise up with wings like eagles and fly in the skies of a new dawn. This was the God of whom Isaiah wished to remind a discouraged people.

Isaiah wanted to show people that reality could be other than the prevailing culture said it was. He wanted to lift their eyes from the dust of the daily scramble to make a success of life in an alien culture, and convince them that if only they seized hold of the dream, it could become real. You have forgotten me, said God through Isaiah. You have turned me into a memory, when I am reality itself. You have reduced me to the level of something you can buy and something you can choose, when I am the beginning and the end of everything, the very source and destination of life. And through Isaiah God began to promise forgiveness, reconciliation, and a renewed and more powerful relationship than the one they had grown used to expecting. "Have you not known, have you not heard?" sings Isaiah. Is this not what you used to believe? That God will open rivers on the bare heights and place fountains in dry valleys, that he will plant trees in the desert and make a way in the wilderness, that he will give drink to his people and do new things which the whole world will see? And that this is his promise; that as the rain and the snow come down from heaven, and do not return there until they have watered the earth, making it bring forth and sprout, giving seed to the sower and bread to the people, so shall God's word be that goes out from his mouth; it will not return to him empty, but it will accomplish that which he has planned, and succeed in the thing for which he sent it. "Wake up", urges Isaiah. It doesn't have to be this way. Stop spending your money on things which are not bread, and your labour on things which do not satisfy. Listen, and you will live.[19]

We don't have to be swamped by the culture.

Stage three: re-imagining the future

Jeremiah and Isaiah tell a tale that is as old as the world itself. Their tale is one of capitulation to voices which tell us we do not need God, and recovery of the knowledge that we do. Their tale is one of rebuke and encouragement, and their vision is one which comes from God himself. It is a vision which must be endlessly recaptured, and which we are called to recapture again now. For we have grown used to providing not wrong but inadequate answers, answers influenced by the modern desire to have everything neatly explained. It isn't the first time that the worshipping community has tried to squash its faith into manageable shapes; and 500 years after Isaiah cried out against conformity, Jesus himself reserved his severest criticism for those who wanted to do it this way – the Pharisees.

The Pharisees, as we saw in Chapter 1, were not bad men. They were a reform movement whose origins dated back, as it happens, to the return of the people from the exile in Babylon, and their desire was to restore the word of God to a central place in the life and experience of Israel by eliminating precisely those godless practices which Jeremiah had so trenchantly exposed. But they hadn't done it Isaiah's way, the way of imagination and hope, the way of waiting and trusting, of dependence and prayer: they had done it the modern way, the way of increased accountability and greater control. In their insistence on holy living they had effectively turned Israel's relationship with the living God into a set of rigidly enforced external rules and observances. They had embraced the faith so thoroughly that they were squeezing the life out of it.

The Pharisees, for their part, were horrified by the irreligious behaviour of Jesus, a man who made blasphemous claims about his own powers, who went to parties in the homes of corrupt tax collectors, who ate and drank with his disciples instead of fasting and praying. One day they faced him up with it and demanded an explanation. Jesus, like Isaiah, responded not with explanation but with metaphor:

> "No one tears a piece from a new garment and sews it on an old garment; otherwise the new will be torn, and the piece from the new will not match the old. And no one puts new wine into old wineskins; otherwise the new wine will burst the skins and will be spilled, and the skins will be destroyed. But new wine must be put into fresh wineskins."
>
> Luke 5:36–38

At first sight it's hard to see what this has got to do with it. Of course you don't cut a bit out of a new shirt to mend a hole in the old one. And of course a competent winemaker doesn't put new wine in old, contaminated wineskins – to do so would wreck the new vintage. But we must remember that Jesus sought not to answer questions but to explode assumptions. These short parables carry some very threatening implications – for wine and garments both have religious associations. The Pharisees' answer is not recorded; but the meaning is clear – that the old religious practices, the ones they themselves upheld, are now to be discarded in favour of something altogether new, something exciting, something that did indeed call for a party. The world was no longer the way the religious people said it was: relating to God wasn't going to be about keeping rules, being respectable, and observing rites. That was the old wine, and it was appropriately kept in old wineskins. But Jesus brought good news, the news that faith in God was going to find expression in completely new and unimaginable ways. That was new wine – and it would need new wineskins.

All that was 2,000 years ago. But we face the same choices, and if we want to revitalise the gospel in our society, to make it accessible to the majority who have heard it only in its tamed, scaled-down version, we need to think carefully about how to proceed. The problem with new wine, as Jesus went on to point out to the Pharisees, is that it tastes a bit raw. There is a lot to be said for a nice, familiar, seasoned claret, matured in oak casks and kept in the traditional way in a cool cellar before being brought out to accompany a candlelit dinner; and there is a lot to be said for the time-honoured forms of traditional religion, reassuring in their predictability, comforting in their familiarity. But all that, Jesus said, is for yesterday. To live the gospel is to drink new wine, and to express it is to use new wineskins. And so we need to ask ourselves some questions.

Firstly: are we really rejoicing in the new wine, or have we without realising it reverted to the carefully nurtured richness of the old? Do we see our own personal journeys through the radical lenses of the gospel, or through the timetabled patterns of what has become a familiar, static faith? Are we open to the challenge which the postmodern world forces upon us, the challenge to seek reality in wider ways, or do we just want to carry on with the packaged familiarities of yesterday's vintage?

Secondly: have we really taken on board the warning that new wine cannot be put into old wineskins, lest they burst, and the wine be lost? What, in what we do as a church, is done simply because that's the way it's always been done? What do we have to stop doing? What do new wineskins actually *look* like, and where do we get them from? How can we, as a gathered community, understand what it means in our changing world to express the gospel together, in a way which effectively communicates its living power to those around us? How are we *now* to pour the oil of the gospel into the wounds of those amongst whom we live? How can we *now* best apply the cutting edge of the truth it conveys to the diseased society of which we form part? And how can we *now* offer the hope it brings into the hidden despair of those for whom life has no real meaning?

In short: do we dare to take the gospel out of the box we have allowed it to settle into, and listen to God's voice afresh? Do we dare to stand before God as he really is – not a sort of kindly patron saint of the church, but the awesome God whom Jeremiah knows, the God who made the earth and established the world, the God whose word is like fire, and like a hammer which breaks the rock in pieces? Do we dare to listen to the God who is hurting because his people have forgotten him, and trusted in lies, and to the God who expects a response, and threatens to shame us by lifting our skirts up over our faces if he doesn't get one?[20] For if we do, God will be there to meet us, to restore and renew us, and to give us once more the waters of the fountain of life. If not, our faith will shrivel and our churches will die.

So it's all change. We are leaving behind the world of modernism, the world of the cut and dried, the world of prose in which the key activity is to explain, and whose language increasingly has come to inhibit the reality which is God. And we are moving into a world of postmodernism, a world of poetry, a world of the possible, a world in which the key activity is to ask questions. The danger is that postmodernism will respond to the inadequacies of a reduced truth by declaring that there is no truth, and so precipitate a whole culture into a vortex of self-indulgent meaninglessness and social disintegration. We will be able to stop this happening only if we are willing to burst out of a restricting framework which with hindsight we should never have embraced, to rehabilitate truth by becoming more real ourselves, and to believe that in the gospel we have a tool which will set people free from the marble which imprisons them.

To do this will be to embark on a journey whose route we cannot yet map. But we have learned in the past that if it is to be successfully communicated, the gospel must be expressed in the language of the culture, focussed into the assumptions of the culture, and offered as an example to the culture. The remaining chapters of this book will attempt to imagine how we might strengthen our resolve to do this by picking up on some of the elements of Jesus' own ministry as we examined it in Part 1. Chapter 8 will look at the personal dimension of our faith as it is received by individuals, Chapter 9 at the spiritual dimension of our faith as we come together in the church, and Chapter 10 at the social dimension as we seek to live out our faith in the world. As we do this we will find ourselves following the strands of the movement from modern to postmodern, and learning to recover a faith which will be experienced rather than taught, spiritual rather than rational, relational rather than institutional, holistic rather than mechanistic, and social rather than individual.

Notes

1 Defined as the mantra of the age by G Kelly, *Get a Grip on the Future*, p.79.

2 Comparisons of the respective characteristics of modernism and postmodernism are given by J Drane, *Faith in a Changing Culture*, p.35; M Riddell, *Threshold of the Future*, ch.7, and G Johnston, *Preaching to a Postmodern World*, p.25–26.

3 R Middleton and B J Walsh, *Truth is Stranger Than It Used To Be*, p.11.

4 The question of what is truth is eloquently explored by Os Guinness, *Time for Truth: Living Free in a World of Lies, Hype and Spin*.

5 I am indebted for these insights to the writings of Walter Brueggemann. See especially *Hopeful Imagination*; *Finally Comes the Poet*; *The Prophetic Imagination*.

6 Jeremiah sets out his main themes in ch.2, but echoes and re-expresses them throughout the book. For this point, see 2:4–8.

7 E E Kellett, *Religion and Life in the Early Victorian Age*.

8 For UK/Romania statistics, see *The Week*, 5 January 2002; for Zambia, see the national profile on www.LonelyPlanet.com.

9 Church membership (adults) in 1900 was 33%, compared with 8% (adults + children) now. 799,000 people go to an Anglican church on any one Sunday (1.4% of the population); P Brierley, *Christian Handbook Religious Trends 2002–03*.

10 See Jeremiah 7:1–11.

11 Statistics taken from various sources, including *Social Trends 1996*; C Bartholomew and T Moritz, *Christ and Consumerism*; R McCloughry, *Living in the Presence of the Future*.

12 Jeremiah 2:13–28 and 10:5.

13 An observation made by S Hauerwas and W H Willimon, *Resident Aliens*, p.63.

14 Marshall Berman, quoted in D Smith, *Crying in the Wilderness*, p.31.

15 A survey of 80,000 schoolchildren found that 80% had been involved in ouija. See J Richards, *But Deliver us From Evil*, p.61. Compare this with our discovery in a Corby comprehensive school that even the three sixth-formers taking Religious Studies A level had never attended a Sunday church service.

16 See especially 2:8.

17 See J Rogerson and P Davies, *The Old Testament World*, p.158.

18 The book we know as Isaiah seems to have been written in three distinct historical periods by three different prophets. The section we are concerned with is known as II Isaiah and runs from chapters 40–55. It is thought to date from about the year 540 BC, 53 years or so into the exile. See B W Anderson, *The Living World of the Old Testament*, ch.14. The quotes that follow are all taken from these fifteen chapters. See especially ch.40.

19 Isaiah 41:18–20; 43:18–24; 55:6–11; 55:2.

20 Jeremiah 5:22–24; 23:29; 4:19–22; 13:26.

PART THREE:
A GOSPEL FOR OUR TIMES

The Individual

In the beginning was the Word, and the Word was with God, and the Word was God.

The Church

What has come into being in him was life, and the life was the light of all people.
The light shines in the darkness, and the darkness did not overcome it.

The World

And the Word became flesh and lived among us.

John 1

CHAPTER EIGHT:

CHANGING INDIVIDUALS:
LIVING IN THE TRUTH OF CHRIST

*In the beginning was the Word, and the Word was
with God, and the Word was God.*

John 1:1

When I was little my friends and I would play the game of
asking one another, "If you had one wish, what would it be?"
My answer was always the same: "To be happy". I had little
idea of what that happiness would actually look like in practice as I grew older, but I knew that it was what I wanted. My
friends were more pragmatic; they would name specific things
that they thought would *make* them happy. But one way or
another, it was a desire we all shared; there is within the
human being an innate desire for happiness. It is a subject
which has occupied philosophers from the earliest times –
already by the fifth century Augustine could remark that
ancient wisdom offered no fewer than 288 different opinions
on the nature of human happiness.[1] The influential thirteenth-
century theologian Thomas Aquinas suggested that this
innate desire for happiness has to come from somewhere
beyond the individual, and that the only place it can come
from is God, who is himself happiness. Aquinas concluded
that true human happiness is to be found by following this
desire back to its source: human beings can be happy only in

relationship with God.[2]

Every society is held together by a web of assumptions about human life and how best to live it. Some of these assumptions recur from one culture to another: in Jesus' time as in ours many people were seeking fulfilment through work, money and sex. Others are peculiar to a particular culture; we have suggested that in the modern period it was thought that technological, political and economic progress would solve the human dilemma, whereas a postmodern generation seeks to slake its thirst by drinking from the cracked cisterns of consumerism and sense experience. What all these approaches have in common, both with one another and with those of the 288 ancient philosophers, is that ultimately they do not work. Now, as then, our whole society is sustained and defined by a web of false assumptions about how to be happy; and we are like flies stuck fast to its almost invisible threads, waiting for the inevitable approach of the spider.

Recovering the truth

> I am the way, and the truth, and the life. No one comes to the Father except through me.
>
> John 14:6

Two thousand years ago Jesus marched into a particular culture, announcing that he had come to bring good news. The good news was that God had taken action, and that the consequence would be release for those in prison, sight for the blind, and freedom for the oppressed. Since then, societies and cultures have come and gone, and the assumptions by which people direct their lives have been endlessly reformulated. But the human condition remains the same: still we are like flies caught on the sticky threads of an invisible web, trapped by the deathliness of our own worldview. Jesus did not come to fiddle with the web or console those stuck on its threads; he came to shout at the top of his voice that the spider's power was now broken – that we would know the truth, and that the truth would set us free.[3]

The problem with freedom is that it is very hard to get hold of. Freedom to choose between brands of baked beans or makes of car or different hairstyles is a safe kind of freedom, to be exercised within the parameters of the known; but the freedom Jesus offers is not of this kind. Jesus offers to take us beyond the boundaries of the known, to turn us from caterpillars to butterflies and transport us from the predictability of our own back garden to the limitless landscapes of an undiscovered continent. This sort of freedom comes not as an event but as a journey, an open door into a new world, a process of discovery which takes us from here to God and from time to eternity. Such freedom cannot be described but only experienced, because it is as different as each person is different. To claim it often hurts; spider's silk is the strongest substance in the natural world, and our entangled wings are fragile and easily damaged. But for those who have the courage to prise themselves free, happiness – defined in Aquinas' terms as relationship with God – becomes a true possibility.

We live in a world which cries out for freedom. Often in the church we fail to offer it, perhaps because we have failed to embrace it ourselves: in our anxiety to find simple ways of expressing the gospel we have reduced it from dream to formula, and at local level the Christian faith often comes across as little more than an institutionally backed and culturally bound belief system, a packaged way of spending a Sunday morning, or of caring for the less privileged, or being respectable. In the context of a postmodern society which no longer has a biblical worldview, many of our human attempts to live out the gospel have the effect of trivialising it by turning what began as a revolutionary message of freedom into a set of things that we say or do. We won't get the gospel to do what Jesus got it to do unless we are willing to realise that it is not so much a package from the Post Office as an octopus in a string bag – a thing both unpredictable and ultimately uncontainable.[4]

If we are to do this we must be clear in our understanding of the truth, what it is and what it does. If a church is to retain its grasp of a truth which can set people free, it needs theologians who are able to avoid becoming entangled in the assumptions of the culture. Increasingly we have them, but for many years we did not. During the last century most theologians adopted the rationalist values of modernism and, in their anxiety for recognition as practitioners of a proper academic discipline, concentrated on the production of dry and detailed research papers instead of acting as resources for the spiritual life and mission of the churches.[5] As physicists split atoms in Swiss research laboratories, so theologians dissected the engine of the Bible, reducing it to its component parts, reassembling it according to the criteria of the culture, and then expressing surprise and sorrow when it no longer seemed to work. Some, like good scientists, sought to explain and defend the Christian faith in rational terms, dismissing those elements which did not seem to lend themselves to such explanations. Others, more in tune with the deconstructionist approaches of philosophical and literary fashion, embraced the postmodern dissatisfaction with the rationalistic strait-jacketing of truth and accepted the view that there is no such thing as truth; truth is an open and inclusive thing, to be personally defined and individually appropriated. Others, staunch in their defence of tradition, have responded in turn with a brandishing of the scriptural rulebook and and calls for a return to disciplined orthodoxy.[6] The result is chaos. Bubbles rise shimmering into the air, and the incarnate reality of Christ in our midst is ignored. Truth was not meant to be dissected; it was meant to be lived.

The power of the truth

For human beings, truth is most readily accessed through relationships. If truth is meant to be lived we will find it most powerfully, as did the individuals of the New Testament, in the context of an encounter with a person, or group of people, in whom it lives already. Truth is not merely factual, as modernism believed – although it does have a factual dimension. Truth is personal. Truth is the reality of God himself. And that is why, when he wished to make that reality accessible to human beings, he did it through a relationship. He sent his Son.

And yet truth also has to come in words, for only in words can it penetrate into our minds and take root within us. And so we say that Jesus is the Word of God, because Jesus came not just to be the truth, but to communicate it, in word and deed. "For this I came into the world: to testify to the truth", Jesus declared to Pilate. "What is truth?" Pilate wondered, without apparently waiting for an answer. "Your word is truth", Jesus prayed in the garden of Gethsemane.[7]

And yet truth, in God's economy, is much bigger and more powerful than just words as we commonly think of them. It is easy for us, the heirs of modernism, to trivialise truth, to reduce it to information carried in black and white marks on a page. But truth is infinitely more than information. When John began his gospel with the phrase "In the beginning was the Word", he did not mean, as we might, that Jesus came to explain something. As I have tried over the years to unpack that phrase, I have found myself following a tantalising trail which my limited mind can only fleetingly grasp. Perhaps I would have given up; but for the fact that as I too have tried to "rightly explain the word of truth" I have seen that truth burst into people's lives with a transforming power which is quite astonishing.[8] For Jesus came to offer freedom, not comfort; and transformation, not good advice. In receiving and offering truth we are wielding the power which made the universe itself. In the beginning was the Word, and the word was a Verb – a doing word. It isn't just that truth *is*; truth *does* something.

Where do we find the truth?

> You Christians look after a document containing enough dynamite to blow all civilisation to pieces, turn the world upside down, and bring peace to a battle-torn planet. But you treat it as though it is nothing more than a piece of literature.
>
> Mahatma Gandhi.[9]

Truth comes in words, and the first place we meet the words of God is in the Bible. The Bible is the word of God, written down – that is what "scripture" means. The word of God is the means by which God communicates himself to us, and the Bible is the vehicle of that communication. From the time of his first giving of the Ten Commandments to Moses, God has communicated with his people through the written word. And yet the words themselves are not the Word; rather they contain it, as a womb contains a baby. This is why the Pharisees got such short shrift from Jesus in their blinkered human attempt to take the words of scripture and turn them into a code of behaviour; and it is why we follow unwittingly in their footsteps if we once allow ourselves to treat the Bible as a collection of rules and instructions, to be embraced or overlooked, depending on how well they fit with the assumptions of our worldview. The Bible is not just a document, but a gateway into spiritual reality. Its words are breathed by God himself, through writers moved by the Holy Spirit, and they offer us not principles or information but a life-changing relationship with the Creator of the universe.[10] As we move from the modern search for rational understanding to the postmodern search for meaningful experience, we have a new opportunity to tear open this long and multiformed letter from God, to let it interact with us at an emotional as well as at an intellectual level, and to accept the transformation that he offers us through it – for the odd thing is that the very words themselves have the power to cut through our desires and thoughts and penetrate beyond our minds to the vulnerable place where soul and spirit meet.[11]

And yet that is not the whole story. The real womb was of course not the Bible but Mary, and the baby was not text but Christ: "In the beginning was the Word, and the Word was with God, and the Word was God, and the Word became flesh and lived among us". If the Bible is the word of God written, Jesus is the word of God made living. Jesus was the human expression of God, God getting down to our level and communicating himself to us in person. This does not contradict our understanding of the Bible as the word of God, for language is not just a set of audible labels which attach themselves to meanings and become indissoluble from them, in a kind of one-on-one relationship between the word and the thing it signifies, but rather a flexible, moving vehicle which serves to carry concepts much bigger than itself. I like to think about the relationship between the word written and the word living by imagining that I have received through the post a photograph of a person I am due to meet at the station. The photograph is not the person, but it is the image of the person, and reflects and expresses who they are. The Bible is like the photograph; it is stamped with the likeness of Christ. And so it is that we may say that the Bible is the word of God, and at the same time that Jesus is the word of God. Both express who God is.

It follows that the word of God is not just an intellectual, rational thing. We may wish to reduce the written word of God to information, to study it to understand him, and to live by it to please him. But we can't do that with the living word. You can't study a living word; you can only let it communicate with you. God's primary intention is not that we should understand him, but that we should know him. "If you know me, you will know my Father also," Jesus said; the Word of God is a person.[12]

If the word of God is a communication from God, it must communicate something in particular. And this is the third way in which we may understand the word: it comes as a message, a statement of fact, a piece of news. "The word is the good news that was announced to you", Peter wrote to the Christians in Asia.[13] To offer a paraphrase, the good news, as Peter might have expressed it, is this: God exists, he loves you, and he wants a relationship with you. The whole of scripture tells you that. God has been writing to you for centuries – letters of love, letters of complaint, letters of guidance, letters of warning. Now God has sent his Son to speak to you. You rejected him and put him to death. But he has been raised from the dead, and he is alive. Still he hasn't given up. He has sent his Holy Spirit to help you to talk to him. Instead of writing his words on tablets of stone, God will now write them on your hearts, and you will know him.[14]

The word of God is in that announcement also.

What does the truth do?

But the trail does not end there. The truth is expressed in the word of God written, the word of God made living, and in the good news that we may be reconciled to God. But what difference does it make? If it is the case that the word *does* something, what is it that it does?

The simple answer Jesus gave is that it grows. The word of God does not come to us as human words do, as a letter or a newspaper article or a text message. It comes as a seed, sown by a farmer, looking for fertile soil in which to put down roots and bear fruit.[15] The word of God is within us. This is what God said to Moses:

It is not in heaven, that you should say, "Who will go up to heaven for us, and get it for us so that we may hear it and observe it?". Neither is it beyond the sea, that you should say, "Who will cross to the other side of the sea for us, and get it for us so that we may hear and observe it?". No, the word is very near to you; it is in your mouth and in your heart for you to observe.

Deuteronomy 30:12–14

James called the gospel the implanted word; John said the truth lives in us. Paul wrote to the Thessalonian church that he was thankful that when they received the word of God from him they accepted it not as a human word but as what it really is, God's word, which was now at work in them.[16] The word of God is not a product but an encounter, not a mailshot but a seed, not information but the nucleus of life itself. And as it grows inside us, it changes us by the generative power of the Holy Spirit, the "Spirit of truth" as Jesus calls him – the one who breathed the written word, implanted the living word, and now dwells in each believer.[17] As the word grows within us, it bears fruit in our hearts – the fruits of love, joy, peace, patience, kindness, generosity, faithfulness, gentleness, and self-control.[18] It brings renewal to our minds, and healing to our bodies. The life of the Christian in whom the word is implanted takes on a new meaning, because he or she is rooted in the principle of the cosmos, Jesus Christ the living word of God. Like the growth of the seed, this is a gradual process. And so the Christian life is best understood as a journey. When we receive the word of God, it is not that a destination has been reached but that a journey has begun, a journey which will be undertaken not alone but in relationship with the Holy Spirit. It is a relationship in which there will be many words, and all those words will change us; for all of us are being transformed into the image of Christ.[19] Quite how this works is deeply mysterious, as Paul himself acknowledged when he said that his task was to make the word of God fully known, the mystery of Christ within us.[20] But it is clear that when we receive the truth, we receive life itself; and when we receive life, we grow.

> You have heard of this hope . . . in the word of the truth, the gospel that has come to you. Just as it is bearing fruit and growing in the whole world, so it has been bearing fruit among yourselves from the day you heard it and truly comprehended the grace of God.
>
> Colossians 1:5–6

Living the truth

We began this book with the image of a pebble falling with a plop into the centre of a pond. This we likened to the way the truth first impinges on our minds. For some it occurs before the time of conscious memory; my children have no recollection of any event they could properly regard as the beginning of their relationship with God. For others it occurs at a specific moment in time which can be dated quite precisely. But whether we can fix the moment of impact or not makes very little difference: it is the subsequent spread of the ripples over the surface of our lives which matters, for this is the process by which we grow into the likeness of Christ, allowing ourselves to be conformed to his image, to develop in the unity of our faith and our knowledge of him, and to come to maturity as the people we were created to be.

What does this look like in practice? Both for me and for those who have allowed me the privilege of sharing in their own journeys, it means that truth has come in successive and ever deeper waves. My initial encounter with the truth came one Saturday afternoon in Cambridge, 20 years ago. As I unpacked a suitcase and read some words I found there, I suddenly knew a whole world was about to end. I gave in to the God I knew existed, acknowledged the futility of trying to hang on to the illusion that I could control my own destiny, and found myself on my knees. As I spoke the inaudible words in which I, Alison Keymer, student, finally gave permission to God, author of the universe, to take control of my life, the earth rumbled and the voice of the God whom for so long I had denied resounded in my head, telling me in words that pulsed with shapeless power what that would mean. I rose rather shaken to my feet, and looked out of the window to see if the world had felt the tremors of the earthquake which had just rearranged my inner being. For a moment I watched the buses passing by as before, the summer flowers painted in the green grass of the park opposite, the people going about their business as they always did. But somehow it all looked different, as if the light had changed. The familiar world was suddenly charged, charged with the grandeur of God, shining like shook foil, as Gerard Manley Hopkins puts it. Reality was painted with droplets of gold, droplets which are always there, if only we know how to see them; and I remembered what it was to be a child and to know that it was my birthday. I suddenly understood the meaning of the phrase I had always thought ridiculous: this is what Jesus had meant when he said that to enter into the kingdom of God we must be born again.

And yet that moment is not what my Christian life has been all about, any more than my birth as a baby has been what my physical life has been all about. People come to faith in all sorts of different ways, and the very fact that "sudden" conversions such as mine take place has often encouraged us to see the state of being a Christian as in some sense having arrived, as standing at the end of a process of enquiry. And yet the reverse is true: becoming a Christian is not an arrival but a departure, the beginning of what will turn out to be a long and complex journey through a world which is bigger than the one we see, and which will find its destination in God. To enter into the truth is both a momentary encounter and a lifelong process; and if we ourselves are not fully engaged in that process we will have nothing to share with those amongst whom we live.

*"You will know the truth, and the truth will make you
free"*   John 8:32

And so my journey began. Life is a messy and often painful
affair, and changing circumstances bring opportunities for the
light of the gospel to shine into freshly exposed areas of darkness. One year after God first spoke to me, I went from life as
a single PhD student in Cambridge to that of a vicar's wife
with three stepsons in Corby, a Midlands town of Scots and
steelworkers. There were many good things, not least the
friendliness of the people amongst whom we had come to
live; but I also began to discover what it means to bite off
more than one can chew. Ghostly voices from the past poured
themselves into a cocktail of expectation, duty, the raging
conflicts of bereaved teenagers and a growing sense of
despair. Brandishing my human imperfections in one hand
and battering at the bars of the cage which surrounded me
with the other, I found that reality no longer sparkled with
drops of gold, and that the ivory towers of fulfilment had
been replaced by the dock of a litter-strewn mental courtroom. Deprived of my identity and surrounded by the accus-
ing voices of inadequacy, my self-esteem shrank and I
wondered at the apparent paradox of a faith which seemed
not so much to set me free as to condemn me.

But time passes. The boys grew up and left home for
university, our son Edward was born, and we moved from
Corby to Leicester. The pain receded. But it proved to be
merely the lull after the storm, for soon the clouds were gathering again, and a fresh storm broke over our heads, this time
within the church itself. Battered and confused, I found that
the new storm merely caused me to start thinking again about
the old one. I felt lost, and I began to talk to a friend about it,
pouring out my pain and asking why.

Into this scenario, one morning after breakfast, stepped
God. In an inner flash I saw myself standing in the dock,

fingers of accusation pointed in eloquent silence towards me. Seated on the bench was God himself, magisterial, red-gowned and grey-wigged, listening. The final moment came. Up went the hammer and, in a timeless descent of aeons, struck the bench with a resounding crash. "Not guilty!" rang the words from the Almighty. And for the second time in my life, reality changed shape. Burdens grew wings and flew away, and I floated through the day knowing at last what it meant that the truth will set you free; that this stuff did actually work, did smash itself into places other than my head and transform them, and that I had been acquitted, despite my shortcomings, by the Creator of the universe himself. Life may be painful, and it may be messy; but I was not responsible. I was free, free from the struggle to define myself amongst the definitions of others – because for the first time I had discovered the definition of God.

"What is truth?"   *John 18:38*

Pilate's question to Jesus is an extraordinarily helpful one to our age. As I have thought about my own life, and as I have talked and prayed with many others, I have concluded that it must be answered on two different levels.

First, truth is something ontological – that is, it applies universally to every member of the human race. It is about the nature of our being, and the meaning of life. As an existentialist this universal truth was hidden from me; I thought I could create my own truth, that truth is relative, and that I could choose a personal truth from a range of options. To make truth relative is perhaps the ultimate refuge from the impossible attempt to understand it, and the sense that "true" is the same as "true for me" has become one of the major and most deathly assumptions of postmodernism. But as Christians we are bound to believe that truth is in some sense absolute; that it is fixed and eternal, and that it resides in God. And so the truth as I embraced it when I became a Christian can be clearly stated: it is that Jesus is the Son of God, the Creator of the universe; that he cannot be separated from God, being the Word which God spoke and speaks; and that through him and with the help of the Holy Spirit I can be restored to a relationship with God which will endure for ever. That is the gospel, the truth as it applies to the whole human race, and all Christians have accessed truth in this sense.

The problem with ontological truth is that it isn't sufficient. It may, in Jesus' phrase, bring life – but it doesn't bring what he went on to call *abundant* life. It may, as he promised, set us free – but we don't necessarily *feel* free. Truth may be universal – but I am an individual, and if it is to mean anything in practice it must be the case that the truth has a personal dimension too. We know that this is so from the many different ways in which Jesus expressed the truth to those to whom he spoke. Truth is like light; it sets off from its source, but it does so in order to flow into particular and specific places of darkness and make them clear. And so I must ask, of myself and of each person to whom I speak: What are the nooks and crannies of my soul into which the truth needs to flow? When God looks at me and my past and my present, what is his perspective? And whatever it is, that is the truth for me individually. I have had life from the day I became a Christian, for from that day I have been in touch with God who is the source of life. But the abundance of my life has increased as I have grasped the implications of the truth for myself as a particular individual with particular experiences and circumstances. I have been free from the day I became a Christian, in that I am no longer subject to the power of death; but I have learned only gradually to take hold of that freedom and allow it to release me from the web of misbeliefs and malpractices which bind me – to be transformed by the renewal of my mind, as Paul puts it to the Romans.[21] For it takes time for the intellect to eddy about a truth, as the poet Robert Frost would observe 2,000 years later.

All Christians have grasped truth in its universal sense – what it *is*, in eternity. But often they haven't grasped it in its personal sense – what it *does*, in the here and now. It is easy to say "The truth will set you free", but not so easy to grasp that that means not from some abstract existential condition, but from the specific things in your life which are causing you not to be free: the values, circumstances, assumptions, experiences and behaviours which separate you from God and cause you pain. It has been estimated that only 15 per cent of Christians learn to embrace truth in this second, personal sense.[22] One of our tasks as ministers of the gospel is to help people grasp the truth as it applies not just to their position as a member of the human race, but as an individual with particular life circumstances and experiences. That was what I discovered that morning in my kitchen.

Receiving the truth as individuals

> Life is not a syllogism of theology, a blueprint of morality, or a scheme of therapy, but an odd tale told by people who have stories of concrete transformation, of facing chaos and receiving new life, of laughing deeply at God's joy and God's gift and God's victory, and of daring to mock the chaos that has lost its power.
>
> Walter Brueggemann[23]

I have known many people whose lives have been dramatically changed by their Christian faith, not in the external sense of church attendance or the making of new friends, but in the deep inner transformation that has taken place in their souls. I think for example of Rob. Rob had been a timid and broken man dominated by his alcoholic wife and dependent on antidepressants; within twelve months of becoming a Christian Rob had changed so dramatically that he had received four promotions at work. Or Liesl, who spent much of her youth incarcerated in mental hospitals suffering from drug addiction and schizophrenia. On one of her periodic escapes from hospital Liesl was drawn into a church where an old lady gave her a cup of tea and told her God loved her. Within months she had given her life to Christ and been completely healed; she has written a book to tell her story.[24] Or Dave. Rejected by his parents, brought up in children's homes, with a history of drugs, a conviction for grievous bodily harm and a rocky marriage, Dave became a Christian. Over the years Dave too has changed – through prayer, through personal support from other Christians, through his own determination to leave the past behind. He and Liz now have four children who pay tribute to the stability of their family life, and Dave works as a carer in a home for disadvantaged adults. Or Marie. Once an irritable person living in a conflict-ridden family, Marie has found such peace since becoming a Christian on an Alpha course that the atmosphere at home has been transformed. Startled by the suddenness of this, her teenage sons began coming to church and her husband decided to join Alpha himself. One of her sons stood up in front of the whole church recently and explained how he no longer needed to steal things because he too had been changed by Jesus.[25]

For some people the transformation in their lives comes immediately. For others, it is more gradual. It has been my privilege to pray with many people since my own encounter with the truth that day in my kitchen. Often I ask them what they think it means that the truth will set them free. Usually they have no idea. But always it turns out that they are believing something that is not true, a belief not rationally held but implictly accepted, an unexamined assumption which has tied up their soul in a tangled distortion of lies. "The truth will set you free", said Jesus; and often I have watched the truth burst into people's minds and hearts in the context of an evening spent in conversation and prayer. Sometimes truth comes as a picture, sometimes as a forgotten memory, sometimes as a new insight or just the flood of an emotional certainty; always it grows as the person welcomes it, absorbs it, and begins to live it – in a way which often demands a conscious effort of some magnitude. I have come to think about this "prayer ministry", as it is often called, in the light of Hebrews 4:12–13:

> The word of God is living and active, sharper than any two-edged sword, piercing until it divides soul from spirit, joints from marrow; it is able to judge the thoughts and intentions of the heart. And before him no creature is hidden, but all are naked and laid bare to the eyes of the one to whom we must render an account.

It is a ministry with a long history. From the earliest times it has been apparent that to enter into a relationship with God is to begin a conversation whose words will gradually help us free ourselves from the things which bind us. The first Christians adopted the practice of public confession of sin as the means of achieving this, but found the task more complex than they had at first anticipated. By the fourth and fifth centuries English and Celtic monks were turning to the first spiritual directors; by the seventh century special penitential books were being written to help the clergy minister freedom and forgiveness to those in their care.[26] By the twelfth century these had grown into what were effectively the first training manuals for prayer ministry, probing the individual's circumstances and inner struggles, and helping him find spiritual disciplines and insights which would assist him in his journey. The modern practices of spiritual direction and prayer ministry are developments of this process, understanding sin not as simple contravention of a commandment – although it is that too – but more widely as everything which prevents us from living as who we are in Christ.[27]

And so it is that when we pray with a person, we are offering not our own wisdom but insight sought in relationship with the Holy Spirit. Such prayer requires a willingness to bare our souls to God, to allow others to accompany us as we seek the kind of understanding which I received that day in my kitchen – an occasion which came not out of the blue but at the end of a process of prayer and reflection undertaken in the company of others. It means opening ourselves up to the Word and the words of God, and being willing to allow him to cut open our souls as thoroughly as any surgeon will ever operate on our bodies. It is an unnerving process, but a rewarding one.

One of the first people I prayed with was Karen. Karen was a happily married mother of two, but struggling with difficult relationships at work. As she shared her story, Karen realised that beneath the undoubted difficulties lay a debilitating and unacknowledged belief from which she had suffered since childhood. Brought up in a loving home, but one where money had been short, all Karen's clothes and toys had been passed down from her elder sister. "Second best" was a voice that had come to echo through Karen's inner being, sapping her self-esteem and greatly magnifying the pain she experienced in the normal ebb and flow of her work relationships. We prayed, and God spoke to Karen through the words of Isaiah: "I have called you by name, you are mine; you are precious in my sight, and honoured, and I love you". Karen meditated on these words day and night until she knew them by heart. She began to smile in a way she never had before; and her colleagues began to treat her differently.

Recently I prayed with George, a gentle man of great ability and integrity, struggling with the legacy of a critical father who had not known how to affirm him. George had poured out his anguish on paper, expressing his self-doubt, his fears about his sexuality, his despair and confusion about the direction of his life. Unable to answer the simple question "What does God think of you?", he allowed us to share with him a picture we received from the scriptures as we prayed of a father running, arms opened wide, to greet his returning son. The next day, alone at home, George was suddenly overwhelmed for the first time in his life with the deep inner knowledge that God was his Father and loved him unconditionally.

And there was Sarah, a kind but rather shy person, outwardly successful but struggling inside with the bitter anger she felt towards two people whom she had been unable to forgive. As we prayed, Sarah began to realise forgiveness meant not saying that it didn't matter – it did – but that she could afford to entrust the people concerned to God, for he was on her side, hurting with her, angry on her behalf. A few days later she walked into her stepfather's house, feeling gigantic in stature, with a vision of an angel on the doorstep beside her, and greeted him confidently and peacefully. A while after that, she met the woman who had damaged her deeply; instead of awkwardness and anger she felt herself being filled with warmth from the head downwards. Sarah has become conspicuous for the peace which shines through her as she prays in her turn for others.

Ministering the truth to others

> Consider your own call, brothers and sisters: not many of you were wise by human standards, not many were powerful, not many were of noble birth. But God chose what is foolish in the world to shame the wise; God chose what is weak in the world to shame the strong.
>
> 1 Corinthians 1:26–27

Rob, Liesl, Dave, Marie, Karen, George and Sarah are all ordinary people, and yet they all have stories of personal transformation to tell, stories of a personal encounter with a truth which they have met not through explanation but through relationship. None of them would be recognised as leaders in the conventional sense of the word, and yet every single one now has a ministry to others.

There have been many others. The details vary; but always the story is the same. In our city centre church we have hospital consultants, street people, teachers, children, single parents, reformed drug addicts, people with criminal records, disabled people, young professionals, students, mentally handicapped people, civic leaders, retired people, business people and, increasingly, asylum seekers. We have people born and bred in Leicester, and we have people from China, Russia, Ethiopia, and Iraq. These people have only one thing in common: their lives are being changed by Christ.

It was from beginnings such as these that the gospel spread through the Roman world. It continues to do so today. Paul explained the gospel to a shy young man called Timothy, urging him to be filled not with the timidity that was his natural inclination, but with the power, love and self-discipline that were his in Christ. Timothy became one of Paul's most effective colleagues, travelling all over the empire, helping to found and pastor churches and ministering the gospel. Twenty-five years ago my husband explained the gospel to a shy young student called John. John responded with enthusiasm, and decided that such was the power of the word of God that he had better make sure it lived within him. Every day John memorised one verse from the Bible. Within months he had become so confident that other students began to seek him out for counsel. He was selected for ordination, and eventually became the vicar of a large international church in Singapore. He went on to spearhead the Anglican attempt to take the gospel into Cambodia, one of only 29 countries in the world where fewer than 1 per cent of the population have embraced the gospel, and where Christians still suffer major persecution.[28]

Another young man who encountered the truth at about the same age is an Argentinian called Hector.[29] By the age of

18 Hector was, in his own words, a drug-addicted delinquent, wanted by the police and a disgrace to his family. Shot while committing a crime, he was taken by his brother to a clinic where a nurse read the words of 2 Corinthians 5:17 to him: "If any man is in Christ, he is a new creation", and asked whether he wanted God to change his life. He said he did. They prayed and she left the room. Instantly the bleeding stopped and the craving for drugs left him. Hector, still with two bullets in his body, joined the church and began to work with drug addicts and young people. He became a pastor, and within a year he had a congregation of 1,000. By 1995, after an astonishing story of radio broadcasts and crowded stadium meetings, he had a Sunday congregation of 15,000, a daily ministry to 10,000 people of whom 200 to 300 were responding to the gospel each day for the first time, and a network of 100 new churches. At that point, aged about 40, he came to England to tell his story. I listened to this man every day for a week; and the most striking thing he said, repeated over and over again throughout his talks, was the single phrase, "And the Lord said to me, 'Hector' . . ." His whole life and ministry were sustained by the simple fact that he heard the Word of God.

For many people the truth is received in the context of an individual encounter or relationship. For others, it comes in a group setting. This is the principle of Alpha in the West, but it is also the principle that underpins the ministry developed in Tanzania between the dioceses of Leicester and of Mount Kilimanjaro, where under the auspices of SOMA a team from Holy Trinity has been working in association with bishop Simon Makundi, assistant bishop John Hayden, and diocesan missioner Stanley Hotay. One of the poorest countries in the world, Tanzania is a land whose spiritual hunger is as great as its material poverty, where many respond to the gospel but few have the education or the resources to help them grow in their faith. The pastors and evangelists of the diocese are a committed and dynamic group determined to improve the quality of life, spiritual and material, of their people. Would it be possible, Stanley had asked, to write a culturally appropriate discipleship course which could be taught by one leader, equipped with one Bible, to a group who could not read, which would cover all the basic areas of the Christian faith, and which would be based on the principles of Matthew 28:19 (go and make disciples) and 2 Timothy 2:2 (who can teach others also)? The result is *Rooted in Jesus*, a two year practical nurture course in Swahili written by a team of clergy, cell leaders and teachers, printed by Springboard and offered to the pastors and evangelists of the diocese at a series of training conferences and seminars in the summers of 2002 and 2003.

Rooted in Jesus has now been in use for two years. Some 2,000 people belong to 180 groups, most of which are led by the dedicated evangelists, many of whom have little training and some of whom did not previously possess a Bible. The results are remarkable. One pastor reports that his church has been transformed as people increase their commitment to Christ and to one another. Others say that the lives of group members are visibly changing as for the first time they receive and apply the word of God. Some have received healing; hundreds have responded to the gospel for the first time; others have found unexpected answers to prayer. Some of the greatest benefits have been reported by the illiterate members, given access for the first time to the power of the truth as it works within them: *the people who are growing the fastest in my group are those who cannot read or write, because they are the ones who have received the memory verses into their hearts*. These are people who face hardships we can only imagine. For many, daily life means spending two hours a day digging two-metre holes in the dry sand of river beds to find water; for some it means malaria or AIDS; for others it means hungry lions prowling at night, the chants and medicines of witch doctors, the perils and hardship of female circumcision, the consolation of "local brews", the empty shelves of the local clinic and the remoteness of thousands of square miles with no secondary schools or tarmac roads. "We want to develop", declared the Member of Parliament for Kiteto, opening a conference in the southern town of Kibaya. "You bring us the word of God. We want to receive what you have for us". And we knew, as together we read, prayed and worshipped God, as people testified to a joy they had never before experienced, received the gifts of the Holy Spirit, found themselves caught up in prayer with a power and fervour that were new both to them and (let's be frank) to us, and as we listened to a promise from God that he will bless his people in this forgotten and neglected place as they continue to open themselves to his word, that develop is exactly what they will do. To hear and embrace the truth is a powerful thing.

Recognising the depth of human need

The reason why it is the truth that makes us free is that it is untruth which causes us not to be free. Often the untruths which bind people are clear and specific, and find their source in a single situation or experience. Others are more insidious, harder to pin down, because they come not from specific traumas but from the pervasive collective voice of a whole society. Every human being is short-sighted, and views reality only through the tinted lenses provided by his culture. We know nothing else; we have no other way of focussing. And so the starting point for effective ministry to the individual is the supposition that he or she is entangled to a greater or lesser extent in the web of false assumptions which govern the world in which we live, whether those be the individualistic assumptions of postmodern England or the tribal traditions of rural Africa. Occasionally we become painfully aware of our own short sight – Ruth's cancer brought me face to face with the fact that the place of success and fulfilment I was heading for was no more than a mirage in the desert, an oasis which I would obediently spend my life moving towards only to find it dissolve into nothing, probably later but maybe sooner. More often we soldier on unaware that we are bound by beliefs we didn't even know we had, pursuing a happiness that seems partially ours and yet never quite within our grasp, and knowing at some level that we have not yet found what we are looking for.

Many people in the West make life work quite well like this, obeying the cultural diktat about where happiness is to be found, until sooner or later something sticks a pin in the bubble and it bursts: a miscarriage, a redundancy, an illness. Others strive for the meaning and fulfilment to be found in the accomplishment of their goals, defeating their stress with dreams. Most settle for living life a day at a time, drowning the inner cry for fulfilment in a wealth of culturally determined distractions. Some succumb to the Western disease of depression, the hopelessness of knowing that their needs are not met and they are hollow within. A few achieve what they have been working for – only to find that the golden trophy, once grasped, crumbles into dust between their fingers. The American journalist Philip Yancey has this to say about those who are most successful at following the voices which define the key to happiness in worldly terms:

> My career as a journalist has afforded me opportunities to interview "stars", including football greats, movie actors, music performers, best-selling authors, politicians, and TV personalities. These are the people who dominate the media . . . Yet I must tell you that ... our "idols" are as miserable a group of people as I have ever met. Most have troubled or broken marriages. Nearly all are incurably dependent on psychotherapy.[30]

Most people have not yet reached the end of the rainbow and made the painful discovery that the crock of gold is not there. Their days are full and their motives unexamined. But their lives are nonetheless governed by a tangle of misbeliefs and misguided strategies. Our culture suggests it is imperative to fill all your needs and make the most of all the opportunities available to you. Many of the whispered needs and opportunities are contradictory or in conflict with those of others, or simply unfillable; and so frustration inevitably results. In a postmodern world where freedom spells choice and choice is expressed in consumption, we find that self-fulfilment means saying yes to everything and being satisfied by nothing: we want meaningful relationships and mobile lifestyles, absorbing careers and happy families, high incomes and lots of opportunities for leisure, city facilities and peaceful country living; personal wealth and social justice, community involvement and individual privacy, and above all, we want the time and the money to pursue hobbies, take holidays, and buy gadgets, listen to music, enjoy meals out.[31] Like jugglers keeping too many balls in the air, our restless busyness is liable to bring not peace and happiness but stress and discontent. For those not given access to the balls, of course, the stress and discontent often takes the form of racial and social conflict, and a life of deprivation and crime. We build, as Jesus would have said, on a foundation of sand; and then we wonder at the instability of what we have built.

And so we must have confidence in the power of the truth we have received. Over the years I have prayed with many people, some more than once, some Christians, some initially not; and I have had the opportunity to watch them grow and change as they, like I, move ever deeper into the truth which sets us free. Always, as Jeremiah warned, there is pain below the surface, even in lives that seem outwardly serene – the pain of being boxed into ill-fitting identities, of striving without reward or recognition, of missed opportunities and unfulfilled longings. Sometimes the pain is acute: I have prayed with people damaged by abusive childhoods, and seen them begin to discover what it feels like to know that they are loved by God; with people suffering specific trauma, who have been able to give and receive forgiveness; and with people enduring situations of great stress at work, who have discovered something of why they are there and what meaning God attaches to their life. I have seen people released from phobias and panic attacks; others from an inherited and inaccurate view of themselves; yet others from family patterns of destructive behaviour. Increasingly it seems that people are seeking to escape from a cage of rationality and get in touch with a more satisfying reality through various forms of alternative spiritual and occult practices – but always with strong negative effects on their personal lives. These effects can range from a sense of spiritual deadness, through nightmares and bursts of irrational anger or anxiety, failed relationships and business deals, to extreme psychic disturbances and even apparent spirit possession. Relief is found in all these situations and many more when the person concerned has been able to step outside the parameters of their own world-locked thinking and experience something of the power of the word of God as it is spoken and prayed into their situation.

Of ourselves, we are powerless to bring about change. I have no rational explanation for what happened to me that day in my kitchen, any more than I am able to bring emotional and spiritual healing into the life of another person merely by clarifying something they had not understood, however clearly and compassionately I may do it. The only explanation I can offer for what I have seen and experienced is that truth as Jesus offers it is not information, proposition, or statement, but the active force of reality itself, universal and personal in its application and spiritual in its essence. This is far removed from the understanding of modernism, which regarded truth as tool or fact, but perfectly compatible with the worldview of postmodernism, which is more aware of the invisible dimension of life. Truth is the self-expression of God, and God is a spiritual being. Spoken by God in creation, made living in Jesus, it is now made available to us through the Holy Spirit, the Spirit of truth himself.[32] Our task is to learn to live and help others to live in the light of the truth and by the power of the Holy Spirit. And when we do that, there really is no telling what might happen.

Notes

1 *City of God* 19,1. "Marcus Varro by careful and minute examination noted such a wide variety of opinions, in his book *On Philosophy*, that by the application of certain criteria of differentiation he easily arrived at a total of 288 . . . possible schools of thought."

2 *Summa Contra Gentiles* I.100–02. The same subject is treated in his *Summa Theologica*, I, I q26. For a discussion of Thomas' thought in this regard, see J Pieper, *Happiness and Contemplation*, especially ch.3.

3 See Luke 4:18–19; John 8:32.

4 Jesus said he had come not just to bring life, but to bring abundant life (John 10:10) and promised that if we live in relationship with him our joy will be complete (John 15:11).

5 See for example A McGrath, *The Future of Christianity*, ch.6; S Hauerwas and WH Willimon, *Resident Aliens*, ch.6. Cultural theology often lies behind the downfall of whole countries. Recent research shows that the Nazis were voted into power in the 1930s by Protestant but not Catholic areas of Germany; and suggests that the genocide of Rwanda could have been prevented by a theology which focussed less on the individual and more on society.

6 The fusion of Christian principles with modern cultural

assumptions is eloquently portrayed by Os Guinness in *The Gravedigger Files*. See also R Niebuhr's classic study *Christ and Culture*, ch.3. The influence of modernism on the evangelical movement in particular is eloquently portrayed by B D McLaren, *More Ready Than You Realize: Evangelism as Dance in the Postmodern Matrix*. This is the subject of what has become known as the "Post-Evangelical Debate" – see the book of that title edited by Graham Cray.

7 John 18:37; John 17:17.

8 2 Timothy 2:15.

9 Quoted in J John and M Stibbe, *A Box of Delights*, p.17.

10 2 Timothy 3:16, "All scripture is God-breathed" (NIV); 2 Peter 1:20–21: "No prophecy [of scripture] ever came by human will, but men and women moved by the Holy Spirit spoke from God." For a discussion of the ways we trivialise the Bible, see M Riddell, *Threshold of the Future*, p.51–56.

11 Hebrews 4:12: "The word of God is living and active, sharper than any two-edged sword, piercing until it divides soul from spirit, joints from marrow; it is able to judge the thoughts and intentions of the heart." For what this means in today's terms, see the study by P Meier which concludes that after three years of meditation on scripture a person's thought patterns and behaviour have changed in such a way as to produce statistically superior mental health and happiness; P Meier, "Spiritual and mental health in the balance", in *Renewing Your Mind in a Secular World*, ed. J Woodbridge, pp.26–28. For how to make this happen in practice, see N T Anderson and R Saucy, *The Common Made Holy: Developing a Personal and Intimate Relationship with God*.

12 John 14:7.

13 1 Peter 1:25.

14 Jeremiah 31:33: "'I will put my law within them, and I

will write it on their hearts; and I will be their God, and they shall be my people. No longer shall they teach one another, or say to each other, know the Lord, for they shall all know me, from the least of them to the greatest,' says the Lord."

15 Mark 4:2–20.

16 James 1:21; 2 John 2; 1 Thessalonians 2:13.

17 John 14:16–17: "I will ask the Father, and he will give you another advocate, to be with you forever. This is the Spirit of truth, whom the world cannot receive, because it neither sees him nor knows him. You know him, because he abides with you, and he will be in you"; Ephesians 1:13: "In [Christ] you also, when you had heard the word of truth, the gospel of your salvation, and had believed in him, were marked with the seal of the promised Holy Spirit".

18 Galatians 5:2–23.

19 2 Corinthians 3:18: "And all of us . . . seeing the glory of the Lord as though reflected in a mirror, are being transformed into the same image . . . for this comes from the Lord, the Spirit."

20 See Colossians 1:25–27: "I became its servant . . . to make God's word fully known, the mystery that has been hidden throughout the ages and generations but has now been revealed to his saints. To them God chose to make known how great . . . are the riches of the glory of this mystery, which is Christ in you."

21 Romans 12:2. The web of misbeliefs and malpractices is what the Bible refers to as sin, which can be defined as "an organic network of compulsive attitudes, beliefs and behaviour deeply rooted in our alienation from God" (L Crabb); or as "behaving in a manner inconsistent with that which we are in Christ Jesus" (D Evrist); see also Galatians 2:14, "When I saw that they were not acting consistently with the truth of the gospel".

22 See N Anderson, *The Bondage Breaker*, pp.107–08.

23 *Interpretation and Obedience*, p.318.

24 Liesl Alexander, *Free to Live*; www.free2live.org.uk.

25 The stories told here are not unusual. Many others have similar experiences. See www.rejesus.co.uk and www.alphacourse.org.uk for more examples.

26 Usually based on the seven capital vices or, as they became known later, the seven deadly sins – first formulated for this purpose by Cassian in the fifth century, along with the concept of the pastor as spiritual doctor whose role is to help the confessant recover the health which he has lost through sin. The history of this literature is discussed, with examples and references, in my *Dante and the Medieval Other World*, pp.113–23.

27 Wholeness Through Christ was founded in the UK in the 1970s to develop the ministry of "prayer counselling". One of its heirs is Christian Prayer Ministries, whose website provides an overview of contemporary prayer ministry. See www.christian-prayer-ministries.org.

28 John Benson. In 2003 John was able to pass the responsibility for the ministry in Cambodia to his colleague Mok Wai Mung.

29 Hector Gimenez's testimony, *The Miraculous Power of God*, can be obtained from Kingdom Faith Ministries (www.kingdomfaith.com).

30 P Yancey, *The Jesus I Never Knew*, pp.115–16.

31 See D Yankelovich, "New rules in American life: searching for fulfilment in a world turned upside down", *Psychology Today* 15 (4) p.36.

32 John 16:12; see also John 14:17.

CHAPTER NINE

RENEWING THE CHURCH: LIVING IN THE POWER OF THE HOLY SPIRIT

What has come into being in him was life, and the life was the light of all people. The light shines in the darkness, and the darkness did not overcome it.

John 1:3–4

On 29 October 1996 my husband, Roger, was hit by a lorry as he crossed the road. Within an hour of breakfast, I found myself sitting in a corner of the resuscitation room of the Leicester Royal Infirmary while they examined him. Within another hour I was receiving the news that he was critically injured. He had a ruptured spleen, four ribs broken in two places each so as to create a whole free-floating section of rib cage, a broken clavicle, a punctured lung, a broken pelvis, a shattered acetabulum, a ruptured left knee ligament, and cuts to his head. They would operate to remove the spleen, and then he would be admitted to intensive care and put on a ventilator. The Accident and Emergency consultant said they would do their best to save him. The anaesthetist said the critical period was the next 72 hours, when his heart might pack up, and then two weeks during which he was likely to develop a lung infection. Either of those would kill him. If he did survive, he would eventually be able to walk, but he would be at risk of serious ongoing problems in his hip, and he would never be able to bend his knee properly. They said they were sorry.

As they spoke the words, the universe changed shape. I suddenly found not only that I believed fervently and unquestioningly in prayer, but that the world in which we live and move is only one plane of a multi-tiered reality: that there is a whole spiritual dimension to our existence which is far more real than the material one we see. I knew that because I was in it. The only way I can describe it is that it was like being catapulted from one world to another, seeing through new lenses into a dimension I had never been in before.[1] In a single instant I learned that reality is not primarily material but spiritual: and I realised that it was in the spiritual realm that Roger would live or die.

So we prayed. And as we prayed, God began to speak. When I went down to the hospital again that night, I found two more members of the church walking round the building, praying. God had given Steve a vision of a punctured football slowly being reinflated; he didn't know that Roger had a punctured lung. The next day Roger came off the ventilator, and a rather startled doctor told me that according to his X-rays he shouldn't be able to breathe without it. Textbook case, he said, you could set it as an exam question.

The next day they moved him out of intensive care into the high dependency unit. He was grey, completely unable to move, badly bruised, able to breathe only with 40 per cent oxygen through a mask, barely able to speak, with blood coming out of a chest drain, monitors everywhere and his leg in traction. He couldn't eat or even absorb liquid food through a gastric tube. They gave him something to help him sleep, which just gave him hallucinations. I prayed God would use the hallucinations. The next day he told me he had had a tremendous, indescribable vision of healing.

Throughout the critical period there was a prayer rota in

the church, which meant that someone somewhere was praying for Roger 24 hours a day, and often whole groups. A week later the surgeons operated on his smashed hip, and we held a prayer meeting. As we prayed, Trevor received a mental picture of two figures working on his hip, with a much bigger figure standing behind, leaning over and touching the area they were treating. The consultant rang me to say that not only had the operation been successful, but they had done it in four hours instead of the anticipated six.

They had put Roger back on the ventilator in intensive care before the operation, and kept him on it afterwards. For days I went every day, always with someone else, to sit by his unconscious body and the machines. Each time we prayed. And each time a nurse came, checked his lung function and turned the ventilator down, from 69 per cent oxygen to 65 to 60 to 55 to 45 to 40. Eventually they took him off it altogether. He couldn't speak, because they'd had to put a tube in his neck so they could clear the gunk out of his lungs. But he could write in the air with his finger. I asked if he'd been aware that I had come every day and prayed. No, he wrote; how many times? Before I'd worked it out, he held up six fingers. He was right. I was too stunned to ask him how he knew, and by the time I did, he'd no memory of the conversation.

It wasn't all plain sailing. He did get a lung infection, MRSA, the dreaded resistant bug: the staff in intensive care broke the news to me with faces of compassion, and drew the curtains round the bed so we could say our goodbyes. But a group praying in South Africa had a vision of Jesus at the entrance of the tomb of Lazarus, seeing the dead body and calling it out to new life. Roger recovered. His clavicle set crooked, and apparently he shouldn't be able to raise his arm above the horizontal; but he can wave it in the air. His knee mended completely, and he can walk and run as before. His smashed hip grew a lot of new bone, and he has had no further problems with it. The only lasting effect is that he has a very slight limp; and God told him there's a particular reason for that.

And so I learned that healing is a spiritual issue. I learned that just as Jesus burst into his world with the power to change reality, so with the help of the Holy Spirit can we. I learned that reality is spiritual before it is physical, and that God speaks in it and through it with words that are not just vehicles for meaning but the active agents of change. It is a lesson I haven't forgotten.

From Word to Spirit

"Do not let your hearts be troubled. Believe in God, believe also in me . . . The one who believes in me will also do the works that I do and, in fact, will do greater works than these, because I am going to the Father . . . And I will ask the Father, and he will give you another Advocate, to be with you forever. This is the Spirit of truth, whom the world cannot receive, because it neither sees him nor knows him".

John 14:1,12,16

After the apparent disaster of the crucifixion the disciples were a dispirited bunch, deprived of their leader and at a loss to know what to do next. Their morale was restored by their encounters with the risen Jesus, and according to John they received the Holy Spirit from Jesus himself at this point. They met together frequently in Jerusalem with 120 other believers, and waited. It was then, as they were gathered together on the day of Pentecost, that the Holy Spirit burst into the public arena and filled them powerfully in a way they had not previously experienced. They were filled again with the Holy Spirit a few days later. From then on, the Holy Spirit was, as Jesus had said he would be, both with them and within them.[2]

Recognising that this had been foretold by the prophets

and promised by Jesus, they found themselves proclaiming the gospel in many languages and praying powerfully for the sick. People were healed, people embraced the gospel, and the Christian church was founded. The Holy Spirit continued to be an ever-present reality amongst the new believers, filling them on numerous subsequent occasions, and enabling them to recognise and experience the power of the truth that unlocks reality and sets people free. The disciples of Jesus were, as he had promised, doing the things that he had done; their words and actions lived as his had – and throughout the Roman empire people began to respond to the gospel as the power of God burst into their familiar world of poverty, sickness, and oppression.

For several centuries this continued to be the normal pattern of the Christian life.[3] And so the church grew, until by the mid-fourth century half the population of the empire was Christian.[4] But as the church became larger and more secular, the unpredictability of the Holy Spirit seemed increasingly to jeopardise the order of the new communities. Reports of signs, wonders and mass conversions died down, and what had begun as a movement gradually transformed itself into an institution, subject to the desire for order and control of those responsible for its well-being. The Holy Spirit continued to work in those willing to receive him; the Franciscans in the thirteenth century, the Huguenots in the sixteenth, the Quakers in the sixteenth, the Jansenists and Wesley's Methodists in the eighteenth all offer examples of New Testament style ministry led and sustained by the Holy Spirit. But gradually this became the exception rather than the rule.

Eventually the modern era began, ushered in by the so-called Age of Reason, reinforced by the success of the industrial revolution, and characterised, as we have seen, by an emphasis on the rational and visible. The Victorian church was strong on Christian morality, respectability and the preservation of the status quo; it fell to Charles Dickens and

Karl Marx to point out the miserable condition of most of the populace and the inadequacy of a church which seemed to regard religion as little more than a kind of drug for the prevention of social uprising.[5] New churches were built, but the gospel was not preached to the poor in any meaningful way. Expected to attend, mostly they did; but gradually they lost faith in a church which lacked spiritual power. The following century saw a slow and gradual decline in church membership, and that decline has continued ever since.[6] The result is that in much of today's church the Holy Spirit is rather like a piece of furniture passed lovingly down the generations, carefully polished and placed in the corner of a room by a family who have forgotten what it is for. Outside the church, the Holy Spirit is little more than a name with no meaning. When I first read the gospel of John, my worldview had so little room for the spiritual that I failed to notice the Holy Spirit altogether. My five-year-old nephew did better: struggling valiantly to get to grips with the new challenges of a Catholic primary school, he came home and explained that he had learned about God the Father, God the Son, and God the Holy Spinach.

And yet without the Holy Spirit we can do nothing. Jesus was the living word of God, the word which spoke the world, the word which shone light into darkness and brought life to the dead. We, by contrast, are mere human beings, equipped with minds and wills but with no spiritual power of our own. We can change nothing, and if we are left to ourselves our churches will be merely institutions, forces for good perhaps, or places of belonging, but no more than that. And so it was that Jesus promised to send the Holy Spirit to those who believed in him, the Spirit of truth by whose power we would continue to speak the words of life and shine light into darkness. We looked at the history of the church in Chapter 4; and perhaps we can now say that it is when the church has been open to the guidance of the Holy Spirit that it has been effective in continuing the work of Jesus, and when it has relied on its own human resources that it has merged with its culture and lost its way.

The Holy Spirit today

Whether the initiative lies with us or with God is sometimes hard to say. But it is clear that about 100 years ago the spiritual climate of the church began to change. In 1901 Christians in a Kansas Bible college were filled with the Holy Spirit and began speaking in tongues. In 1906 it happened to William Seymour, a black evangelist visiting a small church in Los Angeles. By 1922 the Holy Spirit was causing chaos in Kensington, London. On each occasion spiritual revivals took place during which people were healed and converted. Once again the power of God seemed to be present amongst ordinary people to heal the sick, release the oppressed, and proclaim the good news. Dismissed by the mainline churches as rowdy and anti-intellectual, those involved founded a new international movement which became known as Pentecostalism. It grew at an astonishing rate throughout the twentieth century, and it is projected that by 2010 there will be over 150 million Pentecostals all over the world.[7]

In the early 1960s some of these phenomena began to occur within the traditional denominations, both Protestant and Catholic. The charismatic renewal, as it became known, has been characterised by the recovery of the belief that through the agency of the Holy Spirit modern Christians may still expect to speak the gospel with a power which changes people's lives, pray for the sick and see them healed, deliver the oppressed from the forces which afflict them, and learn to live as a community of people who love one another and can reach out effectively to those around them. The result again has been growth, most clearly in parts of the world not affected by the rationalistic legacy of modernism – Africa,

Asia and South America – and least of all in the institution-alised and technological environment of Western Europe. It is now estimated that there are up to 500 million charismatic Christians worldwide.[8] Many have remained within the tradi-tional denominations, seeking to revitalise them; others have left to found new churches and denominations, and many of these have also experienced rapid growth.

Western culture itself is now changing. Perhaps it is not a coincidence that the charismatic renewal of the church began in the context of the swinging rebellion of the 1960s, with its focus on the individual and its desire for experimentation and authenticity. Perhaps it is not a coincidence that new churches and Christian movements have arisen in the context of the postmodern search for the recovery of a spiritual dimension to life.[9] And perhaps we should not think it a coincidence if, in a world increasingly tired of fragmentation and in search of relationship, we find that the church is able to act as a catalyst for the renewal of communities. Spirituality is now respectable, and we have a new opportunity to listen to the voice of Isaiah, to walk in the footsteps of Jesus, and to proclaim the gospel in word and deed to people who have grown tired of a human church offering an institutionalised faith which is, to the postmodern generation, not merely irrelevant but profoundly *boring*. For whatever else Jesus was, he certainly wasn't boring.

The Holy Spirit and the individual

I am the Lord who heals you.

Exodus 15:26

Jesus began with the individual, offering forgiveness of sin and reconciliation with God to each person who wished to accept it. His authority extended not only over the spiritual realm but over the whole created order, and his proclamation of the gospel was accompanied by compelling signs of healing and deliverance. He promised that he would send the Holy Spirit, the Spirit of truth, to his disciples, and that they, and in our turn we, would be guided and empowered by the Holy Spirit to do greater works even than those he had done.[10] If we are to recover the dynamic power of the truth which Jesus came to bring us, we must allow ourselves to be open to the Holy Spirit who alone can make that truth come alive. If we speak seated on our antique furniture, having eaten up our spinach, we will speak to no avail. If we allow the Holy Spirit to be with us and within us, our words will break into the lives of those who receive them with all the healing power of Jesus himself.

This is how Paul prays for the Thessalonians:

> May the God of peace himself sanctify you entirely; and may your spirit and soul and body be kept sound and blameless at the coming of our Lord Jesus Christ. The One who calls you is faithful, and he will do this.
>
> 1 Thessalonians 5:23

The Christian life is about being made whole, or being saved, or being healed – the Greek words are all related. For different people this means different things, for truth is not just ontological but personal; and it may mean different things at different times. But for every Christian it means *something*. And it is in this something that we find the starting point of the church, for the church is not an institution, a museum, or a private club, but rather the community of those who have been and are being healed.

Healing of the body

I have prayed with many people since 1996 both here and abroad. And it has been my experience that when we pray, we may expect things to happen. The healing ministry in our church began many years ago when a child, lying in a coma after a road accident, coughed into unexpected life as members of the church prayed over her. Prayer for healing is now a regular, if rather unpredictable, part of what we do. Recently we have heard from Rob, a young man healed from repetitive strain injury; Nora, a grandmother healed of a frozen shoulder; Alissa, a young mother healed of premature arthritis in the hand; Steven, a boy who complained that no one had told him about "the electricity" he felt running through him when he asked for prayer for his glandular fever; and Mim, whose dislocated knee was restored to normal in two days. Couples unable to conceive have conceived, and people with life-threatening illnesses have got better. Others, of course, have not got better; for healing is but a sign of eternal reality, and not available on demand in a flawed world. I have seen similar things happen in Tanzania. An old woman who had spent all her money on doctors in an attempt to find a cure for the tumours growing in her nose stood up in church the day after she had been prayed for to announce that they had gone. Another with a history of respiratory problems came forward and said she wanted to sing a song to demonstrate that her chest was now clear. In both cases the people told us that these women had indeed been afflicted in these ways; and in both cases the doctor on our team found no signs of illness. These things never fail to surprise me; and yet they keep happening.

Healing occurs not only within the church but, more importantly, outside it. Since the time of Jesus, prayer for healing has been one of the most effective ways of proclaiming the good news to those who have not previously heard it.[11] The spread of the gospel in the Roman empire has been attributed to the healing ministry.[12] In recent times, the unexpected growth of the church in China has been built on a foundation of answered prayer for healing, as witnessed by the story of Brother Yun; and in the United States the growth of the Vineyard movement led by John Wimber has been characterised by signs and wonders of this kind.[13] Closer to home, a recent report commissioned by the Church of England and entitled *A Time to Heal* calls for the recovery of an approach to the healing ministry which will be visionary, prophetic and dynamic. Healing is once again on the agenda.

Healing of the soul

> For this reason I bow my knees before the Father . . . I pray that, according to the riches of his glory, he may grant that you may be strengthened in your inner being with power through his Spirit, and that Christ may dwell in your hearts through faith, as you are being rooted and grounded in love. I pray that you may have the power to comprehend, with all the saints, what is the breadth and length and height and depth, and to know the love of Christ that surpasses all knowledge . . . so that you may be filled with all the fullness of God.
>
> Ephesians 3:14–19

The Holy Spirit is able to bring healing not just to the body but also to the soul, or psyche as it is called in the Greek. For many people this is the cutting edge of the good news: it is often more painful to live out of diseased attitudes and feelings towards the self than it is to live with physical disability, and learning to see ourselves as God sees us can bring personal transformation. Jesus freed the woman caught in adultery from her guilt with a single sentence. In his Sermon on the Mount he taught a whole crowd of people that their suffering and pain could be experienced differently when seen from the perspective of eternity. He helped Peter to replace his fear with steadfastness and his anger with love.[14] If some people experience physical healing, many more experience inner healing. And, like the despised Samaritan woman to whom Jesus chose to identify himself as God, it is often those who experience inner healing who go on to minister most powerfully to others.

One of the cell leaders in our church is a young woman called Jordan. Cheerful, intelligent and outgoing, Jordan is happily married with two young children. She feels called to tell people the good news about Jesus, and she runs her cell group on the basis that that is what they are all trying to do. But Jordan didn't start off like that. One Christmas Eve, four years ago, she decided to come to church. She was single, pregnant, and with a history of debt, drugs and relationships with violent men. Her father was violent and left when she was seven. She was raped as a young child and again as a teenager. Her mother was emotionally and physically abusive, and Jordan left home at fifteen after being beaten up once too often. The men she moved in with treated her little better. As she sat in church, God spoke to her. Jordan began to meet with Roger to learn more. She became a Christian and received the Holy Spirit. Her boyfriend, who wasn't interested either in God or in marriage, left her. Jordan joined a cell group, and the whole cell attended the birth of the baby, to the bewilderment of the hospital. And then she asked us to pray with her about her past. I have now prayed with Jordan seven times over a period of four years. It has been a stunning experience. God has taken us through the rooms of the house she was brought up in, showing her he was there. He's taken us into the cupboard under the stairs where she used to hide. He's helped her deal with the abuse and shown her how he feels about her. He's freed her from the consequences of the occult activities she and her family had been involved in. He's released her from the horrific nightmares which crushed her every night. He's healed her low self-esteem. He's told her to go forwards, to base her life on the truth. He's enabled her to trust the man who is now her husband, a strong Christian who believes in her. We have never prayed through the same issue twice; Jordan takes what God gives her, goes home with it, and receives it into the depths of her being. I asked her if I could share her story. Yes, she said. And tell them it lasts.

Healing of the spirit

> "Not by might, nor by power, but by my Spirit," says the Lord of hosts.
>
> Zechariah 4:6

The other kind of healing made available to us is spiritual healing. In its primary sense, this is what happens to every person when they first become a Christian, in whatever way that comes about; their alienation from God is brought to a close, and new life is infused into their spirit.[15] But for some people the alienation takes a more active form, and a special kind of healing is required. We call it deliverance or, more traditionally, exorcism. It is tempting to believe, in our emphasis on the visible, that evil spirits do not exist, and that Jesus's ministry to those afflicted by them is best understood in some other way. Experience teaches us that this is not so.[16]

Virginia arrived on my doorstep one day. She'd been sent by the local school, where she'd turned up in deep distress talking incoherently about demons and demanding to see a particular teacher whom she knew to be a Christian. I telephoned a colleague, and together we listened to her story. Virginia was a mature PhD student, and her behaviour was certifiable. She hadn't slept for seven days, she was seeing things and hearing voices, any computer she touched went completely haywire, and when we tried to pray with her she spoke in an altered voice and different personality, gave a different name, talked to her dead grandfather whom she said was in the room with us, and remembered nothing afterwards. It turned out that her grandfather had been the top freemason in a whole continent, and that suicide and early death had dogged the family for generations.[17] Even then she'd been fine herself up to this point. But when she arrived in Leicester she'd done two things: she signed up for the Alpha course, which was good, and she went to a psychic fair, which wasn't. She was looking for answers, but instead she found herself the centrepiece of the most spectacular spiritual battle I have ever witnessed. Setting her free took several nights of prayer. Eventually, as she was holding a little wooden cross, she felt something red shoot out of her head and hit the cross, like being struck by lightning in reverse. The instant that happened she looked up and said, "It's gone." She completed her degree, and was last heard of back home leading her family to Christ.

Prayer for deliverance is normally much less spectacular than this, and concerns problems which often people believe to be psychological, but which fail to respond to the normal processes of counselling and prayer for inner healing. We prayed with a young man who was struggling to overcome lustful thoughts towards other women despite being recently and happily married; one simple command to a spirit to leave him alone solved the problem. We have prayed for people with fears that they knew to be irrational, but which nonetheless gripped them; and those fears have gone instantaneously. We prayed for a woman consumed with angry thoughts against her husband. When asked if she was angry with him about anything in particular, she protested no, he was a good man and she loved him, and the anger just kind of swept up on her from nowhere. As we prayed, she had a frightening sensation of something being on her back; she coughed repeatedly and then suddenly burst out laughing as the Holy Spirit brought release to her. Her husband said afterwards she was a different person. Some people for whom we pray, like Virginia, have no Christian background or experience; they come as a last resort, seeking relief from problems for which they have found no other solution. Like Virginia, they respond to the gospel and go out "to start my new life", as one businesswoman put it after being released through prayer. Many of these people go on to share their freedom with others, and to minister the gospel effectively to those around them.

These are the raw materials, the living stones, from which

Jesus builds his church. The church grows one person at a time, as release from illness, inner turmoil and spiritual oppression is brought through prayer. Jesus chose impulsive fishermen, shy youths and dishonest tax collectors to take the gospel all over the empire. He is still choosing them. John Benson took the gospel into war-torn Cambodia. Jackie Pullinger, a young woman who set off alone for Hong Kong armed only with her own determination, learned to preach the gospel and pray for the drug addicts of the Walled City with spectacular results.[18] The ministry of a wizened nun called Mother Teresa who insisted on pouring the love of Christ all over the untouchable and the destitute of Calcutta has had an international impact. Many of those mentioned in these pages are working hard to bring the gospel to their friends and neighbours in Leicester. The revival of the church can be built only on a foundation of the changed lives of individuals who have received the word of God and learned to minister in the power of the Holy Spirit.

The Holy Spirit and the church

> Let anyone who has an ear listen to what the Spirit is saying to the churches.
>
> Revelation 2:7

In 1986 bishop John Taylor published a book which had originally grown out of a series of lectures on the Holy Spirit, given years before when he was the General Secretary of the Church Mission Society. In it he called for each individual to be open to the work of the Holy Spirit, remarking that what matters to God is not whether we are religious or not, but whether we are alive or not. He warned that the church, intended as the community of those into whom the Holy Spirit has breathed new life, easily settles into a framework of systems, structures and institutions; that it is prone to grow the hard crust of self-protection, prone to run away from life, prone to find a bit of insensitivity here, a bit of lethargy there, more comfortable. But Jesus came to bring not just life, but abundant life; and so Taylor called for us to resist the pressure to settle for conformity and instead to learn to trade the traditions of the church for the dreams of its people – not to reject or condemn the church, for the church is us, but to coax it into the renewal which it must choose to embrace in every generation if it is to be faithful to its original calling.[19]

And so, remembering the uncompromising example of Jesus, we try. Jesus burst into his world with a scant disregard for the established ways of doing things. He urged his hearers to pour the new wine of the gospel into new wineskins, rejecting the values and practices of the past which, once necessary, had become restrictive. He quoted the prophets and announced that it was time for things to be done a different way. He took nothing for granted, accepted nothing as inevitable with the exception of that which was willed by his Father, and died, bequeathing his ministry to us and promising that the Holy Spirit would guide and empower us. We need to recognise that his task is now ours, that we too stand at a pivotal point in history, that we too have the power to change things if we dare to use it. We live in a world which increasingly recognises that life cannot be rational alone, that the truth claims of modernism sold us short – a world which has responded by throwing the baby out with the bathwater and declaring that there is no such thing as truth. But it is a world which is once again willing to experiment; and it gives us the opportunity to experiment too, knowing that perhaps as we do so we will help people to get back in touch with a truth which is not incarnated in systems, but lives in the person of Jesus Christ and those who know him.

We will only do this if we dare to dream, and to welcome the Holy Spirit into our dreams. To listen to the Holy Spirit means being open to change. It means daring to try new things, to think in new ways, to be creative and courageous, responsive and flexible. It means learning to think as Jesus thought, allowing our minds to be fired through the exercise of our imagination – for nothing can happen unless it is first imagined. It is in our imaginations that we are most open to the Holy Spirit, who blows like the wind, bursting open the confining patterns of our received worldview and making it possible to see things a different way. To hear his voice is a task which belongs not just to individuals but to churches, for it is in the church that the Holy Spirit is most powerfully present – not the church as building or institution, but the church as the gathering of Christians in one place. And for every church the dream will be different.

The Holy Spirit and the church worldwide: dreaming diversity

As I have travelled through some of the remotest parts of East Africa, far not just from Western civilisation but from the more modest comforts of clean water and adequate shelter, I have been struck by the contrast in the workings of God and of man. Even as we followed the unmapped dirt road which wanders through the arid scrub of the Maasai steppe, we drew up beside a makeshift wooden stall selling the ubiquitous bottles of Coke, Fanta and Sprite to anyone with the cash to buy them – the same Coke bottles planted by the roadside stalls of forgotten Kiteto as on the neon-lit stands of Times Square. All over the planet, human ingenuity breeds uniformity. God, on the other hand, breathes diversity. The emblem of the Holy Spirit is not the Coke bottle but the mustard seed, the microscopic symbol of the faith which lives within us and grows to produce flowers, fruits and homes for the birds of the air. In some places the kingdom of God is like a tiny sapling; in others, like a broad-leafed tree. In some places, finches and sparrows nest in its branches; in others, storks and vultures. Jesus often compared the growth of the gospel to that of a seed. In some places the seed we sow will grow better than in others; but always the power which makes it grow, the sun and the wind and the rain, comes from the creator God himself. The growth comes not from human endeavour but from the inspiration of the Holy Spirit. "He who has ears, let him hear", said Jesus.[20]

Some time at the turn of the second century, John received seven messages from the Holy Spirit for the seven churches of Asia. He wrote them down in what is now the last book of the Bible, the book of Revelation. Each message offered either encouragement or rebuke, and each contained guidance for the future. Each contained the exhortation "Listen to what the Spirit is saying to the churches"; but in each case the message was different. Just as Jesus met each individual in the light of his or her own circumstances, so the Holy Spirit speaks to each church or community in ways appropriate to it alone. In Christian ministry there can be no off-the-peg solutions; we are not opening branches of McDonald's but growing seeds in different climates. The life and ministry of each church will be different, as the Holy Spirit directs.

And so, as we look over the world, diversity is what we find. Take worship. I worship each week in a church which uses sometimes the organ, sometimes a string quartet, and sometimes the band with its drums, screens and electronic amplification. But I have also worshipped to the jumping fireside songs of the Maasai, their rhythm, harmony and sheer guttural energy all harnessed to the same end of expressing their enthusiasm for God, and I have worshipped in the choral harmonies of Handel's *Messiah* at the Royal Festival Hall in London. I have sung to the accompaniment of instruments made of gourds and gut, to the beating call of animal-skin drums, to the ululations of young women, and to the notes of a single piano. Worship is still expressed in the Gregorian chant of the ninth century, or accompanied by robed choirs to the light of candles and the casting of incense. Every generation and every grouping worships in its own way.[21]

If the worship of the church finds different expression in different cultures as the Spirit directs, so does the form of the church. In Olkundulwa, Tanzania, the church is an oval of vertical branches placed at six-inch intervals and left open to the sky, built by a congregation of Maasai who attend in their traditional attire of blankets and beads. In the remoter parts of southern Russia, the church is a river barge which travels up and down the Volga, rekindling the faith suppressed by nearly 100 years of communism. In China, the church is often underground; the Vatican estimates that eight million Catholic Christians meet in secret. Where the church does meet openly, it takes original forms: one church in Shandong province began as a hospital whose founder is also the senior pastor of the church; others run medical clinics as part of their Sunday meetings. In Buenos Aires the Olmos Church has over 1,000 members who meet six days a week; all are convicts, and Olmos is a maximum-security prison. In Willow Creek Community Church, Illinois, the church is a multimedia auditorium equipped with all the latest resources for drama and contemporary music, welcoming 20,000 postmodern Americans in the course of a single Sunday. In South Korea, Pastor Yonggi-Cho's Yoido Full Gospel Central Church began in Seoul in 1958 with five people meeting in a tent. In 1964 Cho divided the congregation into small groups and appointed pastors to look after them. The church is now the largest in the world, with a million members meeting in 50,000 cells for worship, fellowship and prayer; the cell church model has spread all over South-East Asia and many other parts of the world.[22]

With diversity of worship and diversity of form goes diversity of ministry. Reports from around the world tell of the many different ways in which the Holy Spirit is strengthening and guiding Christian groupings, each in ways appropriate to their situation. The fastest growing church in the world is in the Hindu kingdom of Nepal, where until 1990 it was illegal to be a Christian. In 1957 God miraculously healed the brother of a boy named Lok Bahadur, through the prayer of a Nepali who had become a Christian in India. Lok committed his life to Christ, and grew up to plant more than 60 churches all over western Nepal – almost all on a foundation of the physical healing of individuals. Nepal now has 300,000 Christians.[23]

History teaches us that if the gospel is to be embraced, truth must be accurately focussed into the assumptions of each age and culture. It follows that what works in Nepal would not work at Harvard University, where the problem is not physical but spiritual ill-health. At Harvard a group of Christians have founded the Veritas Forum, a regular meeting place where all are welcome to explore any question about truth in relation to Jesus, reviving the idea that truth is a person rather than a concept. Participants are encouraged to ask questions for which there is no space in the academic curriculum, questions to do with life and its meaning, questions like "How can human love last?", "Why does beauty mean something?", "If God is love, why do I suffer?". No question is off limits, and all are answered by a panel of Christians who will respond not just in terms of arguments *about* the truth, but from their own experience of encounter *with* the truth. As in Nepal, this work began with the healing of one individual – an inner healing for one student from the brokenness and sorrow of a disintegrating family.[24]

In Latin America the situation is different again. In 1968, 130 Catholic bishops met in Colombia to discuss the future of the church. Drawing inspiration from the writings of liberation theologians, and aware of the widespread poverty and social deprivation which lay behind them, the bishops stressed Jesus's promise of release for the captives and freedom for the oppressed, and began to call for a faith which addressed the issues people were actually facing. The consequence was the establishment of lay-led "base communities". Formed as peer groups of families meeting to study the Bible, share their problems and press for practical, social and political solutions to their concerns, the base communities changed the way their members experienced their faith – and perhaps paved the way for the ready reception of the charismatic movement in the years that followed.[25]

Sometimes, on the other hand, the Holy Spirit seems to require very little in terms of human thought and planning. In 1994 the Holy Spirit burst into the Toronto Airport Christian Fellowship with a wave of blessing which has since spread all over the world, accompanied by phenomena not dissimilar to those once experienced by the Huguenots in the sixteenth century and the Quakers in the seventeenth. In 1995 a Father's Day service in Pensacola, Florida led to a charismatic revival in which over 100,000 people have since found faith.[26]

Perhaps the most dramatic events in recent times have taken place in Argentina. In 1983 an unknown businessman called Carlos Annacondia held a three-month crusade in the city of La Plata; many people were healed and 40,000 responded to the gospel. As he has moved from one city to another, two million Argentinians are said to have become Christians in the course of his campaigns, of which prayer for healing and deliverance forms an integral part. The Holy Spirit's activity in Argentina has continued to be remarkable; Ed Silvoso, who at the beginning of his ministry was himself healed from an untreatable and fatal illness called myasthenia gravis, has coined the term "prayer evangelism" to describe the response of whole cities to the prayers of Christians who have interceded for the families and businesses listed in a given column of, if you please, *the telephone directory*.[27]

And then there is Africa. In Africa the gospel is spreading at astonishing speeds and in many ways. Reinhard Bonnke and his colleagues preach the gospel and pray for the sick in a tent accommodating up to 34,000 people. The *Jesus Film* is being taken to the remotest villages by teams equipped with a generator, screen and projector; it is an amazing thing to arrive in a dusty community of people far from the nearest town, and see a *Jesus Film* team set up "Cinema Jesus" in the open air, translating into local languages over the top of dubbed Swahili, pausing to lead worship between reels, and praying afterwards for the hundreds who respond, with many healed and delivered. In 2002 in Tanzania alone 147 new churches were founded for those who had met Christ in this way.[28] In Mombasa, Kenya, growth is coming through prayer; after a year of exhausting preaching with only moderate results, Wilfred Lai found himself rebuked by the Holy Spirit for attempting to reach his city himself. Inspired by the biblical example of Daniel, he began to pray and his church to grow. He now requires every member of his church to pray for an hour daily, and every leader for two, beginning with a prayer meeting at 4:30 each morning; and he attributes the spectacular church growth which has followed to this single factor.[29]

But if that sounds a little alarming, there is always the example of the church in Germany which woke itself up and reached out into its community with a seriously funny Christmas pantomime. This is the advice of its reluctant visionary: "The lesson I learned was – find out what you love doing, what you do well, and do it with all your might with a big grin on your face, however mediocre it may seem."[30] It appears that God is as willing to work through the ordinary German toddler as he is through the anointed Kenyan pastor.

The Holy Spirit and the church at home: pictures of change

> I will not cease from mental fight
> Nor shall my sword sleep in my hand
> Till we have built Jerusalem
> In England's green and pleasant land.
>
> William Blake

Every October I drive north with my family to Swaledale to spend a week in an old farmhouse with worn stone-flagged floors and wood-panelled walls, lost in the depths of the upper dale and far from the demands and comforts of the modern world. Our visit straddles autumn and winter, and each year we watch the seasons spin slowly through the dales as the last leaves lift gently from the yellow trees and cold air begins to sink into the deep valleys. We have seen the river swell with floodwater beneath the old packhorse bridge, and woken to find the hills blanketed in fresh white snow; we have listened to the grouse still calling from the moors, and watched fieldfares gusting in on winter winds to feast on the ripe red berries of the rowan trees in the cobbled courtyard. And as our evening fire glows in the grate, time seems to shrink between the cracks in the old stone walls, and we sense the echoes of a pattern of life which has gone on for centuries, in a landscape which never seems to change.

This year, though, one thing was different. Just up the stone track which leads from the valley to the ridge above, the narrow road climbs out of the valley onto the moorland which marks the northern extremity of the dales. It runs beneath weathered drystone walls, grey now and patched with lichen. But this year, turning right to go down towards the Harkers' farm, we found a stretch of new wall, freshly built in the traditional style, with spliced toffee-coloured stone cut from slabs and carefully arranged layer by layer. The central line of bristling stones, turned the other way, still prickled out of the smooth horizontal slabs, and the chunky rocks still straddled the width of the wall to form a rugged top. Who knows, I wondered, why it still needs to be built that way? Who knows how long it took, and how much it cost? To be sure, a wire fence on wooden stakes, or even an electric fence attached to plastic ones, would have been easier. But Mr Harker had built the wall out of the stone which comes from the hillside itself, in the old way of the dales; and it was beautiful.

As I thought about this wall I remembered the words I had read from William Blake that morning, and found myself wondering what it would take to rebuild the church here in England's green and pleasant land. In many places in this country the church still looks like death warmed up. But perhaps here too there are signs that things are changing; that people are indeed daring to dream, daring to rebuild the church in ways that vary just as much as they do in other parts of the world. In many places there have been fresh initiatives, undertaken by people inspired by the Holy Spirit and eager to share the good news with those around them. Some are radical and adventurous; others are simple and unthreatening. But all of them represent attempts to respond in one way or another to the changing world in which we live; and the best are designed like Mr Harker's wall, in such a way as to match their own particular environment, to blend into the landscape and fit with the needs of the community they aim to serve.

And so we dream. We dream new forms of church, for Jesus challenged the people of his day to abandon the fixity of their religious traditions and realise that the new wine of the gospel always needs fresh wineskins if it is not to be spoiled. In the light of their renewed experience of the Holy Spirit, some have formed house churches which have grown from small beginnings to fill warehouses, school halls and community centres. Their emphasis on creative, non-traditional worship has made them attractive to many, and especially to the young.[31] Creative thinking within the Church of England has led to a strategy of planting new churches in areas where there is no living Christian community, many of which have sought to abandon traditional forms of church in favour of café-style gatherings, youth meetings and other "non-institutional" ways of belonging.[32] Other churches have developed young congregations in existing buildings, harnessing new technologies to create visual and participative forms of worship suitable for a postmodern generation, and often drawing on forgotten Christian traditions in a creative blend of the old and the new.[33]

Jesus also challenged his hearers, in a world where social standing went with age, to take note of the child, fluid in mind and spirit, but no longer content in our society to be seen and not heard, or excited by carpet toys and colouring books. Perhaps we are beginning to wake up to the needs of our children: responding to the steep decline in child attendance in recent years, many churches are now appointing specialist youth workers and running culturally appropriate children's programmes. Rural churches from Somerset to Cambridgeshire have reversed a gradual decline by setting out to engage with children, and finding that in this way whole families can be reached with the gospel. In Leicester there is a growing consensus amongst the city centre churches that the future lies in working with children, and schools are beginning to welcome the involvement of Christians in assemblies and after-school clubs; a recent open evening of prayer for the city focussed on education, and we are looking for new ways of supporting teachers in the ministry they have to our young people. We also plan to set up a Schools Trust to resource a Christian group in every school. Local initiatives of this kind draw additional resources from national organisations which have developed exciting teaching materials and offer programmes of adventure holidays staffed by teams of young leaders who aim to deepen and strengthen the children's faith – year after year I have seen my own children return from kayaking in Cornwall or exploring arts and crafts in Brackley increasingly determined to live their lives as Christians in a demanding world.[34]

Dreams take their inspiration not just from the future but also from the past, and as our culture shifts away from a rationalistic approach to life to a more emotional and spiritual one we have an enormous opportunity to recover the depth of some of the spiritual traditions we have lost, and so to offer a faith which embraces all aspects of the human experience. Organisations and movements such as SOMA, Anglican Renewal Ministries and New Wine have sought to bring spiritual renewal within the Anglican communion at home and abroad by encouraging churches to embrace the work of the Holy Spirit in ways relevant to their situation, so that individuals may be renewed, churches equipped and communities transformed.[35] More specialised groupings and associations are responding to the growing hunger for spiritual authenticity and the greater awareness of mystery in the plan of the universe through festivals, pilgrimage, retreat or merely different forms of worship. We live in a mobile society, and people are increasingly willing to travel to find spiritual guidance and refreshment, and increasingly open to new experiences when they get there. Annual Christian festivals have been established in various parts of the country; many churches affiliate to these, and the number of people who attend each year to deepen their faith and learn from the experiments and experiences of other Christians is increasing. At the same time, traditional places of pilgrimage welcome more and more visitors in search of meaningful expressions of faith. Many find that the mist-shrouded monastery on the Hebridean island of Iona brings calm to their souls with its Celtic forms of prayer and worship; others enjoy the companionship of a journey to the shrine at Walsingham in rural Norfolk; yet others visit the Taizé community in France and return with a new vision for contemplative prayer. In a culture of choice, we are no longer compelled to offer a spirituality which is uniform.

We said earlier that language, assumptions and example are all important if we are to successfully offer truth to a world which has forgotten what it is. And so evangelism too must become the subject of our dreaming. Thanks to the "decade of evangelism" and to the efforts of organisations such as Springboard which were founded to resource it, evangelism, like healing, is once again becoming a normal part of the life of the local church.[36] But it has become apparent that the worldview of our culture is so far removed from that of previous generations that methods of evangelism that used to work now make little sense to the average hearer. Many churches have taken advantage of the new courses which enable people to explore the Christian faith at a slower pace, in a venue in which they will feel comfortable and in a way which allows space for questions and exploration; it seems that these churches grow. The best-known course is Alpha, which has now been followed by almost four million people worldwide. Many have become Christians as a result, often taking the final step of commitment on a day at which they are invited to receive the Holy Spirit. Alpha is currently also running in 121 of the United Kingdom's 158 prisons, as well as in prisons in 40 countries overseas; over 21,000 prisoners have completed the course, and many have responded to the gospel. In South Africa it has been found that the reoffending rate of prisoners who have followed Alpha is zero per cent, compared with a national figure of 87 per cent – a powerful witness to the transforming power of the Holy Spirit.[37]

One of the biggest cultural changes of our times is that increasingly we live in the age of the image; it has been said that we are all "screenagers" now.[38] This challenges us to re-examine our word-based ways of doing things, and to embrace the opportunity presented by screen and computer for mission to a generation which tends to think with its imagination. Evangelism, prayer and even church can be done on the internet, and there is an increasing variety of new websites which present the gospel in creative and challenging ways or link people together in prayer chains and cyber-churches. Any church can now have its own website, and increasingly we find people turning up on our doorstep because they have found us in this way.[39]

Many of these initiatives are bold, adventurous and high profile. But up and down the country many individual churches are working, unspectacularly but creatively, in small, Spirit-led ways appropriate to their situations, building the wall with their own materials and bringing growth and renewal at local level. A church in Conisbrough, Yorkshire, decided to reach out to the community in a converted bus called Barney; as Barney travelled round the parish he transformed himself from café to prayer room to children's club to drop-in centre to youth group – and his church has more than tripled in membership. In Southowram, also in Yorkshire, a small, traditional village church decided to host a twelve hour, open air Christian festival which they called "God's Fair"; 2,000 people came, and during the course of the following mini-mission 200 decided to renew their baptism vows.[40] In an East Anglian village, renewal came to the church when a new minister had an experience of the Holy Spirit and decided to follow his leading: a church member was healed in the local electrical shop, little prayer groups were formed, spiritual teaching given, people encouraged to be open to new ways of doing things, services updated; and gradually the village became a place where, as the minister observed, people stopped talking about the church and started talking about Jesus.[41] In urban Leicester we are working to plant a new church in an area of the city where there is little Christian witness; in our first year, services in a local pub, an after-school club and an Alpha course have so far led to a doubling of the number of people we began with. Increasingly, city centre churches like ours are finding that in a rather fragmented and impersonal world of multiple but superficial relationships, people grow in their faith most effectively when given the opportunity to belong to small cell groups which meet regularly to study the Bible, pray together and reach out to those amongst whom they live and work.

The majority of our 800 members, adult and child, now belong to such groups, and the church is slowly expanding as a result.[42]

Perhaps it is as imagination pushes aside the boundaries of convention that the tide of decline will begin to turn. We are all aware of the overall decline in church membership. We are less aware that church growth is increasingly normal. During the 1990s alone 20 per cent of Anglican churches grew.[43] In the case of the Baptist Union, which at the beginning of the 1990s framed some clear policies for church growth, the increase in numbers has affected the whole denomination. And yet there are no formulae; the enormous variety of all these initiatives, big and small, suggests that following the dreams and visions which the Holy Spirit plants within us is the key to success in our diverse and specialised world.

Conclusion

> I will pour out my spirit on all flesh; your sons and your daughters shall prophesy, your old men shall dream dreams, and your young men shall see visions. Then everyone who calls on the name of the Lord shall be saved.
>
> Joel 2:28, 32

The story of our culture is changing, and we must change with it – a complex task, for it means learning to ride the vehicles of the culture without subscribing to the values of the culture. It means taking God at his word when he promised to pour out his Spirit on young and old and to speak to us through prophecy, through dream and through vision. It means starting in the place where we are, and learning to build the church out of local materials quarried from the needs of individual communities.

If we are to do this, we must look at the world with the open eyes of our imagination, the disjointed eyes of parable and metaphor, the eyes which dare to dream beyond the confines of the bubble within which we live. We must dare to imagine that things could be different, to open ourselves in prayer to the inspiration of the Holy Spirit who fills individuals, renews churches and spills out into a world which does not know him – for the ripples which begin when the pebble first strikes the water of a single human life turn out to have no definable end. We must learn to trade the traditions of the church for the dreams of its people; for only if we do so will we succeed in reaching out to the world in which we live. In Christian ministry there can be no blueprints.

Notes

1 The only way I have been able to make sense of this experience subsequently is with reference to 2 Corinthians 12, where Paul relates his experience of being "caught up into heaven".

2 John 20:22; Acts 2:1–4; Acts 4:31; John 14:17.

3 Similar activity of the Holy Spirit is reported by Justin Martyr, Irenaeus and Eusebius in the second century, Tertullian and Novatian in the third, Hilarion and Ambrose in the fourth, Augustine in the fifth and Gregory the Great and Gregory of Tours in the sixth. See J Wimber, *Power Evangelism*, Appendix 2, and R MacMullen, *Christianising the Roman Empire*, ch.4.

4 See R Stark, *The Rise of Christianity*, ch.1. Stark, a sociologist, estimates that 10 per cent were Christians in 300 AD, and 56 per cent in 350 AD (after the cessation of persecution). MacMullen, a historian (see note 3), attributes this to the ministry of healing and deliverance carried out by the Christians.

5 "Religion is the opium of the people" – Marx, *Critique of Hegel's Philosophy of Right*. For a critique of the Victorian church, see E E Kellett, *Religion and Life in the*

Early Victorian Age. This was, however, a period of considerable social reform spearheaded by Wilberforce and other influential Christians – see ch.4.

6 The peak year for attendance per head of the UK population was 1904; since then adult membership of Christian churches has declined from 33% to 8% of the population, and child attendance in the Church of England from 2.3 million to a mere 170,000. See P Brierley, *UK Christian Handbook Religious Trends 3, 2002–03*.

7 P. Brierley, *Future Church*, p.42. A brief history of the Pentecostal movement is given by A E McGrath, *The Future of Christianity*, pp.106–09; and by C Hill, *Prophecy Past and Present*, ch.14.

8 Total world population is 6 billion. Total global number of Christians is 1.5 billion.

9 For an analysis of the spiritual openness of the postmodern generations, see David Hay, "The spirituality of the unchurched", www.martynmission.cam.ac.uk.

10 John 14:12–26 (the promise of the Holy Spirit and of greater works) and 17:20 (for contemporary and subsequent disciples); Acts 1:8 (the power of the Holy Spirit made available to believers for ministry). This was not a promise for the original disciples alone; Paul repeatedly urges all believers to be filled with the Spirit (Ephesians 5:18) and to pray in the Spirit (Ephesians 6:18).

11 It is no coincidence that the Greek word *sozo* means both to save and to heal (see for example Jesus' words to Zacchaeus: "The Son of Man came to seek out and to *save* the lost', Luke 19:10). We must however be aware that physical healing is not promised as of right in the Bible; our primary healing is spiritual, as is made clear in 1 Peter 2:24–25. Physical healing is merely a sign of the spiritual healing which we may all experience. See also Luke 5:18–25, where Jesus regarded it as a higher priority to offer a paralysed man forgiveness than to heal his body.

12 See note 3.

13 For the remarkable story of the church in China, see Brother Yun and Paul Hattaway, *The Heavenly Man*. For the Vineyard movement, see J Wimber, *Power Evangelism*, and C Wimber, *The Way It Was*.

14 For the woman caught in adultery, see John 8; for the Sermon on the Mount, see Matthew 5; for the transformation of Peter, see John 13:38 and 18:27, John 18:10–11, and compare it with his own later writings in 1 and 2 Peter.

15 John 3:16; 3:5; Romans 8:11. See also 1 Peter 2:24, where Peter makes clear that our primary healing is spiritual in nature.

16 The New Testament speaks of the spiritual power of evil, manifested in the entity which it calls the devil or Satan (the name just means "adversary", 1 Peter 5:8). Satan is called the accuser, the deceiver of the whole world (Revelation 12:9–10), the father of lies (John 8:44), the ruler of this world (John 12:31), and the tempter (Matthew 4:3). When we pray for deliverance through the power of the Holy Spirit, we are fighting a battle against "the cosmic powers of this present darkness and the spiritual forces of evil in the heavenly places" (Ephesians 6:10–17). We can expect to be successful because these powers have already been defeated by Jesus on the cross. For more information, see J Woolmer, *Healing and Deliverance*; R Parker, *The Occult: Deliverance from Evil*; N Anderson, *The Bondage Breaker*.

17 Laudable in its aims of mutual support and engagement with good causes, it nonetheless seems to be the case that the practice of freemasonry, particularly at the higher levels which involve various initiation rites and religious ceremonies, is often associated with spiritual deadness, mental illness and ill health in the families of the people

concerned. For an inside view, see J Lawrence, *Freemasonry: A Religion?*

18 Jackie tells her story in her book *Chasing the Dragon.*

19 *A Matter of Life and Death*, pp.18, 76–78.

20 For the parable of the mustard seed, see Matthew 13:31–32; for its growth, see Matthew 17:20. For the parable of the sower, see Matthew 13:1–23.

21 Sixty-four people signed up for a workshop on Gregorian Chant as part of the Leicester Early Music Festival in 2003!

22 The Russian Orthodox floating churches were described in an article in *The Sunday Times*, 18 November 2001; for China, see www.thefcc.org, which tells of other Chinese churches which offer a clinic as part of the normal Sunday morning service, and the Vatican News Agency on www.fides.org. For Olmos, see N Gumbel, *The Heart of Revival*, pp.14–15. The website of Willow Creek Community Church is www.willowcreek.org. An overview of the cell movement is given by Howard Astin in *Body and Cell*. For the church in Asia, see M Green, *Asian Tigers for Christ: The Dynamic Growth of the Church in South-East Asia*.

23 Lok's story is told by Bob Jackson, *Higher than the Hills*. For the statistics, see Patrick Johnstone, *Operation World*.

24 K Monroe, "Finding God at Harvard: Reaching the post-Christian university", in *Telling the Truth*, ed. D Carson. She has written a book, also entitled *Finding God at Harvard*.

25 See R McAfee Brown, *Gustavo Gutierrez*, and P Berryman, *Liberation Theology*. Recent writers suggest that the Pentecostal movement has been as important for the growth of the church in Latin America as the base communities – for a summary, see A McGrath, *The Future of Christianity*, p.35–39.

26 For Toronto, see D Pytches, *Come, Holy Spirit*, Appendix 4; www.tacf.org. For Pensacola, see www.brownsville-revival.org.

27 Ed Silvoso, *That None Should Perish: How to Reach Entire Cities for Christ through Prayer Evangelism*; see also N T Anderson and E L Towns, *Rivers of Revival*, ch.6.

28 The ministry in Tanzania is coordinated by Stanley Hotay and funded by the American *Here's Life* mission based in Fairhope, Alabama. In the period 1997–2002 450 new churches have been planted in Tanzania and Uganda, following showings of the *Jesus Film*. See www.hereslife-missiontoafrica.org.

29 Jesus Celebration Centre. The church secretary informs me by email that following the 4:30 prayer meeting, 5,000 members were added; in the eight years since then the church has grown to 20,000 members.

30 Nicola Vollkommer, writing in *Christianity+Renewal*, December 2002. Nicky and her husband, Helmut, are the founders and pastors of an independent church in Reutlingen; 1,000 people attended the pantomimes, five times the normal congregation, and a great deal of positive feedback has come from the non-churchgoing community. See www.cgr-online.de.

31 Some of these house churches have formed the nucleus of new movements, known collectively as the New Churches. The Ichthus community in London now has 26 congregations and 130 linked churches, and is organised round a structure of small cells, weekly congregations and collective festival and celebration events. New Frontiers places a particular emphasis on evangelism through social action; its 300 churches now in 26 countries reach out to their communities with projects for the unemployed, the indebted, the starving, the orphaned, and those facing unplanned pregnancies or suffering from addiction.

Pioneer has a network of 80 UK churches and 1,000 overseas partners; working in association with others, it sponsored the annual March For Jesus; a recent one-off gathering of 45,000 Christians at Wembley Stadium for praise and prayer; and a large network of hospices for AIDS sufferers. Vineyard, founded in the US by John Wimber, now has over 70 churches in the UK with a strong emphasis on the healing ministry and on contemporary worship. Cornerstone, another growing movement, seeks to make itself accessible to agnostics and atheists as well as to those with a church background. See the churches' own websites: www. ichthus.org.uk; www.n-f-i.org (New Frontiers); www.Pioneer.org.uk; www.vineyard.org.uk; www.cornerstone-evangelical.org. uk.

32 25,000 people have joined such church plants since 1977, equivalent to the addition of a whole diocese. Examples are The Carpenter's Arms, a church plant in Deal which set out to be a Radio 1 style church meeting round tables; its original 35 members worked through contact with local children from unchurched families and after six years had increased to a membership of 140 people; it was then invited to plant another church in Sandwich. Another example is Unit 8, a youth church planted on a council estate near Shipley. For these and other examples, see *Encounters on the Edge*, ed. George Lings at the Church Army's Sheffield Centre. See also the website of Anglican Church Planting Initiatives, www.acpi.org.uk.

33 Examples would be the Late Late Service in Glasgow, Grace in London, and the infamous Nine O'Clock Service in Sheffield, now flourishing again under new leadership. For an analysis of these and other experimental worship forms, see D Hilborn, *Picking Up the Pieces*, pp.124–42. See also www.alternativeworship.org.

34 CPAS and Scripture Union are amongst them (www.scrip-

tureunion.org.uk; www.cpas.org.uk). The Church of England now runs the largest training college for youth workers in Europe! For figures on child attendance and growth of churches with youth workers, see Bob Jackson, *Hope for the Church*.

35 www.somauk.org; www.new-wine.org. ARM was relaunched in 2004 as ReSource, with a mandate to encourage and renew the local church in the power of the Holy Spirit for mission. See www.resource-arm.net.

36 From 1992 to 2004 Springboard has worked all over the country, equipping and encouraging churches to think about their relationship with the community and their presentation of the gospel to outsiders (www.springboard.uk.net).

37 Alpha is an initiative of Holy Trinity Brompton: www.alphacourse.org; www.caringforexoffenders.org. Other courses, such as Emmaus, have a similar response rate of just over 20 per cent.

38 G Kelly, *Get a Grip on the Future Without Losing Your Hold on the Past*, p.114.

39 www.rejesus.co.uk is an example of a new evangelistic website; www.rising.org.uk is a prayer site which aims to coordinate continuous 24-hour prayer across Wales; www.crosswinds.co.uk, aims to establish a 52-week canopy of prayer for the UK, by postal code. The youth-led 24–7 prayer initiative which began in 1999 in a church in Chichester now has a website which coordinates an international network of youth prayer rooms and has no less an aim than "to turn the tide of youth culture back to Jesus". Other sites aim not so much to resource the church as to *be* the church, taking advantage of the freedom of cyberspace from the constraints not just of tradition but also of geography; see for example www.church.co.uk; www.clubberstemple.com – and T Beaudouin, *Virtual Faith*. Holy Trinity can be found on

www.ht-leicester.org.uk.

40 These and other stories from around Europe are given by G Linn in *Hear What the Spirit Says to the Churches*.

41 The story is told by Martin Down, *Speak to These Bones*.

42 There is now a national organisation which supports churches using this model, headed by Laurence Singlehurst: see www.celluk.org.uk.

43 Seven per cent grew by more than 60 per cent. These growing churches were spread over all traditions, sizes and locations. The greatest growth has been seen in the Diocese of London, which increased its overall adult membership by 12 per cent during the 1990s. Statistics from Bob Jackson, *Hope for the Church*, ch.4. For the Diocese of London, see also the report in the *Church Times*, 27 September 2002, which puts the growth at 20 per cent, up from 45,000 in 1990 to 64,000 in 2002.

CHAPTER TEN

RELATING TO THE WORLD: LIVING IN THE LOVE OF THE FATHER

And the Word became flesh and lived among us.
John 1:14

And did you get what
you wanted from this life, even so?
I did.
And what did you want?
To call myself beloved, to feel myself
beloved on the earth.

Raymond Carver[1]

This book has been about what it might mean to minister truth into a changing culture. We began by looking at the life of Jesus, who exposed the lostness of his own culture and proclaimed the truth of the gospel into it in such a way as to bring freedom to one person after another. We looked at ways in which Christians have experienced and expressed their faith in different historical periods since then, and we found that when the gospel has been proclaimed countercult-urally in this way, many have found faith and the church has grown; but that when the gospel has been accommodated to the culture, the church has stagnated. We explored the spirit-ual and philosophical dynamics of our own society, and concluded that we stand at a period of particular change and opportunity as our culture passes from the modern period to what we call postmodernism.

If we are to seize that opportunity, we must be both culturally aware and countercultural. We must move with the culture without being disoriented by it, for it is only at such times of change that it becomes possible for us to assess the ways in which we understand and express our faith, and to ensure that we have not allowed it to become an irrelevance which no longer engages with reality as people experience it. We must learn to let the culture ask the questions and the gospel provide the answer – to focus the truth into the needs of the culture, to express it in the language of the culture, and to offer it as an example to the culture. In a postmodern context, that means expressing a truth which is not just intellectually understood but personally experienced. It means recovering a truth which is not just rational, objective, and scientific, but an expression of the profoundly spiritual nature of ultimate reality. And finally, it will mean offering a truth which is relational, connecting us with one another and with the world around us, and spilling out into the communities of which we form part.

Recovering a relational faith

Relating to God

> Whoever does not love does not know God, for God is love.
>
> 1 John 4:8

I have spent much of my life immersed in the work of the medieval Christian poet Dante. Dante's faith journey begins as he finds himself standing lost and frightened in the midst of a dark and tangled wood, face to face with the realisation that his attempts to make sense of life have largely been a failure. "Abandon hope, all ye who enter here" are the famous words he writes above the gates of hell; but as he is guided through the realm of the lost, up the corrective mountain of purgatory and into the heavenly spheres of paradise, Dante finds that his journey, born of despair, becomes one in which his mind is gradually transformed by the truth which sustains the universe. And yet it is a journey which turns out to be not just intellectual but profoundly emotional. Led by the author he most admires and the woman he most loved, Dante reaches the outermost heaven and finds himself in a realm of light and love: the light which fills the universe, the love which is the source of its energy. Standing beside the flower-studded banks of a river of light, he bends to drink. As he does so, the river becomes a circle, a rose, and finally an amphitheatre filled with the souls of the blessed. Gazing upwards into the source of the light which bathes it, he sees three circles reflected one from another like rainbows, representing God the Father, God the Son and, in an outermost circle of fire, God the Holy Spirit. Glimpsing within this light the shape of a man, Dante's mind bursts with a momentary understanding of divine reality, and he is overcome with the knowledge that the light which illuminates his mind and the warmth which fills his heart are one and the same, equal aspects of the reality which is God. It was like being a wheel, he writes later, a wheel which up to that point had been turning lopsided, but now spins evenly on its axis, powered not just by understanding but also by love, and moving in circles around the God who is both.[2]

Dante's vision is an eloquent expression of what many Christians have come to understand: that the truth which we receive, the truth which was spoken and incarnated in Christ, is not just intellectual but also emotional. We have seen throughout this book that truth is far greater a thing than our modern culture understood it to be, and that in reducing it to facts we stripped it of its power. In recovering the awareness that truth is an expression of spiritual reality itself, and that it is not so much that truth is, as that truth does, we restore to it the power to change our lives. But I think that we need to go further, and realise that the reason it can change our lives is because it draws us into relationship with a God not just who is, but who is love. The truth which fills the universe is love; and it is therefore to be experienced in the heart as well as the mind.

As the Father has loved me, so I have loved you.

John 15:9

Six years after my kitchen encounter with the truth I went to Zambia, rejoicing in the opportunity to leave roles and responsibilities behind, ready to embrace the adventure and to step briefly into the unknown world of sub-Saharan Africa. Stripped from the accretions of the past, healed by God's acquittal and determined to live in the freedom I had been given, I found myself flung into unexpected intimacy with a small team of almost complete strangers. It was an experience which changed my life. As I watched myself slowly take shape in their eyes, it was as if they were holding up a mirror, a mirror of affirmation and encouragement, a mirror which seemed to show me for the first time who I really was – strengths, weaknesses, idiosyncrasies and all. It was an astonishing experience, like going back to the beginning and starting again, and for the first time seeing the real me, the person God had created rather than the one pain had tried to form, and knowing myself to be totally and utterly acceptable, my blemishes covered over by love.

At the end of our stay we were put into pairs during a service to pray for one another, and I found myself with Father James Chungolo. I have no idea what he said, for he prayed in Bemba; but I could feel the Holy Spirit washing over me, prickling and pressing like a physical presence, and it suddenly seemed to me that I was like one of the half built houses we had seen so often as we travelled, made of baked earthen bricks but with no mortar between them. As he prayed I felt cement being poured over the walls, settling down between the bricks and drying in the warmth of the sun – and I understood not only that I was loved, but that in some indefinable way truth and love are the same thing, for both pulse from God with a power which reflects his very being. Paul prayed that the Christians in Ephesus would know the love of Christ that surpasses knowledge; and that was what I discovered that day.[3] I came home reflecting that this new knowing was not so much word-shaped as gut-shaped, not rational but emotional – except that the emotions didn't seem to be in the usual place, but somewhere else, in my spirit perhaps; that they didn't tug or wrench or flood, that they had no beginning or end, that they couldn't be analysed or explained. And that yet they nonetheless *were* a kind of knowledge, a kind of bathing inner certainty, a kind of dissolving of untruth, or the lingering residues of untruth, or perhaps a penetration into parts of my being which I had never properly explored. I concluded that there can be no such thing as a purely objective truth, however much we would like to pretend so. Truth is profoundly emotional. It emanates from an emotional being and it is received by emotional beings. We cannot confine it to our heads alone, but must learn to embrace it in our hearts. We must learn to *feel* truth.

I do not think this step of integration is mine alone. I think it is what people all through our culture are yearning for. We live in a society which has realised that the reduced truth of modernism fails to connect with the personal and emotional dimensions of our being – and yet has no idea what to do about it. Throwing the baby magnificently out with the bath-water, the postmodern conclusion is that truth has no outside point of reference, but is to be located and contained in personal experience. But all too often it seems that experience which is not rooted in reality, in the knowledge and love of God, fails miserably to bring lasting fulfilment. "All you need is love," sang the Beatles in the 1960s; and yet mostly we have not found it. We live now in a culture which looks for gratification but craves belonging, looks for wealth and success but craves relationship. It is a society in which the expectation of love is far greater than the ability of human relationships to meet it, a society in which the greatest public grief is poured out over the abduction and abuse of children whom we seem unable to protect, a society which invests billions in developing drugs to combat the depression, anxiety and emptiness lurking within its members. It is a society of which Princess Diana was the icon, the girl who reached the pinnacle of wealth and success, and yet who cared; who styled herself the Queen of people's hearts. Broken in all the ways people in our culture are broken, Diana represented both our pain and our aspirations. Seeking and offering the love that we crave, she died; and a nation broke down in tears. The truth that we need is love.

> Whoever does not love does not know God, for God is love. God's love was revealed among us in this way: God sent his only Son into the world so that we might live through him.
>
> 1 John 4:8

Diana received a magnificent funeral, watched all over the world. But what would have happened if, as her coffin was drawn through the streets of London to Westminster Abbey, her young sons walking behind it, she had appeared beside them to comfort them? What would have happened had she turned out to have risen from the dead? What would our society be like now had Diana's groping for love been revealed as an expression of God himself? For that, of course, is what happened with Jesus.

In the beginning was the Word, and the Word was God. And the

Word became flesh and lived among us . . . And to all who received him, he gave power to become children of God.

John 1:1ff

Relating to one another

This is my commandment, that you love one another as I have loved you.

John 15:12

The good news announced in the gospel, said the ancient theologians, is simply Jesus.[4] Jesus was born in order to invite us back into relationship with God. He spoke the truth to individuals, drawing them into relationship not just with himself but also with one another; for although the gospel is personal, it is also, like its bearer, profoundly relational. Jesus announced the beginning of a new community which he called the kingdom of God. Sharing every moment of his life with his closest followers, likening his relationship with and amongst them to the organic unity of a vine with its branches and fruits, urging them to serve and love one another, and holding forth the picture of an eternal future as a shared meal of celebration, Jesus constantly stressed the communal nature of the Christian life.[5] After his death, the first Christian community was one which pooled its possessions and cared for its widows. Believers met not in church buildings, for there were none, but in each other's homes: it was 200 years before the first church was built. Paul likened the church to a body in which every member had a part to play, an organic unit in which no part was able to function independently of the others.[6] It was in the body as a whole, and not in the individual members, that the Holy Spirit was most powerfully present; and this continues to be the case today.

Jesus spoke his vision of relationship into a culture of domination and diversity. It has been suggested that our postmodern culture is in many ways similar to the world of the

Roman first century; and it is certainly the case that such a vision of community is profoundly countercultural to the individualistic times in which we now live.[7] We have only to step outside our own culture into that of Africa to realise the shallowness of our relationships not just with God but also with one another. We live now in a society where a third of people have never spoken to their next door neighbours, where the amount of time we spend in one another's homes has dropped by 45 per cent in 30 years, and where family meals have become a memory of times gone by. Disposable income has risen fourfold since the 1950s, but enough prescriptions for antidepressants were issued in the UK in 2002 alone to cover almost half the total population.[8] We have lost our sense of community, and perhaps this is not unconnected with what has been called the 'philosophy of the unencumbered self' – the prevailing notion that happiness is best found in the context of personal freedom and autonomy. We seek to replace community with networks of friends and acquaintances to compensate for the void which our autonomy creates, and yet networks, there to be stepped into and out of again at will, provide no long term solution to the inner craving for relationship implanted in people made in the image of God. Togetherness, belonging, caring community remain the ideals that we strive for – and yet loneliness is the voice of the age.[9]

It is innate in human nature to want to strive for stability and preserve it in systems. Often the church has done this, as we saw in Chapter 4; and perhaps no more so than during the modern period, a period in which society was dominated by institutions. Throughout history the church has had to draw back from an overemphasis on institutional structure and recover the emphasis on relationship with which Jesus began. The gospel was embraced all over England in the eighteenth century not just because John Wesley preached it, but because he organised every new believer into a network of small groups in which they could share their lives and their faith. He called them classes and bands, and by the year 1800 one English adult in 30 belonged to one. The gospel spread through Latin America in the twentieth century because of the foundation of base communities, small local units of Christians who wished to share their faith in the context of their daily struggle to make ends meet. The gospel has spread throughout South Korea because Pastor David Yonggi-Cho decided to organise his growing church into small cells; it now has a million members.[10] In England, research shows that it is little churches, or big churches divided into little units, that are growing the fastest, and a new movement of "cell churches" is gathering increasing momentum, churches in which the primary unit of belonging is not the rather anonymous assembly of billiard-ball relationships on a Sunday morning, but the intimate gatherings of a dozen people in someone's home on a weekday night.[11]

It follows that churches which embody truth most poignantly in the postmodern culture will be churches which are no longer primarily institutional, sustained by the vertical bonds of hierarchy, but relational, formed through the horizontal bonds of peer relationships. They will be churches in which every member is known as an individual, in which every member is needed, in which every member may grow in their understanding of truth and in their experience of love. And above all they will be churches in which the horizontal bonds between the individual members will be strengthened and empowered by the presence of the Holy Spirit, the rainbow of fire, the Spirit of truth who once showed me my identity in Christ reflected in the mirror held up to me by four other people.

For where two or three are gathered in my name, I am there among them.

Matthew 18:20

Relating to the world

> As you, Father, are in me and I am in you, may they also be in us,
> so that the world may believe that you have sent me.
>
> John 17:21

In a modern, rationalistic culture the truth which is most readily grasped is a truth which can be explained. In a postmodern, experiential, network society this is no longer the case, and the truth which is most readily grasped is one which is lived and shared. It is a truth which was incarnated in Christ, which is received by the power of the Holy Spirit, and which now dwells not just in us but amongst us. It is a truth which finds written expression in the Bible, where we find not a list of things to believe, but the rather untidy story of God's involvement in human lives and communities. The Bible is written as story, as picture, as personality; as triumph and disaster, hopes and dreams; it brings us not neat formulae but real-life truth through the stories of people who lived it or who failed to live it. And so it is that we must offer it to others – as an invitation to join us in the relationships we share with one another and with God, as we engage with the business of living.

This should come to us as an enormous relief. We live in a culture where every choice is accompanied by a sophisticated sales pitch, every purchase guaranteed to meet an inner need. We Christians, on the other hand, have no material product to offer, and little confidence in our skills of persuasion. We end up apologising for our ancient gospel, believing in it ourselves, but not expecting others to be very interested. And so it is that the church comes across more as a good cause which is in danger of collapsing for lack of support than as the gateway to eternal reality. But we have no need to apologise. We are not selling a product but inviting people into a relationship; first with us, and through us with God himself. The truth that we have to share is the truth that God loves us;

and the best way of communicating that truth is to invite others into our midst, where the Spirit of truth himself may speak to their hearts and minds.

In Africa this comes as no surprise. Resistant to the health and education packaging of a gospel offered to individuals who were willing to seek out a mission compound, Vincent Donovan found that the Maasai responded readily to the gospel only when it was taken to their whole community, to be discussed by the community and accepted or rejected by the community. In the West it is the Alpha course, and other similar courses, which effectively communicate the gospel, because they offer it in the context of our own Christ-centred relationships. People invited as guests to our own Alpha suppers tell us that they are struck not primarily by the relevance of the talk or even the sincerity of our faith, but by the totally unexpected fact that the church is laid out as a restaurant, with linen cloths and candles, and filled with young people enjoying themselves. "I am known, therefore I am," Donovan summarises the Maasai creed; and so it must be with us, as we seek in a network society to rediscover what it means to belong to one another.[12]

Recovering a holistic faith

> I'm discovering that a spiritual journey is a lot like a poem. You don't merely recite a poem or analyze it intellectually. You dance it, sing it, cry it, feel it on your skin and in your bones. You move with it and feel its caress. It falls on you like a teardrop or wraps around you like a smile. It lives in the heart and the body as well as the spirit and the head.
>
> Sue Monk Kidd[13]

Faith is a journey

If truth must be not just believed but felt and lived, then the process by which we live it is faith. It has been characteristic of the modern age to systematise, and often we have systematised our faith. Faith has been seen as an event, a crossing over point marked by the taking on of a clearly defined package of beliefs; or as a framework, a set of liturgically defined fixed points within which we may live the recurring cycle of our lives. Perfect for the structured and coherent world of modernism, such a faith fits the non-conformist, exploratory atmosphere of the postmodern world about as well as a white glove fits a hungry racoon.[14]

And yet traditionally understood, faith is not so much a set of things we believe or a framework for what we do as a journey, one which departs from a human moment and travels towards the vastness of God. It is a journey which it is open to us to begin again, and which will, if freely embraced, encompass the whole of life, within and without – not just our thoughts and habits but our experiences, emotions, relationships, even our changing selves. It is a journey which invites us to listen to the postmodern cry for meaning and authenticity, and to harness that yearning to the old voices of the poets and the prophets, with their tantalising suggestion that life does indeed offer bigger horizons than we had imagined. It is a journey which is profoundly relevant to the culture in which we live.[15]

And so it was that Jesus offered his hearers not political action or systematic theology but poetry, flinging them into a surprising world of parables and beatitudes, jolting all who would listen out of the settled framework of the predictable, and inviting them to see life another way, as a journey into an alternative reality which he called the kingdom of God. It is a journey which often begins but rarely ends, which like all journeys brings unforeseen encounters and unimagined events. Some have stressed the vertical dimension of this journey as we travel from the world of sense experience to the spiritual realm of God; others the horizontal dimension which moves from birth to death. Some, both ancient and modern, have divided it into stages, matching these to the growth in personality from infancy to old age. Others have written of the spiritual life as being like the gradual ascent of a ladder, or as learning to enter into a "cloud of unknowing" where reality goes far deeper than facts.[16] Dante cast the journey in fictional form, offering perhaps the greatest account to date of the attempt of a single individual to understand the whole of history, universal and personal, in the context of a relationship with God. Amongst contemporary spiritual writers, Paul Tournier has described life as a journey of adventure, a series of new births which bring a gradual integration of our personal adventure with the great adventure of God; and Henri Nouwen has written of the process by which we may seek to integrate our inner spiritual world with the chaotic outer world which surrounds and distracts us, as we move beyond solitude into relationship with God, and through him into meaningful relationship with others.[17]

To embark on such a journey of faith is to enter into a world where nothing can be taken for granted. For the individual it turns out that faith is not so much a hat, to be picked off the shelf and worn only on the head, as a whole stretchy garment, a glittering costume of dance into which gradually we find that we can fit all parts of ourselves – those which we have lost as we moved from one place to another, and those which are yet to grow within us. For the Christian community, it turns out that faith which is experienced as shared journey can move mountains, bursting realities and changing worlds – just as Isaiah cried that it would, if only we dared imagine it. In 1979 people listened in hushed silence as a newly commissioned piece of music filled the Franciscan basilica of Krakow in communist Poland. The composer was Gorecki, the patron Karol Wojtyla, the subject the life of the tenth-century saint Stanislaw – martyred, as it happens, for exposing and opposing an oppressive regime. By the end of the 1980s a whole social and political structure was being dismantled as those same people took to the streets of Warsaw night after night dressed as clowns – daring to live as parable, to imagine, believe, feel and enact the truth which sets us free.[18] It may indeed be that we are the only people in the whole of history who have supposed that a mechanistic and individualistic understanding of life is the way to become fulfilled and whole persons; but nothing now compels us to travel that way.[19]

Faith is about the whole of life

> In the beginning was the Word. All things came into being through him, and without him not one thing came into being. What has come into being through him was life.
>
> John 1:1–3

In the beginning, the earth was a formless void, and darkness covered the face of the deep. A wind from God swept over the face of the waters, and the world was created. Millions of years later Paul would remark to the Romans that ever since that moment God's eternal power and divine nature, invisible though they are, have been understood and seen through the things he has made. Jesus himself lived and taught in a way that was fully aware of the interconnectedness of all things and, like the psalmists and prophets before him, he frequently turned to the created world in order to demonstrate or explain the spiritual realities which it reflects.[20]

A biblical faith is a holistic faith. Within the pages of scripture we find an invitation to recognise that it is not just in Jesus that God is incarnate, but in the whole created world. The world, wrote Hugh of St Victor in the twelfth century, is itself to be understood as a book written by the hand of God in which every creature is a word charged with meaning.[21] It is a book which invites us to consider the beauty of the lily and find there a picture of God's provision for us, to meditate upon the sparrow sustained in its flight by the Spirit of life and understand our own dependence on God. It asks us to look at a tree planted by water, rooted in a living stream which allows it to bear leaves and fruits even when drought eats up the land, and to recognise our relationship with God as having the same life-giving power; and to meditate upon the seed which must die before it bursts forth to new life, and the fragrance of the flowers which are the scent of our faith. It celebrates the sensual wonder of love and invites us to gaze awestruck at the hundred trillion galaxies which we now know to populate the heavens; and commands us to remember Jesus not in concept and dogma but in bread and in wine. It sees our life as part of the life of the whole world, created and sustained by the wind from God which first swept over the face of the waters.[22] It was no coincidence that Isaiah pictured the future in metaphors of stream and flower, green growth in desert places; for the spiritual principle of the universe is embodied in every plant and stream.

This is not how the scientific faith of the modern period has regarded the created world. From the beginnings of scientific materialism in the seventeenth century, the world has been seen as machine, to be used as a tool and understood by reducing it to its smallest constituent parts – and in the church we have gone along with this to such an extent that in a famous article of the 1960s the Christian faith was actually held responsible for the development of a mindset which legitimised the progressive destruction of the environment.[23]

But even among scientists the mechanistic worldview is fading. Progressively challenged by the uncertainties of quantum physics, of relativity and chaos theory, and fuelled by the understanding that we are made of the same stuff as the stars, the modern worldview is increasingly recognised as carrying severe limitations, and is being eclipsed by a holistic and ecological outlook which sees the universe not as machine but as living system, with ourselves as part of it. There is a new craving to reconnect the physical and spiritual dimensions of life, and a myriad of new and recycled spiritualities have grown up to accommodate it.[24]

This is a craving which as Christians we are well placed to satisfy. From the Celts to the Franciscans, from the mystics of the twelfth century to the feminist and creation theologians of recent years, the Christian tradition offers a faith which is genuinely holistic. How do we find God, the God whom over 70 per cent of the UK population say they still believe in? We begin by opening our eyes and unleashing our imaginations; for the most suitable way of seeking God, remarked Calvin in the sixteenth century, is not to attempt with arrogant curiosity to penetrate to the investigation of his essence, but to contemplate him in his works, by which he makes himself near and familiar to us.[25] The author of life reveals himself to us every time we step outside our own front door.

And yet the problem is more profound than that, for in undermining the mechanistic worldview the new physics has undermined our ability to make sense of the world around us. How do we find our place in a universe which cannot decide whether matter is wave or particle, in which space and time are elastic, and whose constituent atoms appear to be governed by completely random internal processes? How do we explain a world which according to the second law of thermodynamics should be in a process of constant decay, and which by mind-defying odds should not exist at all?[26] Darwin felt that the whole subject was too profound for the human intellect; Stephen Hawking confesses himself to be at a loss to understand why it is that the universe bothers to exist.[27] We have come to live in a chaotic world whose incomprehensibility sucks meaning from our lives and leaves us in a void of uncertainty and doubt.

But perhaps within the ancient truths of the Christian faith we may find an answer. Particle physicist James Jeans suggests that the universe is beginning to look more like a great thought than a great machine. Neurophysicist Danah

Zohar suggests that while quantum physics undoubtedly knocks us off the pedestal of certainty, it may also serve to reconnect us with the idea that the universe is in some sense conscious, and that it is relationship which lies at the basis of matter. Or, as the theologian might put it, with the idea that there is a single Spirit which animates the universe, which created and sustains it, and which dwells both in it and in us.[28]

This is not a new idea. "Besides these particular and divided Spirits", wrote Thomas Browne in the seventeenth century, "there may be, for ought I know, an universall and common Spirit of the whole world. I am sure there is a common Spirit that playes within us, yet makes no part of us, and that is the spirit of God, the fire and scintillation of that noble and mighty Essence which is the life and radicall heat of spirits". "To understand the world", said Teilhard de Chardin 300 years later, "knowledge is not enough: you must see it, touch it, live in its presence and drink the vital heat of existence in the very heart of reality . . . Purity does not lie in separation from but in a deeper penetration into the universe. It is to be found in the love of that unique, boundless Essence which penetrates the inmost depths of all things".[29] The basis of matter is relationship.

Many have tried to find non-theological ways of thinking about the spirit of the universe. In the seventeenth century Leibnitz imagined the world to be explained by the existence of spiritual forces called monads, which are inherent in all matter; in the 1920s biologists were postulating the presence of morphogenetic fields which surround all living things; towards the end of the twentieth century Lovelock imagined it as animated by a self-regulating life force which he called Gaia, from the Greek name for Mother Earth.[30] Modern physicists grope for the Grand Theory of Everything, the universal law which will explain life as we know it. But for us, the theory which best explains the continued existence of the universe is the Spirit of God, breathed out at the beginning of time and articulated in a Word who still speaks today.[31]

What does this mean in practice? For many Christians it means, as it has done for mystics throughout the ages, that contemplation of the natural world brings a sense of peace and closeness to God, a reconnection with a reality we easily forget. We live in a take-for-granted world; and yet Jesus tells us to be like little children, inviting us to preserve our wonder at the world around us and our trust in him who made it. And so he offers us that world as metaphor, speaking in the language not of proposition but of poetry. Poetry jolts away our assumptions, untethers the imagination and releases the child within us, the child able still to connect with the presence of the Spirit in something, to feel the traces of the joy that made it, to see the maker through the things he has made. In the fourteenth century Mother Julian gazed at a hazelnut and learned that God is love; for the world speaks the One who made and sustains it.[32]

My own journey has been intimately bound up with such moments. At the age of two I found mself gazing at the fearsomeness of a giant stag beetle as it waved awesome weaponry from the garden stool I had been sent to fetch, and discovering that the familiar world I thought I knew contained rather more than I had bargained for. At 17 I peered into the darkness of a cave on the Isle of Mull, the sun shining cold and clear and waves breaking on the basalt shore behind me, and found myself staring through the fishy stench at a single shag, its feathers glossy green, iridescing with purple as the light caught them, and its eye gazing unfathomably black out of a perfect yellow ring, straight at me; and it began to occur to me that the world was perhaps examining me just as penetratingly as I was investigating it. I am a licensed bird ringer, and a year later I caught and held a long-eared owl. As I looked into its deep orange eyes, probing, questioning, with the unspoken eloquence of its soft feathers puffed over the insignificance of the scrawny body hidden inside, I wondered what it was that it saw with those eyes, so much bigger, more magnificent than mine. And at 23 I sat on a Devon hillside, looking down over a patterned jigsaw of fields and hedges, trying to make sense of the world I knew, and watching a soaring buzzard riding the thermals. I could see it cocking its head and gazing down with a clarity of vision that I knew that I would never have, and it occurred to me that I never would have more than part of the picture, a picture seen in its totality only by God. It was through moments such as these that I became a Christian.

We live in a world of dislocated meaning, a complex world in which we struggle to find a place for ourselves. Perhaps we strain too hard. Perhaps, as the ancient mystics knew, we should begin with the humblest creatures and learn to ascend the ladder which rises from their simple one-celled existence to reality itself. Perhaps we should learn that if we want to understand the world, knowledge is not enough – that we must see it, touch it, and begin to live in its presence. As my journey has continued I have repeatedly found the created world to reveal its maker, because his handwriting is in his words, his sense of order and humour and love, beauty and power and anger. A single wren fusses deep in a bush, and life speaks in its throat. Red-winged blackbirds sing from the rafters of a church, and people begin to be healed inside. A waterfall plunges with frothing brown water into a limestone gorge, and strength speaks with the paradox of both life and death through the roar of its voice. Even in natural disasters we find God, for it is deep within the fissures in the sea bed, where earthquakes and volcanic eruptions have their source, in the midst of the most destructive powers of the planet, that the chemicals without which life itself would not exist are released from the depths of the earth into the living world.

And so it is that we must learn to look at life with eyes of wonder, and to know that wonder is where the laws of the universe pulse and glide into alternative worlds, worlds seen with the inner eye, the eye of the imagination, the eye of a reality which is so much bigger than human life alone. As we do so we find ourselves to be a small part of a delicate and powerful balance, held in delight in the midst of forces which we can neither understand nor control. The whole world beats with the creative, sustaining power of the Spirit; withdraw the Spirit from any living thing and it would dissolve immediately into death. This is the world to which we belong and into which we may draw others; and it is a far cry from the mundane world of utilitarianism, the blinkered existence of career-spun hamster wheels and package-laden shopping trolleys.

When once we have rediscovered our place in a world created by God, we may use our experience as a bridge over which others may cross. In a world which has lost its understanding of sin and yet which is deepening its awareness of creation, evangelism can take surprising forms. In Blackheath, London, a church was planted when a community came together to dig out an overgrown pond. In Southall a partnership has formed between Christians and the community to regenerate a piece of waste land as a country park. Research shows that the mental health of a population is proportionate to its access to green spaces; and in helping a community care for the created world we help them to find life: for the physical world is but a reflection of spiritual reality, and reality is there not to be explained, but to be discovered.[33]

Faith is about the invisible as well as the visible world

He is the image of the invisible God, the firstborn of all creation; for in him all things in heaven and on earth were created, things visible and invisible, whether thrones or dominions or rulers or powers – all things have been created through him and for him.

Colossians 1:15–16

Flying back from a holiday in Portugal I am struck again by the peculiar abnormality of the Western worldview, as the hostesses of the budget airline enact the assumption that passengers need to pass the time by buying things, offering not lunch but duty-free goods loaded onto special trolleys and hoisted 33,000 feet into the air for the purpose. At the same time, reading the paper I discover that a new survey suggests that the value of a happy marriage is equivalent to a £72,000 annual pay increase. We live in a world which knows that happiness is intangible, yet which stumbles on blindly trying to buy it – like the fabled Irishman found looking for his wallet in Piccadilly Circus not because he lost it there but because the lights are on and it makes the search easier. Jesus on the other hand knew that reality is spiritual, that the most real in this world is the most invisible; and that lasting happiness is therefore to be found not in material things but in forgiveness from sin, in reconciliation with God and with one another, and in healing and deliverance from the invisible powers which beset us. These are the things which he offered to those who came seeking his help.

If we have overlooked the spiritual dimension of the visible world, our culture has been even more resistant to this idea of the invisible. As children we learn to place it in the realm of myth and make-believe, casting the spiritual powers of which Paul repeatedly warned the early churches into the safer garb of witches and wizards, elves and fairies. Assured by adults that such things do not exist, we grow up to belong to a church which doesn't believe in them either, dedicating ourselves instead to a variety of good causes, and wondering why people prefer to experiment with the occult than to attend our services. And yet the culture is changing. People are increasingly willing to acknowledge what other societies have always known to be true: that there is more to life than that which can be bought or measured. A recent Gallup poll suggests that two-thirds of Americans now declare themselves aware of the existence of spiritual entities which they identify as angels and demons. Research into psychical and paranormal phenomena has become respectable, and many people engage in spiritual practices of one kind or another, from yoga to tarot. Many of these are not as harmless as they seem; one study suggested that as many as 80 per cent of schoolchildren try ouija or seances, and that adverse psychological and spiritual effects are common.[34]

Sometimes it is possible to experience this other, unseen, reality directly. Plato was so convinced of its supremacy that he spoke of reality as a world of eternal ideas, of which the material things we see are merely shadows. The surrealist painters tried to jolt us into it by their disjointed representations of the world we take for granted, and many have sought entry to it through the use of recreational drugs. All religions have their spiritual practitioners, whether they be whirling dervishes and shamans or mystics and intercessors. Paul described his experience of the invisible world as being caught up into paradise in a vision so real that he was unsure whether he was in the body or out of it. I had my first conscious experience of this world as they whisked the grey and crumpled body of my husband into the intensive care unit and I realised that life and death were spiritual issues; I experienced it again as I stood on the dusty hillside of Chipili watching the sun rise amongst a people who knew their lives to be framed within an invisible world of meaning and power. And I have been there often since then as I have tried to minister to those affected by some of the invisible agents of this world, the rulers and authorities, the spiritual forces of evil who dwell in the heavenly places and who may be defeated only, but always, by the power of the Holy Spirit made available to us, in any culture, by Christ. In the Tanzanian village of Matui I met a man injured in an accident, treated by witch doctors, diagnosed mentally ill after that, asking for the help of Christ and coughing out his afflictions, shaking, as we prayed for him. The next day he came, smiling and well, clasping a scrap of paper on which he had written "1991", indicating his release from eleven years of suffering.[35] Closer to home, I once lived in an eighteenth-century Northamptonshire cottage, joined to a large house inhabited by a young family and two ghosts. One, a man, would stand at the top of the stairs in the evening, when even the family dog would refuse to go up them, and the other, a fair-haired girl, used to walk out into the garden in the early morning. Enquiry from an old villager found that a man had once been shot at the house during a dinner party, and a girl had hanged herself in the orchard. After prayer for their release, neither was seen again.

This is the world in which we now find ourselves, a world in which people are increasingly spiritually aware, but where the traditional framework of interpretation has been lost. It is a world in which scientists now tell us that 90 per cent even of *physical* matter is invisible to us, and in which mathematicians postulate the existence of no fewer than ten dimensions, the four we know plus another six of what they refer to collectively as hyperspace.[36] It is a world of strange and invisible forces, full of the mysterious, the unpredictable and the unexplained, and far bigger than the mapped certainties of modernism suggested. And it is a world in which we as Christians already live.

Recovering a social faith

Gospel and culture: bursting the bubble

> In Christianity, neither morality nor religion come into contact with reality at any point.
>
> Friedrich Nietzsche[37]

Since the Age of Reason the common view has been that faith is a private matter which has little to do with public reality.

Postmodernism, with its cheerful kaleidoscope of pick'n'mix truth, does little to challenge this perception. And yet what Jesus came to offer was not a lifestyle choice or a differently packaged way of doing things, but a dialogue – a dialogue which varies in character with time and place, which ranges over the full spectrum of possible subjects, and which reflects and repeats a process that began at the beginning of time with the creation of the world itself. As we enter into this dialogue with the Word of God we find that far from being an add-on to our daily lives, a new splodge on the canvas of our culturally determined picture, faith changes our whole perception of reality. First to change is our interior life, the place of thoughts and feelings and our sense of self. Our relationships follow, and our understanding of the outer world, visible and invisible, comes next. We become part of a new community, a community which heralds the coming kingdom of God, and we learn that we too are part of the dialogue, and that we can carry it to others still outside that community.

But what difference does it make to the world we live in? Jesus promised a new kingdom. Is that kingdom, in the old phrase, a kingdom which is not yet, or is it one which could be now? Is Isaiah's vision of a desert bursting into flower one which we may expect to witness within the societies in which we live, or is it just a picture of the eternal reality to which we now belong? And if we can claim Isaiah's promises for now, what would that mean in practice? For to adopt the teaching of Jesus, as Rabbi Klausner warned, would mean no less than to remove ourselves from the whole sphere of ordered national and human existence. The implications of Jesus's attitudes towards marginalised groups would have been the total dismantling of the prevailing social and political structures, remarks historian Richard Cassidy.[38] And indeed it has sometimes been so. Wesley's determination to preach the gospel and disciple believers ultimately did result in social changes which transformed a culture, finding expression amongst other things in the abolition of slavery and in a marked improvement in the living and working conditions of the poor. Something similar is under way in Uganda today. In modern New Guinea, the acceptance of the gospel by the Sawi people signalled the end of a culture based on cannibalism. The Church of South India is struggling now to express the gospel into a society based on the exploitation of the Dalit people within the Hindu caste system. There have been many examples throughout history of the impact of the gospel on a culture.

And yet there have also been failures. The Crusaders of the medieval period began not with Christ but with the political and social needs of the time, and we are still reaping the consequences of their missions to the Middle East. The Popes of the Renaissance confused spiritual and temporal power, and sought land and influence according to the politics of the day, rather than to offer good news to the poor. The Christianity of the modern West has in many ways, particularly in the United States, become indistinguishable from the materialist society of capitalism, democracy and consumerism within which it lives, and this also is causing a dangerous identification of the two in the mind of the outsider.[39] And even when we are not confused ourselves, our attempts to minister the gospel into a culture can boil down to little more than an endorsement of the politically correct social agendas of the ruling worldview. We can easily become a bubble protection agency rather than a bubble bursting one, ministering compassionately to the oppressed but stopping far short of setting them free.[40]

Gospel and culture: impacting society

I began this book with an image. Jesus said, "I am the way, the truth and the life". That statement for me has been like a pebble dropped into a pond: it landed, splash, in the centre, clear and visible, at the moment of my first encounter with Jesus; and yet its arrival was like a beginning, not an end, for from the point of impact sprang concentric ripples which have been slowly moving over the surface of my life in ever-increasing and interdependent circles.

It is the same in the life of the church. Over the last 50 years or so we have been more receptive to the Holy Spirit in the West, and many people have experienced personal renewal and transformation as they have received his blessing. As these people have prayed for others, the ripples have spread over the surface and renewal has come to whole churches. All the signs are that the renewal is now beginning to spread further and affect the communities in which those churches are set, sometimes on a small scale, sometimes on a scale and with a speed which surpass anything we have seen for centuries. It is not primarily by disapproving of abortion or by running socially relevant care programmes or by up-dating our image that we will bring the gospel to a culture (justly concerned though we may be about all these things): it is by allowing the Holy Spirit to change us, and, through us, others. The church is the place in which the kingdom begins.

> You are the light of the world. Let your light shine before others, so that they may see your good works and give glory to your Father in heaven.
>
> Matthew 5:14–16

Jesus taught that we are to live as salt and as light, not seasoning our own food and lighting our own homes, but bringing flavour to the tasteless meat of a secular culture and shedding light into the dark places of the world we inhabit. As the church has come to life and we have deepened our understanding of the truth, many Christians have experienced a growing desire to be salt and light to their communities. The society of the unencumbered self suffers from a devastatingly high rate of family breakdown, and in Modesto, California, the united ministry of the churches to the married resulted in a 40 per cent drop in divorce over a period of ten years. A benefit culture spawns whole communities plagued by vandalism and violence, and the prayer-led ministry of an estate church in Birmingham saw the end of gang warfare, an open door into the local schools and a great growth in the number of those turning to Christ. A local headteacher said that she had come to realise that the greatest problem on the estate was not lack of facilities but the undeveloped souls of the children; a confirmation of the ministry of a church which saw its task not as meeting social needs but in being a prophetic signpost to the community in which it was set.[41]

Sometimes the vision has been even more ambitious. In Little Rock, Arkansas, one church noticed that despite excellent teaching and genuine worship, sensitive pastoral care and culturally relevant evangelism, many members suffered a loss of enthusiasm after four or five years. When encouraged to take their faith into the community in order to offer themselves as living proof of the love of God, they met with an enormous response from people who had not previously regarded the church as being relevant to their needs in any way. Mentoring children, building houses, painting schools, facilitating adoptions, offering financial advice – all these became ways of building bridges between the church and the city, living out Jesus's command to "let your light shine before men so that they may see your good deeds and praise your Father in heaven" (Matthew 5:16). An upsurge of interest in the gospel has followed – which the switched-on churches of Little Rock do not, of course, forget to explain in words as well as deeds.[42]

The examples given above illustrate what can happen in a community with a renewed church at its centre. But sometimes the impact is proving even greater, and communities are being not just changed but transformed through the ministry of the church. The story as we are increasingly hearing it told begins in Cali, Colombia, centre of the infamous drugs cartels and a city riven by corruption and violence. A group of ministers began to meet for prayer, a meeting which led eventually to the nervous hiring of the city stadium in May 1995 for an all-night prayer vigil. Thirty thousand people turned up to pray for release from the violence which dominated the city, and two days later the newspaper ran the unimaginable headline: "No Murders". A second meeting was attended by 40,000 people, praying this time against corruption. Following this meeting, 900 policemen were fired for their links with the cartels, the military closed the city and seized all the drug leaders, and explosive church growth began. Cali's problems are certainly not over – recession hit the city with the end of the drugs trade, and a leading pastor was assassinated in the middle of it all. But the people have no doubt that transformation has come to Cali not merely by wanting it or even working for it, but by Christians praying for it in the name of Jesus.[43]

The story of Cali has spread. Similar united and fervent prayer has been offered by large gatherings of Christians in Cape Town, South Africa, and in Woodbridge, Virginia. In both cases the results have been measured not by the church but by the press. In Cape Town the papers reported that over a two-year period the crime rate had fallen by 55 per cent. In Woodbridge the issue has been the racial divisions which dominate church and town alike; 50 churches, black and white, are now meeting together for prayer, and the local headlines have been "Churches practise what they preach". There have been other examples; George Otis tells similar stories from Kenya, Uganda and Guatemala.[44] In all these places there appears to be a consistent pattern: the problem dominating the community has been recognised as having spiritual origins which underpin its human manifestation; Christians of all denominations have come together in persistent prayer to tackle this specific problem; prayer has been backed up by determined action in the community with those most affected; and many people have responded to the gospel as a result of the transformation they have witnessed in the life of their neighbourhood. In all these instances negative social conditions have been seen as underpinned by spiritual realities which need to be tackled on their own terms. As Paul reminded the Ephesians, even life and death themselves are spiritual issues:

> Our struggle is not against enemies of blood and flesh, but against the rulers, against the authorities, against the cosmic powers of this present darkness, against the spiritual forces of evil in the heavenly places.
>
> Ephesians 6:12

What would happen if we were to pray for our own communities in this way?

Gospel and culture: a sign of the kingdom

> If you continue in my word, you are truly my disciples, and you will know the truth, and the truth will make you free.
>
> John 8:31

So the ripples continue to spread, and everything is part of a process. Sometimes it is one which takes not just a lifetime but several generations. We are, said the mystics of the twelfth century, like dwarfs standing on the shoulders of giants, adding our own pint-sized contributions to their achievements and so seeing further than ever before. The events of Cali must be seen in the context of the development of the base communities of the Catholic liberation theology movement, which first banded ordinary Christians together into cells of prayer and social concern, and then of the Pentecostal movement which swept the continent after that, bringing spiritual renewal to individuals and churches. The renewal in Cape Town and other South African townships must be seen in the context of the long struggle against apartheid in a country where racial divisions have perhaps run deeper than anywhere else in the world. The transformation in social and political structures currently taking place in Uganda follows on from the desperate years of Idi Amin when many Christians went underground and continued to pray for their country, culminating in its public dedication to Christ by the President's wife on the eve of the millennium.[45] The kingdom of God is most readily available to those who know they need it.

And so it is open to us to be part of the life-changing purposes of God. We will never fully experience the reality of his kingdom on this earth, for all these things are meant to be to us as signs. Every healed person goes on to die, and every transformed community remains subject to the forces which seek to destroy it. Ultimately they will not succeed, for when Jesus died on the cross, the veil which kept people out of the holy part of the temple was ripped, and a new reality revealed – a reality which we may experience as individuals, as churches and even as communities, a reality painted in the beatitudes and the parables, a reality grasped in the brokenness of our ministry as we speak the words of life: and a reality which has no end.

> For God so loved the world that he gave his only Son, so that everyone who believes in him may not perish but may have eternal life.
>
> John 3:16

Notes

1 "Late fragment", *All of Us: The collected poems*, p.294.
2 *Paradiso* XXX 61–127; XXXIII 82–145.
3 Paul prays twice for the Ephesians, firstly, that they

would receive a spirit of wisdom and knowledge of God, 1:17–19; secondly, that they would know the love of Christ that surpasses knowledge, 3:16–19.

4 For example, Origen in his commentary on John; see M Green, *Evangelism in the Early Church*, p.60.

5 John 15:1–11; John 13:3–16; Matthew 22:1–14.

6 The first church building we know of was erected in Edessa in ca 200 AD; see O Chadwick, *The History of Christianity* p.29. The Greek word *ekklesia* literally means the "called out".

7 H Snyder, *Radical Renewal: The Problem of Wineskins Today*, ch.2.

8 Statistics taken from *The Sunday Times* 5 March 2000 (neighbours); *The Week* 9 December 2002 (time spent in others' homes in the US), *The Sunday Times* 19 January 2003 (9 million antidepressant prescriptions in 1991; 22 million in 2002).

9 An excellent analysis of the problem of loneliness in our culture is given by H Nouwen, *Reaching Out*, especially ch.1–2.

10 For Wesley, see H Snyder, "In a class of their own", *Cell UK* magazine 13; for the contemporary cell movement in the UK, see also www.celluk.org.uk. For the Latin American base communities, see M Nazir-Ali, *Shapes of the Church to Come*, pp.104–06; P Berryman, *Liberation Theology*. For the church in South Korea, see M Green, *Asian Tigers for Christ*, and H Astin, *Body and Cell*, ch.13.

11 See B Jackson, *Hope for the Church*, ch.11 "Acting small whatever your size".

12 V Donovan, *Christianity Rediscovered*, ch.10.

13 *When the Heart Waits*, p.71, quoted by M Yaconelli, *Dangerous Wonder*, p.91.

14 An excellent analysis of this problem is given by A Jamieson, *A Churchless Faith: Faith Journeys Beyond the*

Churches.

15 For a discussion of faith as journey, see J Fowler, *Stages of Faith*; A Jamieson, *Faith Journeys Beyond the Churches*.

16 Bonaventure in the thirteenth century, *Itinerarium Mentis in Deum*, and J Fowler in the twentieth, *Stages of Faith*, both describe the journey of faith as having six stages, vertical and horizontal respectively. For the ladder, see for example Honorius of Autun, *Scala Coeli Major*; for the cloud, see the anonymous fourteenth-century work *The Cloud of Unknowing*.

17 Paul Tournier, *The Adventure of Living*; Henri Nouwen, *The Way of the Heart*; *Reaching Out*; and other writings.

18 For the clowns, see J Drane, *The McDonaldization of the Church*, pp.121–22; for Gorecki, see C Colson, *How Now Shall We Live?*, pp.433–38.

19 J Drane, *The McDonaldization of the Church*, p.20.

20 See Genesis 1 and Romans 1:20.

21 Quoted by E Mâle, *The Gothic Image*, p.29.

22 Matthew 6; Matthew 11; Psalm 1; 1 Corinthians 15:36; 2 Corinthians 2:14–16; Song of Songs; Psalm 8; 1 Corinthians 11:23–26; Psalm 104. The number of galaxies is estimated by astronomers using the Hubble space telescope.

23 For the transition from world as organic to world as machine in the seventeenth century, see C Merchant, *The Death of Nature*, especially ch.4 and ch.7; for its development and consequences for our worldview, see W Barrett, *Death of the Soul: From Descartes to the Computer*. The article is that by L White, "The religious roots of our ecological crisis", *Science* 155 (1967).

24 The transition is described by F Capra, *The Turning Point*. The best known rebellion against the modern scientific approach is perhaps that of James Lovelock in his book *Gaia: A New Look at Life on Earth*. See also R Sheldrake, *The Rebirth of Nature: The Greening of*

Science and God; and P Davies, *God and the New Physics*. For what we commonly refer to as New Age beliefs and practices, see DR Groothius, *Unmasking the New Age*.

25 Calvin, Institutes IV 9.

26 These odds are so great that scientists have coined the term "anthropic principle" to account for the fact that the universe is apparently designed in such a way as to make possible the existence of life on earth. See J Polkinghorne, *Science and Creation*, and A McGrath, *Science and Religion* for a discussion of these and other issues.

27 For Darwin, see J Polkinghorne, *Science and Christian Belief*, p.76; for Hawking, see DAS Fergusson, *The Cosmos and the Creator*, p.43.

28 Jeans quoted by G Otis, *The Twilight Labyrinth*, p.95; D Zohar, *The Quantum Self*. For a theological discussion of the relationship between the Holy Spirit and the created world, see W Pannenberg, "The doctrine of the Spirit and the task of a theology of nature", in *Toward a Theology of Nature: Essays on Science and Faith*.

29 Sir Thomas Browne, *Religio Medici*, p.99; P Teilhard de Chardin, *The Spiritual Power of Matter*, p.65.

30 For Leibnitz, see W Barrett, *Death of the Soul: From Descartes to the Computer*, ch.2. For morphogenetic fields, see R Sheldrake, *The Rebirth of Nature*, p.87. Lovelock expresses his theory thus: "If Gaia does exist, then we may find ourselves and all other living things to be parts and partners of a vast being who in her entirety has the power to maintain our planet as a fit and comfortable habitat for life", *Gaia*, p.1.

31 Lovelock remarks that Tribus and McIrvine showed in *The Scientific American* (1970) that the beneficence of the sun could be regarded as a continuous gift of 10^{37} words of information per second to the Earth – rather than as the conventional 5×10^7 megawatt hours of power per

second; *Gaia*, ch.8.

32 Julian of Norwich, *Revelations of Divine Love*, V; see also Psalm 19:1–4.

33 The Pond Church is a plant of St Michael's, Blackheath Park; see G Lings, *Encounters on the Edge 6*. The Southall project is managed by Dave and Anne Bookless of the Christian conservation organisation A Rocha (www.arocha.org; see also the article in CMS *Yes* magazine April–June 2001, and on their website www.cms-uk.org). Research finding from a study undertaken by the King's Fund, a medical research charity.

34 See J Richards, *But Deliver us from Evil*, p.61.

35 Ephesians 6:12: "Our struggle is not against enemies of blood and flesh, but against the rulers, against the authorities, against the cosmic powers of this present darkness, against the spiritual forces of evil in the heavenly places."

36 Researchers using a NASA telescope demonstrated in 1992 that over 90 per cent of the universe must consist of "cold dark matter" which we cannot see, feel or detect; reported in *The Times*, 25 April 1992. More than 5,000 scientific papers were published in the ten-year period 1984–94 on the six dimensions of "hyperspace" postulated by mathematicians. See G Otis, *The Twilight Labyrinth*, p.61.

37 Quoted in Lewis, *The Church of Irresistible Influence*, p.216.

38 For Rabbi Klausner see ch.1 n.86. Also R J Cassidy, *Jesus, Politics and Society*, ch.6, "Was Jesus dangerous to the Roman empire?"

39 Analyses of the capitulation of faith to culture in the US are given by D Bosch, *Believing in the Future: Towards a Missiology of Western Culture*; S Hauerwas and W H Willimon, *Resident Aliens: Life in the Christian Colony – a provocative assessment of culture and ministry for people who know that something is wrong*; and C Colson

and N Pearcey, *How Now Shall We Live?* For summaries of these and other relevant works, see www.alisonmorgan.co.uk.

40 H A Snyder remarks that "too often the church presents a theology of political and/or social causes so hopelessly tied to passing cultural fads that its demise precedes that of its promoters", *Radical Renewal: The Problem of Wineskins Today,* p.23.

41 For Modesto and many similar stories of the impact of church on culture, see C Colson and N Pearcey, *How Now Shall We Live?*, ch.33 and elsewhere. For Birmingham, see W and M Brown, *Angels on the Walls: The Risk-Taking Faith that Reclaimed a Community.*

42 R Lewis, *The Church of Irresistible Influence.*

43 The story of Cali is told by G Otis in his book *The Twilight Labyrinth,* ch.11, and in the video entitled *Transformations: A Documentary,* available in the UK from Gateway Christian Media.

44 John Guernsey of Woodbridge and Trevor Pearce from Cape Town told the story of the transformation of their communities at a Consultation organised by SOMA, ARM and Springboard in November 2002. Annual stadium prayer meetings now take place all over Africa; on 1 May 2003 there were 71 such meetings in South Africa and a further 60 elsewhere on the continent (see www.transformationafrica.org). For more information on community transformation, see George Otis, the foremost researcher in this area, who has written a number of books, including *The Twilight Labyrinth* quoted above. For a general introduction, see J Leach, *Community Transformation: A Beginner's Guide.*

45 Since then, an increased willingness of Christians not only to pray for their country but to become actively involved in its community and political life has brought a complete turnaround in Uganda's fortunes. Once a byword for

corruption and cruelty, Uganda is now the only country in Africa where AIDS is decreasing; inflation has fallen from 380 per cent to 6–8 per cent, and economic recovery is well advanced. This has been achieved through a nationwide initiative of prayer and fasting and a new government campaign for integrity and morality; a Christian anti-corruption minister was appointed and an ethical sex campaign introduced. A new Uganda Christian Alliance has been formed, and the churches are growing rapidly. Uganda's story is told in the second of the two *Transformations* videos mentioned above.

BIBLIOGRAPHY

Adam, P: *Speaking God's Words: A Practical Theology of Preaching*, IVP, Leicester 1996

Alexander, Liesl: *Free to Live*, New Wine Press, Bognor Regis 1988

Allison, D C: *The Sermon on the Mount: Inspiring the Moral Imagination*, Crossroad, New York 1999

Anderson, B W: *The Living World of the Old Testament*, 3rd edition, Longman, London 1978

Anderson, N T: *The Bondage Breaker*, Monarch, London 1996

Anderson, N T and R Saucy: *The Common Made Holy: Developing a Personal and Intimate Relationship with God*, Monarch, London 1997

Anderson, N T and E L Towns, *Rivers of Revival*, Regal, Ventura, California 1997

Astin, H: *Body and Cell: Making the Transition to Cell Church*, Monarch, London 1998

Attwater, D: *The Penguin Dictionary of Saints*, Harmondsworth 1965

Bainton, R H: *Here I Stand: A Life of Martin Luther*, Mentor, New York 1955

Bainton, R H: *The Medieval Church*, Van Nostrand, Princeton 1962

Bammel, E and C F D Moule (eds): *Jesus and the Politics of His Day*, Cambridge University Press (CUP) 1984

Barnes, T D: *Tertullian: A Historical and Literary Study*, Oxford University Press (OUP) 1971

Barrett, W: *Death of the Soul: From Descartes to the Computer*, OUP 1987

Bartholomew, C and T Moritz (eds): *Christ and Consumerism: Critical Reflections on the Spirit of our Age*, Paternoster Press, Exeter 2000

Baynes, N H: *Constantine the Great and the Christian Church*, OUP, 1972 (1934)

Beatrice, P F: *Introduzione ai Padri della Chiesa*, Edizioni Istituto S Gaetano, Vicenza 1983

Beaudoin, T: *Virtual Faith*, Jossey-Bass, San Francisco, California 1998

Berryman, P: *Liberation Theology: Essential Facts About the Revolutionary Movement in Latin America and Beyond*, Tauris, London 1987

Blanch, S: *Encounters with Jesus*, Hodder & Stoughton, London 1988

Blanchard, K and T Waghorn: *Mission Possible: Becoming a World-Class Organization While There's Still Time*, McGraw-Hill, New York 1997

Bonaventure: *The Soul's Journey into God and the Life of St Francis*, ed. E Cousins, SPCK, London 1978

Borg, M J: *Jesus: A New Vision: Spirit, Culture and the Life of Discipleship*, HarperCollins, New York 1987

Bosch, D J: *Believing in the Future: Towards a Missiology of Western Culture*, Trinity Press International, Harrisburg, Pennsylvania 1995

Bowker, J (ed.): *The Complete Bible Handbook*, Dorling Kindersley, London 1998

Brierley, P: *Future Church: A Global Analysis of the Christian Community to the Year 2010*, Monarch, London 1998

Brooke, R B: *The Coming of the Friars*, G. Allen & Unwin, London 1975

Brown, R M: *Gustavo Gutierrez: An Introduction to Liberation Theology*, Orbis, Maryknoll, New York, 1990

Brown, W and M: *Angels on the Walls: The Risk-Taking Faith that Reclaimed a Community*, Kingsway, Eastbourne 2000

Browne, Sir T: *The Major Works*, ed. C A Patrides, Penguin, London 1977

Bruce, F F: *Paul: Apostle of the Free Spirit*, Paternoster Press, Exeter 1977

Brueggemann, W: *Biblical Perspectives on Evangelism: Living in a Three-Storied Universe*, Abingdon Press, Nashville, 1993

Brueggemann, W: *Finally Comes the Poet: Daring Speech for Proclamation*, Fortress Press, Minneapolis, 1989

Brueggemann, W: *Hopeful Imagination: Prophetic Voices in Exile*, SCM, London 1996

Brueggemann, W: *Interpretation and Obedience: From Faithful Reading to Faithful Living*, Fortress Press, Minneapolis 1991

Brueggemann, W: *The Prophetic Imagination*, Fortress Press, Philadelphia, 1978

Brueggemann, W: *Texts that Linger, Words that Explode*, Fortress Press, Minneapolis, 2000

Brueggemann, W: *Texts Under Negotiation: The Bible and Postmodern Imagination*, Fortress Press, Minneapolis, 1993

Burke, P: *The Italian Renaissance: Culture and Society in Italy*, Polity Press, Cambridge 1999

Burton, J: *England Needs a Revival*, SCM, London 1995

Buttrick, D: *Preaching the New and the Now*, J Knox Press, Louisville, Kentucky 1998

Buttrick, G A: *The Interpreter's Dictionary of the Bible*, Abingdon Press, Nashville 1962

Carroll, R P: *Wolf in the Sheepfold: The Bible as Problematic for Theology*, SCM, London 1997 (1991)

Carter Heyward, I: *Our Passion for Justice*, Pilgrim Press, Cleveland, Ohio 1984

Cassidy, R J: *Jesus, Politics and Society: A Study of Luke's Gospel*, Orbis, Maryknoll, New York 1978

Chadwick, H: *The Early Church*, Pelican, London 1967

Chadwick, O: *A History of Christianity*, Phoenix Illustrated, London 1997

Chadwick, O: *The Reformation*, Penguin, London 1964

Chadwick, O: *Western Asceticism: Selected Translations with Introductions and Notes*, SCM, London 1958

Chitty, D J: *The Desert A City*, St Vladimir's Seminary Press, Crestwood, New York 1966

Collingwood: *The Idea of Nature*, OUP 1945

Colson, C and N Pearcey: *How Now Shall We Live?*, Marshall Pickering, London 2000 (1999)

Cragg, G R: *The Church and the Age of Reason 1648–1789*, Pelican, Harmondsworth 1960, reprinted 1970

Cray, G: *The Gospel and Tomorrow's Culture*, CPAS, Warwick 1994

Cray, G (ed.): *The Post-evangelical Debate*, Triangle, London 1997

Croft, S: *Ministry in Three Dimensions: Ordination and Leadership in the Local Church*, DLT, London 1999

Crossan, J D: *Jesus: A Revolutionary Biography*, HarperCollins, New York 1994

Dale, A T: *Portrait of Jesus*, OUP 1979

Dalrymple, John: *Simple Prayer*, DLT, London 1984

Davies, P C W: *God and the New Physics*, Dent, London 1983

Delumeau, J: *Sin and Fear*, St Martin's Press, New York, 1990 (translated from the French edition of 1983)

Derrett, J D M: *Jesus's Audience: The Social and Psychological Environment In Which He Worked*, DLT, London 1973

Dodd, C H: *The Parables of the Kingdom*, London 1935, reprinted Fount Paperbacks 1978

Dodds, E R: *The Greeks and the Irrational*, University of California Press 1973

Dodds, E R: *Pagan and Christian in an Age of Anxiety*, CUP 1965

Donahue, J R: *The Gospel in Parable*, Fortress Press, Philadelphia 1988

Donovan, V J: *Christianity Rediscovered: An Epistle from the Masai*, SCM, London 1978

Dowley, T (ed.): *The History of Christianity*, Lion, Tring 1977

Down, M: *Speak to these Bones*, Monarch, London 1993

Drane, J: *Faith in a Changing Culture: Creating Churches for the Next Century*, Marshall Pickering, London 1994

Drane, J: *The McDonaldization of the Church*, DLT, London 2000

Eagleton, T: *The Idea of Culture*, Blackwells, Oxford 2000

Eden, M and D F Wells (eds): *The Gospel in the Modern World: A Tribute to John Stott*, IVP, Leicester 1991

Ela, J-M: *African Cry*, Orbis, Maryknoll, New York 1986 (Paris 1980)

Ela, J-M: *My Faith as an African*, Orbis, Maryknoll, New York 1988, & Chapman, London 1989

Eliot, T S: "Notes towards the definition of culture", in *Selected Prose of T S Eliot*, ed. F Kermode, Faber, London 1975

England, E (ed.): *Living in the Light of Pentecost*, Highland, Godalming 1990

Fergusson, D A S: *The Cosmos and the Creator: An Introduction to the Theology of Creation*, IVP, Leicester 1998

Fowler, J: *Stages of Faith*, Harper Row, New York 1981

Frend, W H C: *The Early Church*, Fortress Press, Philadelphia 1982 (1st edition 1965)

Gibbs, E and I Coffey: *Church Next: Quantum Changes in Christian Ministry*, IVP, Leicester 2001

Gibellini, R (ed.): *Paths of African Theology*, SCM, London 1994 (Brescia 1994)

Gifford, P: *African Christianity: Its Public Role*, Hurst & Co, London 1998

Gimenez, H A: *The Miraculous Power of God*, Kingdom Faith Ministries, Weatherford, Texas 1995

Goldsmith, M: *Jesus and His Relationships*, Paternoster Press, Exeter 2000

Green, M: *Asian Tigers for Christ: The Dynamic Growth of the Church in South East Asia*, SPCK, London 2001

Green, M: *Evangelism in the Early Church*, Highland, Crowborough 1984 (Hodder & Stoughton, London 1970)

Groothius, D R: *Unmasking the New Age*, IVP, Leicester 1986

Guinness, O: *The Gravedigger File*, IVP, Leicester 1983

Guinness, O: *Time for Truth: Living Free in a World of Lies, Hype and Spin*, IVP, Leicester 2000

Gumbel, N: *The Heart of Revival*, Kingsway, Eastbourne 1997

Gunstone, J and B Brandon (eds): *A Time to Heal*, Church House Publishing (CHP), London 2000

Gurevic, A: *Medieval Popular Culture: Problems of Belief and Perception*, CUP 1988

Hall, D J: *The End of Christendom and the Future of Christianity*, Trinity Press International, Harrisburg, Pennsylvania 1995

Hastings, A: *Church and Mission in Modern Africa*, Burns & Oates, London 1967

Hauerwas, S and W H Willimon: *Resident Aliens: Life in the Christian Colony*, Abingdon Press, Nashville 1989

Hay, D: *The Medieval Centuries*, Methuen, London 1964

Hay, D: *The Italian Renaissance in its Historical Background*, 2nd edition, CUP 1977

Hilborn, D: *Picking Up the Pieces*, Hodder & Stoughton, London 1997

Hill, C: *Prophecy Past and Present: An Exploration of the Prophetic Ministry in the Bible and the Church Today*, Eagle, Guildford 1995

Horsley, R A: *Archaeology, History and Society in Galilee: The Social Context of Jesus and the Rabbis*, Trinity Press International, Harrisburg, Pennsylvania, 1996

Horsley, R A (ed.): *Paul and Empire: Religion and Power in Roman Imperial Society*, Trinity Press International, Harrisburg, Pennsylvania, 1997

Howse, C (ed.): *AD: 2000 years of Christianity*, SPCK, London 1999

Jackson, B: *Higher Than The Hills*, Highland, Godalming 1999

Jackson, B: *Hope for the Church: Contemporary Strategies for Growth*, CHP, London 2002

Jamieson, A: *A Churchless Faith: Faith Journeys Beyond the Churches*, SPCK 2002

Jeremias, J: *The Parables of Jesus*, SCM, London 1963

Johnston, G: *Preaching to a Postmodern World: A Guide to Reaching Twenty-first-Century Listeners*, Baker, Grand Rapids, Michigan 2001

Johnstone, P: *The Church is Bigger Than You Think: Structures and Strategies for the Church in the 21st Century*, Christian Focus, Fearn 1998

Johnstone, P and J Mandryk, *Operation World*, 21st century edition, Paternoster Lifestyle, Carlisle, 2001

Jones, A H M: *Constantine and the Conversion of Europe*, Penguin, Harmondsworth, 1972 (EUP 1949)

Jones, B: *The Radical Church: Restoring the Apostolic Edge*, Destiny Image, Shippersberg, PA, USA 1999

Kee, H C: *Medicine, Miracle and Magic in New Testament Times*, CUP 1986

Kellett, E E: *Religion and Life in the Early Victorian Age*,

Norwood, London 1938

Kelly, G: *Get a Grip on the Future Without Losing Your Hold on the Past*, Monarch, London 1999

Kitzberger, I R (ed.): *Transformative Encounters: Jesus and Women Reviewed*, Brill, Leiden 2000

Lawrence, C H: *Medieval Monasticism*, Longman, London 1984

Lawrence, J: *Freemasonry: A Religion?* Kingsway, Eastbourne 1987

Leach, J: *Community Transformation: A Beginner's Guide*, Grove Books, Cambridge 2002

Leach, J *et al.*: *Renewing the Traditional Church*, Grove Books, Cambridge 2002

Le Goff, J: *Time, Work and Culture in the Middle Ages*, University of Chicago Press 1980

Lewis, R: *The Church of Irresistible Influence*, Zondervan, Grand Rapids, Michigan 2001

Lindblom, J: *Prophecy in Ancient Israel*, OUP 1962

Linder, R D: *The Student Church History Timeline*, Candle, Carlisle 2000

Linn, G: *Hear What the Spirit Says to the Churches*, WCC, Geneva 1994

Lortz, J: *How the Reformation Came*, Herder & Herder, New York 1964

Lovelock, J: *Gaia: A New Look at Life on Earth*, OUP 1979

MacMullen, R: *Christianising the Roman Empire AD 100–400*, Yale University Press, 1984

Maddocks, M: *The Christian Healing Ministry*, 3rd edition, SPCK, London 1995

Magonet, J: *The Subversive Bible*, SCM, London 1997

Magonet, J: *A Rabbi's Bible*, SCM Press, London 1991

Male, E: *The Gothic Image: Religious Art in France of the Thirteenth Century*, Harper, London 1972 (1913)

Markus, R: *The End of Ancient Christianity*, CUP 1990

Marsh, H: *The Rebel King: The Story of Christ as Seen*

Against the Historical Conflict Between the Roman Empire and Judaism, Albyn Press, Edinburgh 1975

Mayer, H E: *The Crusades*, 2nd edition, OUP 1988

Mayne, M: *This Sunrise of Wonder*, Fount, London 1985

Mbiti, J F: *African Religions and Philosophy*, Heinemann, London 1969, reprinted 1990

McCloughry, R: *Living in the Presence of the Future*, IVP, Leicester 2001

McFague, S: *The Body of God: An Ecological Theology*, SCM Press, London 1993

McGrath, A E: *A Life of John Calvin: A Study in the Shaping of Western Culture*, Blackwell, Oxford 1990

McGrath, A E: *Bridge-building: Effective Christian Apologetics*, IVP, Leicester 1992

McGrath, A E: *Science and Religion*, Blackwell, Oxford 1999

McGrath, A E: *The Future of Christianity*, Blackwell, Oxford 2002

McLaren, B D: *More Ready Than You Realise: Evangelism as Dance in the Postmodern Matrix*, Zondervan, Grand Rapids, Michigan 2002

McManners, J (ed.): *The Oxford History of Christianity*, OUP 1990

Merchant, C: *The Death of Nature: Women, Ecology and the Scientific Revolution*, HarperCollins, London 1982

Meyer, B F: *The Aims of Jesus*, SCM Press, London 1979

Middleton, R and B J Walsh, *Truth is Stranger Than It Used To Be*, SPCK, London 1995

Miller, B: *John Wesley*, Dimension Books, Minneapolis, no date

Miller, B: *William Carey: The Father of Modern Missions*, 2nd edition, Bethany House, Minneapolis 1980

Milne, B: *The Message of John*, IVP, Leicester 1993

Minear, P S: *Matthew: The Teacher's Gospel*, DLT, London 1984

Montefiore, H (ed.): *The Gospel and Contemporary Culture*,

Mowbray, London 1992

More, T: *Utopia*, eds G M Logan and R M Adams, CUP 1989

Morgan, A: *Dante and the Medieval Other World*, CUP 1990

Morris, L: *The Gospel According to John*, Eerdmans, Grand Rapids, Michigan, 1971

Moynagh, M: *Changing World, Changing Church*, Monarch, London 2001

Nazir-Ali, M: *Mission and Dialogue: Proclaiming the Gospel Afresh in Every Age*, SPCK, London 1995

Nazir-Ali, M: *Shapes of the Church to Come*, Kingsway, Eastbourne 2001

Newbigin, L: *Foolishness to the Greeks: The Gospel and Western Culture*, SPCK, London 1986

Newbigin, L: *The Gospel in a Pluralist Society*, SPCK, London 1989

Niebuhr, R: *Christ and Culture*, Faber & Faber, London 1952

Nineham, D: *Christianity Medieval and Modern: A Study in Religious Change*, SCM, London 1993

Nouwen, H: *Making All Things New*, reprinted HarperCollins, London 2000 (1981)

Nouwen, H: *Reaching Out*, reprinted HarperCollins, London 1998 (1975)

Nouwen, H: *The Way of the Heart*, 3rd ed., DLT, London 1999 (1981)

Nouwen, H: *The Wounded Healer: Ministry in Contemporary Society*, reprinted DLT, London 1994 (1979)

Oden, T C: *Two Worlds: Notes on the Death of Modernity in America and Russia*, IVP, Leicester 1992

Oppenheimer, H: *Finding and Following: Talking with Children about God*, SCM, London 1994

Osborn, L: *Restoring the Vision: The Gospel and Modern Culture*, Mowbray, London 1995

Otis, G: *The Twilight Labyrinth: Why Does Spiritual Darkness Linger Where It Does?* Chosen Books, Grand Rapids, Michigan 1997

Ozment, S: *Protestants: The Birth of a Revolution*, Fontana, London 1993

Pannenberg, W: *Toward a Theology of Nature: Essays on Science and Faith*, John Knox Press, Louisville, Kentucky 1993

Parker, R: *The Occult: Deliverance from Evil*, IVP 1989, reprinted 1992

Payne, L: *The Healing Presence: Curing the Soul Through Union with Christ*, Baker, Grand Rapids, Michigan 1995 (1989)

Peacocke, A: *God and Science: A Quest for Christian Credibility*, SCM Press, London 1996

Pieper, J: *Happiness and Contemplation*, St Augustine's Press, Indiana 1998 (1958)

Pirani, F and C Roche: *The Universe for Beginners*, Icon, Cambridge 1993

Polkinghorne, J: *One World: The Interaction of Science and Theology*, SPCK, London 1986

Polkinghorne, J: *Science and Christian Belief: Theological Reflections of a Bottom-Up Thinker*, SPCK, London 1994

Polkinghorne, J: *Science and Creation: The Search for Understanding*, SPCK, London 1988

Pullinger, J and A Quicke: *Chasing the Dragon*, Hodder & Stoughton, London 1980

Punton, A: *The World Jesus Knew*, Monarch, London 1996

Pytches, D: *Come Holy Spirit: Learning How to Minister in Power*, Hodder & Stoughton, London 1985

Rack, H D: *Reasonable Enthusiast: John Wesley and the Rise of Methodism*, 2nd edition, Epworth Press, London 1992

Redig de Compos, D: *Art Treasures of the Vatican*, Spectrum, London 1975

Richards, I A: *The Philosophy of Rhetoric*, OUP, London and

New York 1936

Richards, J: *But Deliver Us From Evil: An Introduction to the Demonic Dimension in Pastoral Care*, DLT, London 1974

Richardson, D: *Peace Child*, Regal, Ventura, California 1975

Riches, J: *Jesus and the Transformation of Judaism*, DLT, London 1980

Riddell, M: *Threshold of the Future: Reforming the Church in the Post-Christian West*, SPCK, London 1998

Roetzel, C J: *The World that Shaped the New Testament*, SCM, London 1987 (1985)

Rogerson, J and P Davies: *The Old Testament World*, CUP 1989

Sampson, P *et al.*: *Faith and Modernity*, Regnum, Oxford 1994

Schaff, P: "Monasticism" in *History of the Christian Church* III, Michigan 1910

Schott, R: *Michelangelo*, Thames and Hudson, London 1963

Sheldrake, R: *The Rebirth of Nature: The Greening of Science and God*, Century, London 1990.

Shorter, A: *The Church in the African City*, Chapman, London 1991

Silvoso, E: *That None Should Perish: How to Reach Entire Cities for Christ through Prayer Evangelism*, Regal, Ventura, California 1994

Smith, D: *Crying in the Wilderness: Evangelism and Mission in Today's Culture*, Paternoster Press, Carlisle 2000

Smith, G T: *Courage and Calling*, IVP, Downers Grove, Illinois, 1999

Snyder, H A: *Radical Renewal: The Problem of Wineskins Today*, Touch, Houston, Texas 1996

Southern, R: *Western Society and the Church in the Middle Ages*, Penguin, London 1970

Southern, R W: *The Making of the Middle Ages*, Hutchinson, London 1953, reprinted 1967

Spear, T and I N Kimambo (eds): *East African Expressions o Christianity*, James Currey, Oxford 1999

Stark, R: *The Rise of Christianity: A Sociologist Reconsider. History*, Princeton University Press 1996

Stewart, R (ed.): *Ideas that Shaped our World*, Marshall London 1997

Stott, J and R T Coote (eds): *Down to Earth: Studies ir Christianity and Culture*, Eerdmans, Grand Rapids Michigan, 1980

Stott, J R W: *Christian Counter-Culture: The Message of the Sermon on the Mount*, IVP, Leicester 1978

Stott, J R W: *The Message of Ephesians*, IVP, Leicester 1991

Tacitus, P C: *The Annals of Imperial Rome*, translated by Michael Grant, Penguin, London 1996

Taylor, J V: *A Matter of Life and Death*, SCM, London 1986

Taylor, M: *Not Angels but Agencies: The Ecumenica. Response to Poverty*, SCM, London 1995

Teilhard de Chardin, P: *Hymn of the Universe* HarperCollins, London 1965

Theissen, G: *The Shadow of the Galilean: In Quest of the Historical Jesus in Narrative Form*, SCM, London 1987 (1986)

Theissen, G and A Merz: *The Historical Jesus: A Comprehensive Guide*, SCM, London 1998

Tournier, P: *The Adventure of Living*, Highland. Crowborough 1983 (1965)

Ullmann, S: *Language and Style*, Blackwells, Oxford 1964

Walker, A: *Telling the Story: Gospel, Mission and Culture,* SPCK, London 1996

Warren, R and B Jackson: *There Are Answers*, Springboard Resource Paper 1, Abingdon 2001

Way, R (ed.): *The Cloud of Unknowing and the Letter of Private Direction*, Anthony Clarke, Wheathampstead 1986

Wenham, D: *The Parables of Jesus: Pictures of Revolution,* Hodder & Stoughton, London 1989

Westermann, C: *The Parables of Jesus in the Light of the Old Testament*, T&T Clark, Edinburgh 1990

Wimber, C: *John Wimber: The Way It Was*, Hodder & Stoughton, London 1999

Wimber, J and K Springer: *Power Evangelism: Signs and Wonders Today*, Hodder & Stoughton, London 1985

Woolmer, J: *Healing and Deliverance*, Monarch, London 1999

Wright, T: *The Original Jesus: The Life and Vision of a Revolutionary*, Lion, Oxford 1996

Yaconelli, M: *Dangerous Wonder: The Adventure of Childlike Faith*, Zondervan, Grand Rapids, Michigan 2000

Yancey, P: *The Jesus I Never Knew*, Marshall Pickering, London 1975

Yancey, P: *What's So Amazing About Grace?* Zondervan, Grand Rapids, Michigan, 1997

Young, B: *Jesus and His Jewish Parables: Rediscovering the Roots of Jesus' Teaching*, Hendrickson, Peabody, Massachusetts 1989

Young, B: *The Parables: Jewish Interpretation and Christian Tradition*, Hendrickson, Peabody, Massachusetts 1998

Yun, Brother and P Hattaway: *The Heavenly Man*, Monarch, London 2003

Zacharias, R: *Deliver Us From Evil: Restoring the Soul in a Disintegrating Culture*, Word, Dallas 1996

Zohar, D and I Marshall: *The Quantum Self*, Flamingo, London 1991

Zohar, D and I Marshall: *SQ – Spiritual Intelligence: The Ultimate Intelligence*, Bloomsbury, London 2000